BIOGRAPHY OF A SUBJECT

BIOGRAPHY OF A SUBJECT
An Evolution of Development Economics

Gerald M. Meier

OXFORD
UNIVERSITY PRESS

2005

OXFORD

UNIVERSITY PRESS

Oxford   New York
Auckland   Bangkok   Buenos Aires   Cape Town   Chennai
Dar es Salaam   Delhi   Hong Kong   Istanbul   Karachi   Kolkata
Kuala Lumpur   Madrid   Melbourne   Mexico City   Mumbai   Nairobi
São Paulo   Shanghai   Taipei   Tokyo   Toronto

Copyright © 2005 by Oxford University Press, Inc.

Published by Oxford University Press, Inc.
198 Madison Avenue, New York, New York 10016

www.oup.com

Oxford is a registered trademark of Oxford University Press

Library of Congress Cataloging-in-Publication Data
Meier, Gerald M.
Biography of a subject: an evolution of development economics / Gerald M. Meier.
p. cm.
Includes bibliographical references.
ISBN 0-19-517002-4; 0-19-517003-2 (pbk.)
1. Economic development. I. Title.
HD75.M439 2004
338.9—dc22   2004049281

9 8 7 6 5 4 3 2 1

Printed in the United States of America
on acid-free paper

Another fifty years

Preface

Universities introduced the subject of "economic development" some 50 years ago, just when I was a graduate student. Since then, the subject has been my closest intellectual companion, but its biography has been ever-changing. Now I want to capture in this book the essence and some highlights in the life of the subject.

I do so not only to provide perspectives in the present but also for the future. After a half century of development efforts, there is now widespread interest in assessing the development record—what has gone right and what has gone wrong. The successes and disappointments, however, derive from the ideas underlying development policies and strategies. An understanding of the evolution of development thought may help to influence future policy.

By assessing this evolution in the ideas of the first generation of development economists (roughly 1950s–1970s), the second generation (1970s–1990s), and the new third generation, we may recognize how the subject has evolved with increasing rigor in its analytics. And we may judge how policy implications have become more definitive. This evolution in thought and policy should offer more insights into three essential questions: (1) What are the sources of economic growth and change in a developing economy? (2) What accounts for the variation in cross-national development performance? (3) What policies are most appropriate for promoting development?

The literature on development is enormous. I have tried to reduce it to the basic organizing principles of the subject, to convey many specialized articles in less technical language for nonspecialized students, and to keep the whole picture in mind.

This is therefore an integrative type of book that synthesizes the ideas of many authors. I am obviously indebted to many development economists whose writings underlie much of this book. Specific citations are frequently made, and the reader may undertake detailed reading in the original work.

Among association with many development economists, I have been especially influenced by the thoughts of at least Lord Peter Bauer, Jagdish Bhagwati, Paul Collier, Paul Krugman, Sir Arthur Lewis, Michael Lipton, Ian Little, Hla Myint, Nicholas Stern, Frances Stewart, Joseph Stiglitz, and Paul Streeten. In my editing of *Emerging from Poverty* (1984), *Pioneers of Development* (1984) and *Frontiers of Development Economics* (2001), I have learned much from both the first and second generations of development economists.

Several of my own writings have been related to different periods of development thought. I now borrow from my various editions of *Leading Issues in Economic Development* (1964–2000), *Pioneers of Development* (1984), *Emerging from Poverty* (1984), and *Frontiers of Development Economics* (2001). I am grateful to Oxford University Press for permission to use and adapt sections from my earlier books.

Moreover, many thoughts have been inspired by students at Stanford University and Oxford University. I am also indebted to the librarians at these universities for particular references.

With exceptional efficiency and utmost kindness, Yuri Woo has processed this entire typescript. Without Yuri, it could not have been forthcoming.

Gerald M. Meier
Stanford University

Contents

BIOGRAPHY OF A SUBJECT

1

Thinking About Development

Do development economists really know how to put things right? Although the development record exhibits many achievements, there are also failures. Beneath the statistics of the development record lie vigorous controversies in ideas. There are also historic endeavors to translate the thinking of development economists into problem-solving and policy action. We want to appraise the evolution in development thought, its effects on policy, and the successes and disappointments.

Like the biography of a person, this biography of the subject of economic development tries to capture the essence and highlight in the life of the subject. Heralding a "revolution of rising expectations," the subject was born at the end of World War II during a period of decolonization and has been from its beginning a policy-oriented subject. Its motivating question is what can be done to accelerate the pace and quality of the development process in poor countries in order to alleviate their poverty. Over the past 50 years, during the life of the subject, two generations of development economists in academia, government, and business have continued to think long and hard about how to reduce international poverty.

Although the first two generations of development economists have made much progress in the subject, we want to rethink development and want to be forward-looking in focusing on unsettled questions and central issues that still need to be resolved. It is distressing that two centuries after the Industrial Revolution, almost half of the world's people (2.8 billion) live on less than $2 a day, and a fifth live on less than $1 a day.[1] (See appendix B for data on income poverty in regions and individual countries.)

While policies to eradicate poverty are being revised, ever more ambitious goals are being set, such as those established at the U.N. Millennium Summit to reduce the proportion of people living on less than $1 a day to half the 1990 level by 2015. Tables in appendix B indicate the goals of 2015 for poverty reduction, universal primary education, gender equity, and reduction in child mortality rates. Whether the goals will be attained will depend in large part on how ideas influence policy for higher rates of growth and less inequality.

THE MEANING OF "ECONOMIC DEVELOPMENT"

Clear thinking about development depends on clarification of the meaning of "economic development." From the time of its initial use, the term itself has conveyed a persuasive definition—a desirable objective. Over the past half century, however, with changing political economy contexts and the lessons of experience, the meaning has been refined and deepened. In general, it has always meant an increase in living standards. To achieve this, development policies during the 1950s and early 1960s focused on the maximization of growth of GNP (gross national product) or GDP (gross domestic product). In recognition of population growth, an index of per capita real income was also used. It was later realized that intercountry comparisons of levels of income are often misleading when they are made by converting the incomes of the various countries into a common currency—say, the U.S. dollar—through the use of official exchange rates. These nominal exchange rates do not reflect the relative purchasing power of different currencies, and thus international comparisons of income are misleading. Purchasing power parities (PPPs), rather than official exchange rates, are therefore used as the correct converters for translating GNP per capita or GDP per capita from national currencies to "international dollars."[2] In developing countries where domestic prices are relatively low, the GNP and GDP per capita based on PPPs will be higher than those obtained from official exchange rates. For example, GNP per capita in India in 2001 at official exchange rates was $460, but GNP per capita measured at PPP was $2,450. In Kenya, it was $340 and $1,020; in the Philippines, $1,050 and $4,360; in the United States, $34,870 and $34,870.

Some may wish to attach conditions to the rise of per capita income as an index of development. What if at the same time that average income per head in international dollars rises, the number of people in poverty also increases? Years before the start of the United Nations' first Development Decade in the 1960s, Jacob Viner (1953: 99–100) had warned:

> Suppose that someone should argue that the one great economic evil is the prevalence of a great mass of crushing poverty, and that it is a paradox to claim that a country is achieving economic progress as long as the absolute extent of such poverty prevailing in that country has not lessened or has even increased? If its population has undergone substantial increase, the numbers of those living at the margin of subsistence or below, illiterate,

diseased, undernourished, may have grown steadily consistently with a rise in the average income of the population as a whole.

Two decades after Viner's warning, Hollis Chenery (1974) introduced the World Bank's influential study *Redistribution with Growth* with this statement:

> It is now clear that more than a decade of rapid growth in underdeveloped countries has been of little or no benefit to perhaps a third of their population. Although the average per capita income of the Third World has increased by 50 percent since 1960, this growth has been very unequally distributed among countries, regions within countries, and socio-economic groups. Paradoxically, while growth policies have succeeded beyond the expectations of the first Development Decade, the very idea of aggregate growth as a social objective has increasingly been called into question.

This questioning became common among development practitioners. In assessing development, the condition has been imposed that even if per capita real income rises, there should not be at the same time an increase in the absolute number below a poverty line. Following two earlier World Development Reports on poverty, in 1980 and 1990, the World Bank's *World Development Report* of 2000/2001 continued to emphasize its message of "attacking poverty."

Many analysts also like economic development to incorporate human development, insofar as the objective is a reduction of absolute poverty. As Robert McNamara (1972) emphasized, there is always likely to be relative poverty—rich and poorer—but below an absolute poverty line, one confronts a "condition of life so degraded by disease, illiteracy, malnutrition, and squalor as to deny its victims basic human necessities." Robert McNamara (1973: 27) therefore urged that a major part of the Bank's efforts should be directed at the poorest 40 percent of the population, with the objective of eradicating absolute poverty.

The United Nations Development Program (UNDP) later introduced the concept and measurement of human development or quality of life in terms of a human development index (HDI). The HDI combines into a single index not only real GDP per capita but also social indicators of life expectancy at birth, adult literacy, and school enrollment. Accordingly, a ranking of countries by their HDI can differ markedly from that by per capita income. For example, in a 1997 ranking of countries the Sudan ranked 17 places lower by HDI than by GNP per capita. The United Arab Emirates ranked 50 places lower by HDI. India, however, ranked 12 places higher by HDI capita than by GNP per capita. Sri Lanka was exceptional in ranking 45 places higher by HDI.

Parallel to the quantitative measurement of economic development, there are qualitative considerations that go beyond the narrow quantitative measures. The first major study of economic development was W. Arthur Lewis's book *The Theory of Economic Growth* (1955). Economic development was to be measured by growth of output per "head of the population" that could be considered as "progress" or "development" (Lewis 1955: 10). To Lewis, "the advantage of economic growth is not that wealth increases happiness, but that it increases the range of human choice" (Lewis 1955: 420). This was also emphasized by Peter Bauer and Basil Yamey (1957: 149–150): "We believe that the widening of effective choice is the most valuable single objective of economic development as well as the best single criterion of its attainment."

Moreover, Lewis said that "the case for economic growth is that it gives man greater control over his environment, and thereby increases his freedom" (421). Half a century later, the Nobel laureate Amartya Sen has refined and extended the principle that development should be seen as a process of expanding substantive freedoms that people have. Emphasizing "development as freedom," Sen (1999a: 291) says that "since freedom is concerned with processes of decision making as well as opportunities to achieve valued outcomes," the interest in development "cannot be confined only to the outcomes in the form of the promotion of high output or income. . . . Such processes as participation in political decisions and social choice . . . have to be understood as constitutive parts of the ends of development in themselves." And poverty should be seen as a serious deprivation of an individual's basic capabilities (Sen 1999b: 360).[3] Development releases people from the unfreedom of poverty and expands the "capabilities" of persons to lead the kind of lives they value. In short, their escape from the poverty trap gives people another chance in the world.

Because the realization of economic opportunities also depends on political liberties, the term "development" has increasingly encompassed political development as well as economic development. Sen (1999a: 38) emphasizes political freedoms as instrumental freedoms:

> Political freedoms, broadly conceived (including what are called civil rights), refer to the opportunities that people have to determine who should govern and on what principles, and also include the possibility to scrutinize and criticize authorities, to have freedom of political expression and an uncensored press, to enjoy the freedom to choose between different political parties, and so on. They include the political entitlements associated with democracies in the broadest sense (encompassing opportunities of political dialogue, dissent and critique as well as voting rights and participatory selection of legislators and executives).[4]

Recognizing that as the subject has matured, there have been various interpretations of the meaning of economic development, we should not settle for any aggregate or even per capita index of development. Instead we should recognize the several dimensions of economic development. And rather than seek development as an end, we should view it as a means—as an instrumental process for escaping from the poverty trap, achieving human development, and acquiring freedom.

The subject of development goes far beyond a simple description of the characteristics of a less developed country. In broadest terms, development is a process that encompasses economic growth plus structural transformation. Not simply growth in the quantitative sense but also an array of institutional, political, and sociocultural changes that embody the qualitative traits of modernization. Growth plus change leads to the structural transformation of the economy, in the sense that the structure of production is transformed from primary to secondary production, and the traditional subsistence sector of the economy is absorbed into a modern sector. Parallel to the transformation of the economy is the modernization of society.

DEVELOPMENT ECONOMISTS

Economists of the past have been called "the worldly philosophers" (Heilbroner 1953). A Nobel laureate calls contemporary economists the "guardians of rationality" (Arrow 1974: 16). Regarding development economists, however, another Nobel laureate observes that "most of the people in the world are poor, so if we knew the economics of being poor we would know much of the economics that really matters" (Schultz 1980: 639).

We focus on development economists in their role as "trustees for the poor." They may combine some traits of the worldly philosophers and guardians of rationality, but their preoccupation is to reduce poverty for the 80 percent of the world's people living in some 140 developing countries.

Why are poor countries still poor? What can be done to remove their persistent poverty? Simply stated, these are the two fundamental questions confronting the trustees for the poor. As given by the subject of development economics, however, the answers are continually evolving. They are evolving on three levels—the theoretical, empirical, and normative.

My task is to interpret this evolution. In doing so, I look at the intellectual biographies of the trustees for the poor through the biography of their subject—the progress in their ideas for promoting development in poor countries. This may be best realized through an understanding of the core ideas for development, their translation into policy, and their consequences for development performance.

The most significant period for the study of economic development is the past half century of 1950–2000. Since the end of World War II, the international community has devoted unprecedented efforts to accelerate the development of poor countries, from Afghanistan to Zimbabwe. In 1776, on the threshold of Britain's industrial expansion, Adam Smith offered an optimistic analysis of the "wealth of nations." Now in Latin America, and in the Caribbean, Africa, Asia, and the Middle East, policy makers must still overcome the pessimism that envelops the *poverty of nations*.

The responsibility of being a trustee for the poor weighs heavily when the economist realizes what poor people suffer. Almost 11 million children, most of them babies, die each year—30,000 every day—of preventable causes. Malnutrition causes about 60 percent of the deaths. Life expectancy of the average person in the less developed countries is 20 years shorter than in the more developed countries. Safe water is unavailable to one-fourth of the developing world's people, and 13,000 people die every day from water-related disease. Fifty percent of people in developing countries lack access to basic sanitation. The adult literacy rate in 1998 was 35 percent for males and 59 percent for females in South Asia, and 32 percent for males and 49 percent for females in Sub-Saharan Africa. The average income in the richest 20 countries is 37 times the average in the poorest 20—a gap that has doubled in the past 40 years; more than 80 countries have per capita incomes lower than they were a decade ago. The poorest 20 percent of the world's population account for only 1 percent of world output. World income inequality is high: the richest 1 percent of people in the world in 1993 (50 million people) received as much as the bottom 57 percent (2.7 billion). The statistics of deprivation are voluminous, but even this short list must evoke empathy and compassion.

As the World Bank recognizes, the poor themselves are the true poverty experts. Even more sobering than the statistics of poverty are the studies sponsored by the World Bank entitled *Voices of the Poor*, a series that elicits from over 60,000 poor people their own psychological experiences of powerlessness, lack of voice, and lack of freedom of choice and action.

However, as moving as the statistics and voices are, the responsibility of being a guardian of rationality weighs equally heavily when the economist realizes that the fundamental fact of scarce resources is inescapable; the forces of the market cannot be ignored. The transfer of resources from rich to poor countries must be productively utilized; and the leading international development agency, the World Bank, is, in the words of its former president, Robert McNamara, "not the Robin Hood of the international financial set, nor a giant global welfare agency," but "a development bank using the most sophisticated techniques available to facilitate development while providing unmatched protection and strength for creditors and shareholders." The logic of the economic calculus does not succumb to sentiment.

As trustee for the poor, the economist respects the values of altruism and economic justice. As guardian of rationality, the economist respects self-interest and efficiency—in economic jargon, "rational choice models" and "maximization under constraints." But does not the future course of development depend in large part on the capacity to combine these seemingly incompatible values of the trustee and the guardian? Can the professional developer combine a warm heart with a cool head?

An answer to this question involves a wide consideration of how moral conviction, technical economic analysis, and policy action can shape the course of development. This book's auditing of development thought and experience thus becomes an inquiry into the possibility of change—through vision in ideas and persuasion in policy guidance.

IDEAS FOR DEVELOPMENT

Development studies are essentially problem solving and policy oriented. Ideas for development are therefore not fixed once and for all. As the interpretation of development has widened and become more complex, economists have introduced new concepts and new policy objectives. The subject has not evolved in a linear fashion. As I shall show, changes in the organizing principles of the subject and shifts in development thinking have arisen in response to advances in general economic theory, phases in the political economy of the policy environment, and the lessons of diverse development experiences.

Logical reasoning, model building, empirical data, and country cases shape ideas for development. Development economists in academia concentrate on the economic theory of development. But their words, diagrams, and equations underlie development applications and policy making as practiced by those in government, the World Bank, International Monetary Fund (IMF), United Nations, and nongovernment organizations (NGOs).

In the emergent nations after World War II, the economics of development was initially an economics of discontent—discontent with the old order, discontent with the legacy of colonialism, and discontent with economic dependence. The former colonies became aspiring nations that sought to move the world quickly toward both political and economic equality. Their aspirations were now to meld with the activities of the new international institutions of the World Bank and International Monetary Fund and the efforts of the international development community.

Development, however, cannot come merely from emotional desire. Nor is an economics of resentment against a former colonial relationship equivalent to the type of economics needed to promote development. Economic development cannot be legislated or voted on as can political independence. As countries became independent and as the new international institutions were formed, there arose a need for policy advice on development problems. Economists were called on for such advice. Ideas for development mattered.

But has the economics of development itself developed sufficiently to provide the appropriate policy guidance? Can the economist as advisor offer more than the policy strictures derived from neoclassical economics? In advising nations how to develop, can the economist be more than the guardian of rationality? Can the economist also be a trustee for the poor—solving development policy problems that extend beyond the constraints of conventional neoclassical economics?

The causes of underdevelopment, inequality, and absolute poverty are interrelated, and so too must be policies for their removal. But the guardian of rationality may fear that the trustee for the poor has gone too far in advocating a concern for such policies. Even though John Maynard Keynes maintained that "economics is essentially a moral science and not a natural science," he chided the venerable Cambridge economist Alfred Marshall for being "too anxious to do good." The guardian of rationality may well fear that "anything goes" when the trustee for the poor seeks a "better" income distribution or the provision of basic human needs. The moral fervor of the social reformer who is concerned with objectives and values at the normative level may run away with the scientific discipline at the positive level.

This tension is not new among economists. The positive–normative distinction exists for all economic problems, but a sharp distinction between what "is" and what "ought" to be cannot be readily drawn as long as economics intends to be an applied subject that deals with urgent, real-world economic problems.

Valiant efforts have been made to maintain the distinction for advanced economies, but the distinction is exceedingly difficult to draw for the problems of a developing economy because of the limits of welfare economics, the intrinsic concern with growth and distribution when economists are concerned with development, and the close interconnection of politics and economics in a developing country.

Through the application of welfare economics, economists in developed countries have been able to deal with the normative while maintaining a rigorous, systematic, logically valid discipline. In what would now be an uncharacteristic statement, A. C. Pigou, who was to write the classic *Economics of Welfare* (1920), did not hesitate to say in his inaugural lecture at Cambridge University that the most valuable kind of motivation for the economist was not so much that he might be

> interested by Professor Edgeworth's *Mathematical Psychics* or Dr. Fisher's *Appreciation and Interest*, but rather that he should be possessed by "social enthusiasm"—because he has walked through the slums of London and is stirred to make some effort to help his fellow men. . . . Social enthusiasm, one might add, is the beginning of economic science.

Again, in considering the objective of economic welfare, Pigou declared:

> It is not wonder, but rather the social enthusiasm which revolts from the sordidness of mean streets and the joylessness of withered lives, that is the beginning of economic science. Here, if in no other field, Comte's great phrase holds good: It is for the heart to suggest our problems; it is for the

intellect to solve them. . . . The only position for which the intellect is primarily adapted is to be the servant of the social sympathies.

Pigou's *Economics of Welfare* emphasized forces that affected the production of the "national dividend" and its distribution. But subsequent refinements in welfare economics narrowed the subject considerably. Now desiring to avoid interpersonal comparisons of utility, the "new welfare economics" can say much less about the distribution of income than did the old welfare economics of Pigou. Criteria of "efficiency" still dominate the notion of an economic "improvement." Distributional issues are sidestepped by the condition that a policy that leads to an "improvement" would allow the gainers from the policy to compensate the losers and still leave gainers better off after the "improvement." No welfare weighting according to the distribution of income is given to the measurement of GNP. No greater "social enthusiasm" is expressed for the betterment of the lowest 40 percent of the population who are in absolute poverty than for the top 10 percent who already receive 50 percent of the GNP. Being constricted by the theory of exchange, welfare economics has had little to say about long-term growth and income distribution, and has had little influence on the analysis of development problems.

In its narrow sense, neoclassical economics is primarily devoted to static market conditions of economic efficiency, and an equilibrium is a Pareto equilibrium. Problems of development, however, are dynamic in nature, subject to multiple equilibria, market failures, issues of distribution beyond efficiency, and social-political considerations. As a trustee for the poor, the development economist has to be concerned with growth plus welfare or well-being.

The outstanding welfare economist Nobel laureate John Hicks (1981: xvii), however, concluded that he was "trying to show that 'Welfare economics,' as I would now regard it, is composed of a series of steps, steps by which we try to take more and more of the things which concern us into account. None of our 'optima' marks a top of that staircase. We must always be prepared to push on, if we can, a little further."

Being unable to be shielded by the fig leaf of welfare economics, the development economist has to be exposed to more explicit and forthright policy pronouncements. When growth, underemployment, absolute poverty, and income distribution are of more concern than conditions of efficiency, development economists must be more than guardians of rationality. But they are always restrained from "anything goes" by retaining growth as an indispensable policy objective. Their compassion is constrained by competence. As long as they practice their competence, they will assess alternative policies in terms of trade-offs among objectives. And in doing that, they must exercise the logic of choice—albeit now in terms of social choice and public policy.

As guardians of rationality, economists are concerned with instrumental rationality—that is, how to achieve most economically a given objective. On the given objective, however, they pass no judgment—only the means of achieving the objective are scrutinized in economic terms. What then can the economist say when "economic development" is defined in terms of several objectives—growth in GNP, income distribution, alleviation of absolute poverty, basic human needs, or employment? Might not these objectives conflict? Indeed, they may. A redirection of resources, in the interest of income distribution, may be at the expense of growth in GNP. Or more labor-intensive techniques designed to utilize more labor may reduce the rate of growth. The pursuit of any one of the other objectives may at the same time be at the expense of a higher rate of growth in GNP.

What policy advice can the economist then offer? The economist's sense of instrumental rationality can be cogent in pointing out the trade-offs between the objectives and in indicating how the trade-offs might be avoided or minimized. The achievement of efficient labor-using techniques, for instance, is the economists' responsibility, as they denote techniques that will raise the use of labor input per unit of output without decreasing the productivity of capital. The economist may also indicate that in fulfilling the basic need of education, concentration on primary education may yield higher returns with less reduction in GNP growth. In reformulating development policies, the economist must therefore delineate ever more precisely the various trade-offs that might result from alternative policy instruments.

Because the public sector and public policy making are so prominent in a less developed economy, a nonpolitical economics is unrealistic. When political economy gave way to economics, it did so at a time when the interconnections and interdependencies between politics and economics were at an all-time low. This was far different from conditions now prevalent in the less developed countries. If a strongly developed market economy already exists, if the economy's organizational framework is in place, if a well-developed price system is a given—if these conditions exist, then the role of government will be correspondingly diminished, and political and ethical issues will not be of so much concern. But these conditions are not fulfilled in many of the less developed countries (LDCs). In these countries, the very process of attempting to establish market institutions and a more refined price system is in itself a political and ethical undertaking.

In the mix of politics and economics, therefore, the larger problems of political economy and the old growth economics are again being raised by the challenge of development. The challenge to the contemporary economist, in turn, is now to analyze these problems with the more rigorous techniques of modern economics.

It was not until the 1950s that development economics emerged as a special subdiscipline of economics. Lauchlin Currie (1967: 30–31) recalls that when he directed the first World Bank country mission to Colombia in 1949, "there were no precedents for a mission of this sort and indeed nothing called development economics. I just assumed that it was a case of applying various branches of economics to the problems of a specific country, and accordingly I recruited a group of specialists in public finance, foreign exchange, transport, agriculture, and so on."

The total in the subject of development, however, was to be more than the sum of the parts. During the 1950s, university courses in development economics multiplied.[5] Development economists began to envisage development as a complex dynamic process of structural change. There was also to be a respect for unique histories of development. A special subdiscipline arose that, while acknowledging a set of basic economic principles, went further in recognizing that their particular application to any one country will depend on the economic structure, institutions, political regime, administrative capacity, and history of the particular country. As Christopher Bliss (1989: 1188) writes,

> those parts of economic theory and method which apply more or less universally (such as the notion of opportunity cost) are among the most useful tools in the subject. However, alone they tell us less than we need in a particular application. To give them life they have to be enlarged and translated. When this is done a specialty is created. Development economics consists in part of the refinement of general economics to deal with questions which arise in the context of development, and partly of certain special ideas which have proved useful in studying developing countries.

Against the background of 50 years of development thought, the overriding theme now is that the creation and implementation of ideas are fundamental to understand and guide the development process. No formula exists for development. Aid alone cannot yield development. As a former chief economist of the World Bank (and now president of Harvard) observed,

> more than ever before, the central priority for the World Bank ... is to create and help implement improved strategies for economic development. These strategies must rely, to a greater extent than before, on the transfer and transformation of knowledge, so as to compensate for the expected paucity of development assistance. ... To put it bluntly, since there will not be much development money over the next decade, there had better be a lot of good ideas. (Summers 1991: 2)

Recognizing that the knowledge gap between rich and poor countries is as significant as the savings gap or foreign exchange gap, the World Bank's 1998/99 *World Development Report* was devoted to the theme "knowledge for development." Another chief economist of the Bank also observes:

> One of the major ways in which less developed countries are separated from more developed countries is by their level of knowledge. Successful development thus entails not only closing the gap in physical or even hu-

man capital, but also closing the gap in knowledge. That is why the World Bank is increasingly thinking of itself as a Knowledge Bank, not just a bank for facilitating the transfer of capital to developing countries. It is not just knowledge of production processes that matters; good institutions and policies are an essential ingredient of successful development efforts. One feature of good institutions and policies is that they not only facilitate the transfer of knowledge, but also enhance the likelihood that such knowledge will be used effectively. (Stiglitz 1998b: 11)

Further, a growth economist also claims

that ideas should be our central concern. . . . [I]deas are extremely important economic goods, far more important than the objects emphasized in most economic models. In a world with physical limits, it is discoveries of big ideas, together with the discovery of millions of little ideas, that make persistent economic growth possible. Ideas are the instructions that let us combine limited physical resources in arrangements that are ever more valuable. (Romer 1992: 64)

Development economics is unlike a natural or physical science in which the latest theory is necessarily the most valid and the "best." Although progress in ideas for development does replace earlier ideas and does refine old ideas, nonetheless some ideas of an earlier period might still be more relevant than current ideas. For some development issues, the earlier analysis by an Adam Smith can still be relied on by a present-day Amartya Sen. As the subject evolves, its continuity and differentiation are both important.

We therefore begin the next chapter with a review of the heritage of classical growth economics and its early contribution to the subject of development. In that and subsequent chapters, we consider how development economists have tried to understand the forces of development and design appropriate policies in support of these forces. Our overall objective is to examine the interplay between economic thought and development policy and relate the evolution of development thought and policy to the achievements and disappointments in the development record. In so doing, this biography of the subject should be of value from both a retrospective and prospective viewpoint.

2

The Heritage of Classical Growth Economics

Development as a subject entered mainstream economics only some 50 years ago. Its major ancestors, however, were the classical economists of the eighteenth and nineteenth centuries—Adam Smith, Thomas Malthus, David Ricardo, J. S. Mill, Karl Marx. Following the emergence from feudalism of the nation state, the Enlightenment of the eighteenth century, and the extension of science, technology, and industrialization, the classical economists were concerned with the "progressive state"—economic growth.[1] After World War II, development economics as a policy-oriented subject was to expand beyond the growth economics of the classicists, but some of the old insights formed a background for the new subject.

SMITH AND THE PROGRESSIVE STATE

Why the classical interest in growth? Let the first word be from Smith's *Enquiry into the Nature of Causes of the Wealth of Nations* (1776).[2]

> It is in the progressive state, while the society is advancing to the further acquisition, rather than when it has acquired its full complement of riches, that the condition of the labouring poor, of the great body of the people, seems to be the happiest and the most comfortable. It is hard in the stationary, and miserable in the declining state. The progressive state is in reality the cheerful and the hearty state for all the different orders of society. The stationary is dull; the declining melancholy. (Smith 1776: bk. 1, ch. 8)

Smith denotes more specific objectives of development when he writes that the objects of "Political Economy, considered as a branch of the science of a statesman or legislator" are "first, to provide a plentiful revenue or subsistence for the people, or more properly to enable them to provide such a revenue or subsistence for themselves; and secondly, to supply the state or commonwealth with a revenue sufficient for the public services" (Smith 1776: bk. 4, introduction).

With his emphasis on the "progressive state," Smith—for the first time in the history of economic thought—adopts production per head, as distinct from aggregate production, as the central criterion of development. "According . . . as this produce, or what is purchased with it, bears a greater or smaller proportion to the number of those who are to consume it, the nation will be better or worse supplied with all the necessaries and conveniences for which it has occasion" (Smith 1776: 1: 1).

Smith maintained an optimistic outlook on the progressive state. Not only would it be for the professor of moral philosophy "the cheerful and hearty state," but one could identify and promote various sources of growth that would support the "progress of opulence." According to Smith, the level of output per head, together with its growth, "must in every nation be regulated by two different circumstances: first, by the skill, dexterity, and judgment with which its labour is generally applied; and secondly, by the proportion between the number of those who are employed in useful labor, and that of those who are not so employed. (Smith 1776: 1: 1).

Smith's concern with rising per capita income was partly for its own benefit and partly as a means of encouraging population expansion and consequently the extension of the productive or capitalist sector of the economy. As Hollander comments (1973: 254), expansion of the productive sector, in turn, was recommended in part because of the productivity advantages of large scale, and in part because of the desirable social and personal characteristics engendered in the capitalist sector.

It is a misreading of classical economics to believe that the central problem of the classicists was to demonstrate the conditions of "allocative efficiency." As Myint (1948: 87) explained:

> The nature and significance of the classical welfare analysis cannot be fully appreciated except by considering it against its proper background of the man-against-nature conception of the central economic problem. . . . It now becomes clear that the principal welfare objective of classical economics is to attain a continuous state of economic expansion, rather than to "tighten" up the equilibrium allocation of resources within a given static framework. This of course follows from the view that the welfare of society, as measured by the measuring rod of labour, may be regarded as being roughly proportional to the volume of output and economic activity. The allocative approach accepts given labour supply, capital equipment, and technique as data and tries to make the best of them to satisfy given consumers' preferences. The classical economists, on the other hand, accepted land as given; they believed that instead of accepting the rest of the data as given, far-reaching additions to the welfare of society can be made by changing these data into component parts of an expanding framework, even if it entails interfering with the given time preferences of individuals. . . . Hence the entire classical economic policy was primarily directed towards the attainment of the ideal "balance of production and consumption."

In a similar vein, Hicks (1966: 258) observes that

> The "static" state of mind . . . was not original to economics. It was itself
> the product of an evolution. . . . The modern growth theorist does find stuff
> that interests him in Adam Smith and Ricardo, such as he does not find in
> Marshall and Marshall's contemporaries. It is fair to say that classical eco-
> nomics is actually, from one aspect, an Old Growth Economics, which has
> something of the same relation to modern Growth Economics as Greek
> geometry to modern mathematics. In the neoclassical epoch, it was just put
> to bed.

When Smith called his work *An Inquiry into the Nature and Causes of
the Wealth of Nations*, he began a type of an inquiry that economics, ever
since that day, has been committed to—namely, the search for "laws" or
generalizations, on the basis of which we can assert something about the
cause of events (Hicks 1979: 9). Smith sought the "why" of growth and
by implication the policies for growth.

According to Smith, the major sources of growth or the causes of
growth are (1) growth in the labor force and stock of capital (machinery
and equipment), (2) improvements in the efficiency with which capital
is applied to labor through greater division of labor and technological
progress, and (3) foreign trade that widens the market and reinforces the
other two sources of growth.

Smith assigned a major role to capital accumulation or investment in
the growth process. For capital is the main determinant of "the number
of useful and productive laborers" who can be set to work. Labor is "put
into motion" by capital. Capital accumulation allows population and the
labor force to increase, provides workers with better equipment, and,
most important, makes possible a more extensive division of labor. Capital accumulation therefore serves to increase both total output and output per worker (labor productivity). An economy's rate of progress is
proportional to its rate of investment: more investment leads to more
employment and output, and faster growth in living standards.

> When we compare, therefore, the state of a nation at two different periods,
> and find, that the annual produce of its land and labor is evidently greater
> at the latter than the former, that its lands are better cultivated, its manu-
> factures more extensive, we may be assured that its capital must have in-
> creased during the interval between those two periods. (Smith 1776: 343)

Underlying the process of capital accumulation is thrift or saving—
Smith's stipulation that "the exchangeable value of the annual produce"
must exceed "that of the annual consumption." "Capitals," he says,

> are increased by parsimony and diminished by prodigality and miscon-
> duct. Whatever a person saves from his revenue he adds to his capital, and
> either employs it himself in maintaining an additional number of produc-
> tive hands, or enables some other person to do so, by lending it to him for
> an interest, that is, for a share of the profits. As the capital of an individual

can be increased only by what he saves from his annual revenue or his annual gains, so the capital of a society, which is the same with that of all the individuals who compose it, can be increased only in the same manner. (1776: bk. 2, ch. 3)

What is saved is then invested, provided that a "neat or clear profit" can be earned: "Every prodigal appears to be a public enemy, and every frugal man a public benefactor" (Smith 1776: 340). But even though wages exceed subsistence in a progressive state, the margin is hardly sufficient to allow saving by laborers. Most of the addition to a nation's capital stock must therefore originate with "undertakers" (businessmen) or with landlords. In the Smithian trade-off between growth and equity, the national product could not be raised while at the same time giving the poor a larger share. A rise in the share of profits was the key to increasing the saving rate, and security of property is necessary for capital accumulation.

As for the policy of forcing savings through taxation by the state, Smith gave no support to this. Indeed, public prodigality was considered the enemy of private parsimony. "Great nations are never impoverished by private, though they sometimes are by public prodigality and misconduct. The whole, or almost the whole public revenue, is in most countries employed in maintaining unproductive hands." In contrast, Smith believed that capital accumulation would proceed most rapidly when capital was "employed in the way that affords the greatest revenue to all the inhabitants of the country, as they will thus be enabled to make the greatest savings." Such employment would result when investors were left free to invest according to their self-interest in seeking the best attainable returns. It was "the highest impertinence and presumption, therefore, in kings and ministers . . . the greatest spendthrifts in the society . . . to pretend to watch over the economy of private people" (Smith 1776; bk. 2, ch. 3).

Considering "the different employments of capitals," Smith emphasized the differential employment-generating capacities of investment in agriculture, manufacturing, and trade of various kinds:

When the capital of any country is not sufficient for all those three purposes, in proportion as a greater share of it is employed in agriculture, the greater will be the quantity of productive labour which it puts into motion within the country; as will likewise be the value which its employment adds to the annual produce of the land and labour of the society. After agriculture, the capital employed in manufactures puts into motion the greatest quantity of productive labour, and adds the greatest value to the annual produce. That which is employed in the trade of exportation has the least effect of any of the three. (Smith 1776, bk. 2, ch. 5)

This sectoral ranking of investment seems to derive from the influence of the physiocrats, with their emphasis on the singular importance of agriculture. Although the analysis may appear muddled,[3] Smith did not want to encourage manufacturing at the expense of agriculture.

Classical economists also viewed education and the growth of knowledge as a form of investment.[4] Smith classified "the acquired and useful abilities of all the "inhabitants or members of society" as one of the forms of fixed capital.

> The acquisition of such talents by the maintenance of the acquirer during his education, study, or apprenticeship, always costs a real expense, which is a capital fixed and realized, as it were, in his person. Those talents, as they make part of his fortune, so do they likewise of that of the society of which he belongs. The improved dexterity of a workman may be considered in the same light as a machine or instrument of trade which facilitates and abridges labour, and which, though it costs a certain expense, repays that expense with a profit. (Smith 1776: bk. 2, ch. 1)

Once begun, the growth process becomes self-reinforcing in the progressive state. As long as the growth in wealth (GNP) favors profits, there are savings and additional capital accumulation, hence further growth. And with capital accumulation, the demand for labor rises, and the growing labor force is absorbed in productive employment.

Smith attributed overwhelming importance to the division of labor, in the broad sense of technical progress: "It is the great multiplication of the productions of all the different arts, in consequence of division of labour, which occasions, in a well-governed society, that universal opulence which extends itself to the lowest ranks of the people." The division of labor entails improved efficiency of labor, and increasing specialization leads to rising per capita income. By increasing the division of labor, improvements in production would reduce the amount of input per unit of output.

> This great increase of the quantity of work, which, in consequence of the division of labour, the same number of people are capable of performing, is owing to three different circumstance; first, to the increase of dexterity in every particular workman; secondly, to the saving of the time which is commonly lost in passing from one species of work to another; and lastly, to the invention of a great number of machines which facilitate and abridge labour, and enable one man to do the work of many. (Smith 1776: bk. 1, ch. 1)

Smith also emphasized that the extent of the division of labor is limited by the extent of the market. "When the market is very small, no person can have any encouragement to dedicate himself entirely to one employment, for want of the power to exchange all that surplus part of the produce for his own labour, which is over and above his own consumption, for such parts of the produce of other men's labour as he has occasion for" (Smith 1776: bk. 1, ch. 3).

An increase in the division of labor improves productivity, and this in turn widens the market, which enables the division of labor to be carried further forward. An increase in buying power through a rise in average income and numbers would enlarge the division of labor, and this enlargement would further expand buying power. This view of the progressive and cumulative changes associated with increasing division of labor is the basis for Smith's optimism with regard to economic growth.

Smith's analysis became dynamic when he recognized that "the annual produce of the land and labour of any nation can be increased in its value by no other means, but by increasing either the number of its productive labourers, or the productive powers of those labourers who had before been employed"—and this, in turn, depends not only on the extent of the market but also the supply of capital (Smith 1776: bk. 2, ch. 3). Because an inadequate supply of capital limited the division of labor, Smith's distinction between "productive" and "unproductive" labor led him to conclude that growth of capital depended on the most extensive use of funds in the employment of productive labor.

Accordingly, he based his encouragement of agriculture on the superior productivity of capital when combined with land. This conformed to his contemporary mid-eighteenth-century experience of agriculture being the main source of Britain's growth. Smith did recognize however, that at a later stage of development when "there is either no uncultivated land, or none that can be had upon easy terms, every artificer who has acquired more stock than he can employ in the occasional jobs of the neighborhood, endeavours to prepare work for more distant sale" (Smith 1776: 359). That is, the profit rate in manufactures for foreign trade would then exceed that in agriculture or manufactures for the home market.

Although Smith argued that in a closed economy the size of the nonfarm population depends on the size of the agricultural surplus, he recognized that in an open economy, the towns are no longer limited by the size of the domestic agricultural surplus; they can import and export instead, leaving it to the agricultural community to do the same. This opportunity, "though it forms no exception from the general rule, has occasioned considerable variations in the progress of opulence in different ages and nations" (Smith 1776; bk. 3, ch. 1). The constraint on a country's growth is thus shifted from the size of its agricultural surplus to its potential foreign exchange earnings (Lewis 1988: 29).

Some passages in the *Wealth of Nations* may be interpreted as suggesting that agriculture is in some absolute sense "advantageous." But the agricultural emphasis should not be exaggerated: Smith recognized that there can be too much agricultural investment as well as too little, as his discussion of the interdependence between country and town indicates. Moreover, Smith certainly did not exclude industrialization in favor of agriculture but recommended that while industrialization should proceed in landed states, it should do so only in "due time" and not by artificial government interventions (Hollander 1973: 291).

Analysis of the distributions of means also relates to the classicists' concern with the changing relationship between agriculture and industry. To the classicists, the relation to the means of production defined the classes of society—capitalists, laborers, and landlords. The task of political economy was not only to illuminate the process of national economic development but also to explain how in the course of a country's development its national income is distributed in the form of profit for capital, wages for labor, and rent for landlords. If capital accumulation was the fundamental force in development, profit was the key to capital accumulation.

How do the relative income shares change as development proceeds? And why can the dynamic process of development terminate in a stationary state? Considering first a recently settled region, rich in natural resources, Smith postulates a high rate of profit because the capital stock is small in relation to resource opportunities. Furthermore, because the rate of capital accumulation is then high, wage rates are also relatively high. But as more capital is accumulated, the rate of profit falls. Finally, as the population grows, and the capital stock becomes very large, the economy attains "that full complement of riches which the nature of its soil and climate, and its situation with respect to other countries, allowed it to acquire" (Smith 1776: 94–95). When the economy reaches this state, the rate of capital accumulation slackens, and, therefore, wages decline, but rents have become relatively high as more land has been brought into use. A stationary state is ultimately reached in which investment ceases.

In David Ricardo's analysis, capitalists also play the major dynamic role. In undertaking production, they rent land from the landlords, provide the laborers with fixed capital, and advance as wages the circulating capital consumed by the workers during the production period. A rate of profit above zero encourages capitalists to save a portion of their income and to hire additional workers in order to expand production. If the wage rate is assumed to be initially at its "natural" price, the addition of the savings to the wages fund causes the wage rate to be bid up above its "natural" price. Population then increases, the price of food rises, rents rise, and the real wage rate eventually returns to its customary, near-subsistence level. But in money terms, the wage rate is higher because the prices of agricultural commodities are higher, and this implies that the rate of profit is lower. Ricardo recognizes that technological improvements can mitigate the downward pressure on the rate of profit. But he contends that, in mature economies, the profit rate is eventually squeezed in agriculture and manufacturing. Again, as in Smith, the lower profit rate curtails investment, and the rate of growth in national income declines. Finally, when the rate of profit is too low to afford adequate compensation for the trouble and risk involved in capital accumulation, the economy becomes stationary. Rents are then high, the real wage rate is at its minimum, and the profit rate is near zero.

Paul Samuelson (1978: 1416) has formalized the classical, long-run theory by noting that just as the classicists had a long-run horizontal supply curve for the subsistence wage, "so they had a long-run horizontal supply curve for capital at the *minimum-effective rate of accumulation*, that profit rate just low enough and just high enough to cause capital to be *maintained* with zero net algebraic saving."

The pessimistic outcome of the stationary state in classical economics depends, however, on two assumptions: historical diminishing returns and the Malthusian principle of population. Fortunately, subsequent history has belied both assumptions, and the dismal science has had to defer to the classicists' initial optimism of the progressive state.

INTERNATIONAL TRADE AND DEVELOPMENT

Classical economists gave special attention to how the gains from trade contribute to growth. The gains from trade take several forms. As an extension of the division of labor on an international scale, Smith viewed overseas trade as a way to allow a country to purchase goods more cheaply:

> It is the maxim of every prudent master of a family, never to attempt to make at home what it will cost him more to make than to buy. . . . What is prudence in the conduct of every private family, can scarce be folly in that of a great kingdom. If a foreign country can supply us with a commodity cheaper than we ourselves can make it, better buy it of them with some part of the produce of our own industry, employed in a way in which we have some advantage. (1776: bk. 4, ch. 2)

Smith also viewed foreign trade as providing a "vent-for-surplus":

> When the produce of any particular branch of industry exceeds what the demand of the country requires, the surplus must be sent abroad, and exchanged for something for which there is a demand at home. Without such exportation, a part of the productive labour of the country must cease, and the value of its annual produce diminish. The land and labour of Great Britain produce generally more corn, woollens, and hardware, than the demand of the home-market requires. The surplus part of them, therefore, must be sent abroad, and exchanged for something for which there is a demand at home. It is only by means of such exportation, that this surplus can acquire a value sufficient to compensate the labour and expence of producing it. (bk. 2, ch. 5)

> In every period, indeed, of every society, the surplus part both of the rude and manufactured produce, or that for which there is no demand at home, must be sent abroad in order to be exchanged for something for which there is some demand at home. (bk. 3, ch. 1)

In another passage, Smith relates the vent-for-surplus phenomenon to the gains from trading on a wider market:

> Between whatever places foreign trade is carried on, they all of them derive two distinct benefits from it. It carries out that surplus part of the produce of their land and labour for which there is no demand among them, and brings back in return for it something else for which there is a demand. It gives a value to their superfluities, by exchanging them for something else, which may satisfy a part of their wants, and increase their enjoyments. By means of it, the narrowness of the home market does not hinder the division of labour in any particular branch of art or manufacture from being carried to the highest perfection. By opening a more extensive market for whatever part of the produce of their labour may exceed the home consumption, it encourages them to improve its productive powers, and to augment its annual produce to the utmost, and thereby to increase the real revenue and wealth of the society. (1776: bk. 4, ch. 1)

In recognizing the significance of the width of the market, Smith also presents a productivity theory of trade. If growth in productivity is due to the division of labor, which, in turn, is limited by the extent of the market, then trade on world markets has the advantage of enabling a small country to overcome the diseconomies of small size.

Smith's vent-for-surplus theory of international trade differs from Ricardo's comparative cost theory. In his two-country, two-commodity, one-factor (labor) model, Ricardo demonstrated that under conditions of free trade, a country will specialize in the production and export of those commodities for which its costs are comparatively lowest, and will import commodities it can produce only at high relative cost. The cost of "indirectly producing" imports through specialization on exports is less than if the country directly produced the importables at home. In following its comparative advantage, each country maximizes output (imports) per unit of input (exports). The welfare result, according to Ricardo, is that "the extension of foreign trade . . . will very powerfully contribute to increase the mass of commodities, and therefore, the sum of enjoyments." And these gains from trade will accrue to each trading nation: trade is symmetrically beneficial.

Smith's vent-for-surplus theory contrasts with the Ricardian analysis in two ways: first, the comparative cost theory assumes that a nation's resources are given and fully employed before the nation enters international trade. After being opened to trade, the country faces a new set of relative prices on world markets and reallocates its given resources more efficiently between expansion of export production and contraction of domestic production. In contrast, according to the vent-for-surplus theory, the country enters into international trade with surplus productive capacity over domestic consumption requirements. The function of international trade then is not to reallocate given resources but rather to provide the new effective demand for the output of surplus resources that would have remained unutilized without trade. Export production can thus be increased without reducing domestic production; exports become a virtually costless means of acquiring imports and expanding domestic activity. This was how Smith used the theory to support free trade.

Ricardo formulated his theory of comparative advantage to provide a persuasive case for free trade in order to secure repeal of the Corn Laws. He wanted this policy outcome not simply because it would reduce the price of food so as to increase "the mass of commodities and, sum of enjoyments"—the static gains from trade—but because it would also re-distribute income from landowners, who absorb their rents in luxury consumption, to capitalists, who save and invest. If the wage good (food) could be kept low through free trade, profits could be high, savings and investment increase, and economic growth in Britain could accelerate as the capitalist sector expanded.

Regardless of their various interpretations of the gains from trade, the classical economists agreed that all the trading countries benefit from free trade. And the gains are not only the static gains of efficiency as in the Ricardian model but also dynamic gains of growth.

Smith's productivity theory of trade—based on his dictum that "the division of labor is limited by the extent of the market"—links devel-opment to international trade by interpreting trade as a dynamic force based on economies of scale.

John Stuart Mill noted that trade according to comparative advantage results in a "more efficient employment of the productive forces of the world," and this is to be considered the "direct economical advantage of foreign trade. But there are, besides, indirect effects, which must be counted as benefits of a high order" (1848: vol. 2, bk. 3, ch. 17, sec. 5). One of the most significant "indirect" benefits, according to Mill, is "the tendency of every extension of the market to improve the processes of production. A country which produces for a larger market than its own, can introduce a more extended division of labour, can make greater use of machinery, and is more likely to make inventions and improvements in the processes of production."

Further, Mill observed that another result "principally applicable to an early state of industrial advancement" is that

> the opening of a foreign trade, by making [people] acquainted with new objects, or tempting them by the easier acquisition of things which they had not previously thought attainable, sometimes works a sort of industrial revolution in a country whose resources were previously undeveloped for want of energy and ambition in the people: inducing those who were sat-isfied with scanty comforts and little work, to work harder for the gratifi-cation of their new tastes, and even to save, and accumulate capital, for the still more complete satisfaction of those tastes at a future time. (1848: vol. 2, bk. 3, ch. 17, sec. 5)

Or again, "it is hardly possible to overrate the value in the present low state of human improvement, of placing human beings in contact with persons dissimilar to themselves, and with modes of thought and action unlike those with which they are familiar. . . . Such communication has always been and is peculiarly in the present age, one of the primary sources of progress" (Mill 1848: vol. 2, bk. 3, ch. 17, sec. 5).

Mill also emphasized that trade benefits the less developed countries through

> the introduction of foreign arts, which raises the returns derivable from additional capital to a rate corresponding to the low strength of accumulation; and the importation of foreign capital which renders the increase of production no longer exclusively dependent on the thrift or providence of the inhabitants themselves, while it places before them a stimulating example, and by instilling new ideas and breaking the chain of habit, if not by improving the actual condition of the population, tends to create in them new wants, increased ambition, and greater thought for the future. (1848: vol. 1, sec. 1, ch. 13)

Given the gains from trade, any restriction on free trade should therefore be generally opposed. As Smith argued, the "mean and malignant" trade regulations of the earlier mercantilist system should be disbanded in favor of trade liberalization that would widen the extent of the market and promote growth.

Only a few exceptions to free trade—under limited conditions—were recognized. Smith acknowledged "defence before opulence." But while the infant industry case for protection had appeal for some, Smith rejected it on the grounds that it would retard capital accumulation and fail to maximize current national income: "the immediate effect of every such regulation is to diminish its revenue, and what diminishes its revenue is certainly not very likely to augment its capital faster than it would have augmented of its own accord, had both capital and industry been left to find out their natural employments" (1776: bk. 4, ch. 2). And again: "No regulation of commerce can increase the quantity of industry in any society beyond what its capital can maintain. It can only divert a part of it into a direction into which it might not otherwise have gone; and it is by no means certain that this artificial direction is likely to be more advantageous to the society than that into which it would have gone of its own accord" (bk. 4, ch. 2).

In answer to Smith, however, John Rae argued that "individuals, as well as nations, acquired wealth from other sources than mere saving from revenue . . . skill is as necessary, and consequently as valuable a co-operator with the industry of both as either capital or parsimony." Nonetheless, Rae cautions that the legislator

> is never justified in attempting to transfer arts . . . from foreign countries to his own, unless he have sufficient reason to conclude that they will ultimately lessen the cost of the commodities they produce, or are of such a nature, that the risk of waste to the stock of the community from a sudden interruption to their importation from abroad, is sufficiently great to warrant the probable expense both of the transfer and of maintaining the manufacture at home. (1834: 61, 367)

Mill also recognized the infant industry exception.

> The superiority of one country over another in a branch of production often
> arises only from having begun sooner. . . . A country which has . . . skill and
> experience yet to acquire may in other respects be better adapted to the
> production than those which were earlier in the field. . . . But it cannot be
> expected that individuals should, at their own risk, or rather to their certain
> loss, introduce a new manufacture, and bear the burden of carrying it until
> the producers have been educated up to the level of those with whom the
> processes are traditional. A protecting duty, continued for a reasonable
> time, might sometimes be the least inconvenient mode in which the nation
> can tax itself for the support of such an experiment.

Nonetheless, after witnessing the abuses of protection, Mill said: "I
am inclined to believe that it is safer to make it [infant industry support]
by an annual grant from the public treasury, which is not nearly so likely
to be continued indefinitely, to prop up an industry which has not so
thriven as to be able to dispense with it" (Robbins 1968: 15).

MARKET AND STATE

If for the classicists the market was to determine a free trade strategy, so
too were the domestic forces of competition and the virtues of the capitalist sector to limit the role of government in national development
policy. To Smith, the system of natural liberty permits change and development, while government intervention would handicap the positive
forces of growth. Enjoying the "obvious and simple system of natural
liberty," individuals should be free to act on "their propensity to truck,
barter, and exchange one thing for another" and to pursue self-interest.
Competition and market forces would act as an invisible hand to bring
self-interest into harmony with public interest.

> As every individual, therefore, endeavors as much as he can both to em-
> ploy his capital in the support of domestic industry, and so to direct that
> industry that its produce may be of the greatest value; every individual,
> necessarily labours to render the annual revenue of society as great as he
> can. . . . He generally, indeed, neither intends to promote the public interest,
> nor knows how much he is promoting it . . . he intends only his own gain,
> and he is in this, as in many other cases, led by an invisible hand to pro-
> mote an end which was no part of his intention. (1776: bk. 4, ch. 2)

Yet Smith did not simply assume a "spontaneous" identity of interest
and did not rely merely on "competition" in the abstract but instead
went beyond this to evaluate the effectiveness of different institutional
forms in enforcing the identity of self-interest and public interest (Rosenberg 1994: 59). Recognizing that individuals are also influenced by
certain impulses, motivations, and behavior patterns that could thwart,
rather than reinforce, the beneficent operation of market forces, Smith

gave considerable attention to specifying the institutional conditions under which a competitive market system would operate most effectively. Robbins (1952: 56) puts it well:

> in the classical system of economic freedom, the invisible hand which guides men to promote ends, which were no part of their intention, is not the hand of some god or some natural agency independent of human effort; it is the hand of the lawgiver, the hand which withdraws from the sphere of the pursuit of self-interest those possibilities which do not harmonize with the public good. There is absolutely no suggestion that the market can furnish everything; on the contrary, it can only begin to furnish anything when a whole host of other things have been furnished another way.

The ideal institutional order would allow the individual to behave with maximum industry and efficiency when the reward for effort is neither too low nor too great (monopolists, large landowners). Further, institutional arrangements should not allow income to be pursued without contributing to the public interest. This principle underlay Smith's attack on mercantilism. He condemned that system for its dispensation of monopoly grants, the arbitrary bestowal of "extraordinary privileges," and the "extraordinary restraints" put on different sectors of industry through government policies.

Smith therefore sought the establishment of appropriate institutions that would increase both the motivation and the capacity of the human agent (Rosenberg 1960: 560–561). For example, he opposed apprenticeship laws that diminished the incentive to industry and hard work, advocated certain systems of land tenure, argued that the ideal unit of agricultural organization is the small proprietorship, and opposed the joint-stock company.

Given his critique of mercantilism, Smith advocated that individuals should be freed from governmental policy that had the distortionary effects of limiting capital formation, using capital unproductively, conferring monopoly privileges, and sapping the vitality of competitive forces. Public spending should be kept to a minimum, and production in the public sector should be limited to that small share that could not be supplied by private enterprise. Narrowly restricting the activities of government, Smith declared that the sovereign's duties were limited to defense, administration of justice, and the maintenance of certain public institutions and certain public works (1776: bk. 4, ch. 9). According to Smith, "little else is requisite to carry a state to the highest degree of opulence from the lowest barbarism, but peace, easy taxes, and a tolerable administration of justice."

Smith was especially emphatic in criticizing any state allocation of investment:

> What is the species of domestic industry which his capital can employ, and of which the produce is likely to be of the greatest value, every individual, it is evident, can, in his local situation, judge much better than any states-

man or lawgiver can do for him. The statesman, who should attempt to direct private people in what manner they ought to employ their capitals, would not only load himself with a most unnecessary attention, but assume an authority which could safely be trusted, not only to no single person, but to no council or senate whatever, and which would nowhere be so dangerous as in the hands of a man who had folly and presumption enough to fancy himself fit to exercise it. (1776: bk. 4, ch. 2)

David Hume, however, had argued in *A Treatise on Human Nature* (1739) that a large number of individuals might find it impossible to agree to execute a project of public interest, but "political societies" may accomplish what individuals cannot:

Thus, bridges are built, harbours opened, ramparts raised, canals formed, fleets equipped, and armies disciplined, everywhere, by the care of government, which, though composed of men subject to all human infirmities, becomes, by one of the finest and most subtle inventions imaginable, a composition which is in some measure exempted from all these infirmities. (1739: bk. 2, p. 304)

Smith too saw as a major responsibility of government the provision of certain public works of such a nature that "the profit could never repay the expense to any individual or small number of individuals, and which it therefore cannot be expected that any individual or small number of individuals should erect or maintain" although "they might be in the highest degree advantageous, to a great society" (1776: bk. 5, ch. 1, pt. 3). His examples are of transport infrastructure—roads, bridges, canals, and harbors.

Not only did Smith limit governmental activities but he also promulgated a strong principle for the guidance of public administrators: "Public services are never better performed than when their reward comes only in consequence of their being performed, and is proportioned to the diligence employed in performing them" (1776: bk. 5, ch. 1, pt. 2). The diligence, of course, was to be directed, to only a restricted set of public duties that met Smith's criteria for the proper role of the state.

As for agriculture, this too should be free of government policies except insofar as the provision of public works might benefit agricultural development. Selective forms of taxation on the rents of landlords were also advocated to encourage landlords to take a more "active part in agriculture."

If capital accumulation, division of labor, and foreign trade are sources of a nation's economic growth, then growth can be promoted through the extension of market institutions and the activity of competition. Competition promotes economic evolution. Growth is enhanced by competition that extends the division of labor and expands markets, hence leads to the establishment of new trades. Technological development is promoted by expanding markets that facilitate the further exploitation of technology, land, and improvements in machinery and in techniques of production. The strategic class that is to be the agent of development comes from society's middle and lower ranks, which stand to benefit most. Not to a few creative entrepreneurs innovating in a bold manner did Smith look for his agents of change. Instead, economic change is primarily the product of a vast number of minor changes introduced by a multitude of comparatively small "undertakers."

To appreciate Smith's emphasis on the market in *The Wealth of Nations*, it is important to recognize that the market was not a static conception for the analysis of value and distribution: instead it was to be conceived in a dynamic sense (Robbins 1968: 101). In supporting the division of labor, free markets also promote invention and improvement; and, if economic freedom allows opportunities to be pursued, the force of self-interest disturbs existing equilibria and promotes progress.

Slight, if any, attention, however, was given to the process by which markets actually arise. The classicists focused their main attention on the spontaneous elements in economic society—on the way in which the private interests of individuals guided by the impersonal mechanisms of the market achieved an orderly system of social cooperation and some of the prerequisites of economic growth. "They saw markets and the organization of production arising, like language itself, without any act of conscious collective choice. They saw the main influences which bring about economic development operating without central initiative" (Robbins 1968: 161).

Within his own system of thought, Smith's optimistic view of development might be justified. But Smith wrote before the Reverend Thomas Malthus raised the specter of population outstripping the supply of resources. Smith did not worry about population. In Smith's progressive state, the demand for labor is increasing, and the supply of labor is increasing, but with a time lag, so that an expanding economy was likely to be associated with rising real wage rates.

Nor did Smith believe that machinery would displace labor. The introduction of machinery was regarded as a complement of, rather than a substitute for, labor. Indeed, the division of labor depended on a prior increase in the labor supply, and the number of workers also increased with the division of labor. No Malthusian overpopulation, no Marxian reserve army of the unemployed, no Keynesian problem of less than full employment worried Smith. Capital would simply outdistance population in the progressive state. The benefits of growth would be shared by all orders of society. No problem of inequality would arise.

Smith's analysis was also restricted to Western capitalist countries about to enter the Industrial Revolution. Only a few casual references were made to China and India, and then only to illustrate that these countries were either in a stationary state or declining state. Other members of the British classical school of thought were to remain as parochial. But their thought is worth recalling for the ways they extended Smith's analysis of growth.

MALTHUS AND REDUNDANT POPULATION

The doctrine of Thomas Malthus that population could outstrip the means of subsistence was to reduce economics to a dismal science.[5] Without food there could not be population, but food output was believed to be subject to diminishing returns. For growth, there had to be the right balance between agriculture, industry, and public expenditure.[6]

Earlier writers had anticipated Malthus's leading idea, but with the exaggerated emphasis of a simple metaphor Malthus captured the public's attention by arguing that population was actually and inevitably increasing faster than subsistence, and that this was the reason for the misery observed: "Population, when unchecked, increases in geometrical ratio. Subsistence increases only in an arithmetical ratio." He illustrated this by the juxtaposition of the series:

1, 2, 4, 8, 16, 32, 64, . . .
and
1, 2, 3, 4, 5, 6, 7, 8, . . .

for population and food, respectively. The underlying basis for these series is not clearly enunciated (Eltis 2000: 109). That food increases only in an arithmetical ratio is a different view from Malthus's predecessors. Smith did not assume rising costs and diminishing returns in agriculture.

Population had to be kept in line with the supply of food through positive or preventative checks. Only through the operation of "misery and vice" could there be "a strong and constantly operating check on population from the difficulty of subsistence." This was Malthus's view in the first edition of his *Essay on the Principle of Population* (1798). In his second edition (1803), however, he offers an entirely different theory. For now Malthus introduces the prudential check of "moral restraint." (It may be that Malthus discovered from his own experience that a deferment of marriage until the year following the second edition, when he was 38 years old, did not involve either misery or vice.) The possibility of "moral restraint" meant that, given suitable institutions and social habits, the possibility of improvement could not be absolutely denied as under the population specter of the first edition.

Keynes rightly makes a distinction between the first and second editions of the *Essay on the Principles of Population* and points out that, whereas in the first edition the stress is on the *difficulty* of curtailing the supply of labor, in the later editions the emphasis is on the *importance* of curtailing its supply. As Malthus said in the second edition:

> The structure of society, in its great features, will probably always remain unchanged. We have every reason to believe that it will always consist of a class of proprietors, and a class of laborers; but the condition of each, and the proportion which they bear to each other, may be so altered as greatly to improve the harmony and beauty of the whole. It would, indeed, be a melancholy reflection, that, while the views of physical science are

daily enlarging, so as scarcely to be bounded by the most distant horizon, the science of moral and political philosophy should be confined within such narrow limits, or at best be so feeble in its influence, as to be unable to counteract the increasing obstacles to human happiness arising from the progress of population. But however formidable these obstacles may have appeared in some parts of this work, it is hoped that the general result of the enquiry is such, as not to make us give up the cause of the improvement of human society in despair. The partial good which seems to be attainable is worthy of all our exertions; is sufficient to direct our efforts and animate our prospects. (bk. 4, ch. 14)

By "moral restraint" Malthus did not mean deliberate control of conception. By his classification, contraceptive practices amounted not to "moral restraint" but "vice." Other classical economists, however, advocated birth control as the way to emancipation and progress by restraining population growth below the rate of capital accumulation. As Francis Place said in his *Illustrations and Proofs of the Principle of Population* (1822),

If it were once clearly understood, that it was not disreputable for married persons to avail themselves of such precautionary means as would, without being injurious to health or destructive of female delicacy, prevent conception, a sufficient check might at once be given to the increase of population beyond the means of subsistence; vice and misery, to a prodigious extent, might be removed from society, and the object of Mr. Malthus, Mr. Godwin, and of every philanthropic person, be promoted by the increase of comfort and intelligence and of moral comfort, in the mass of the population. . . . It is time that those who really understand the cause of a redundant, unhappy, miserable, and considerably vicious population, and the means of preventing the redundancy, should clearly, freely, openly and fearlessly point out the means.

In addition to dealing with the rate of growth of population, Malthus also emphasized the role of demand in determining the rate of growth. A sufficiently high level of effective demand was necessary to maintain "proportionality" with supply. He maintained that

the three great causes most favourable to production are accumulation of capital, fertility of soil, and inventions to save labour. They all act in the same direction; and as they all tend to increase supply, without reference to demand, it is not probable that they should either separately or conjointly afford an adequate stimulus to the continued increase of wealth. (1798: 360)

RICARDO AND THE STATIONARY STATE

The most elegant of the British classical theorists was David Ricardo.[7] Concentrating on three major groups of actors on the economic scene, capitalists, laborers, and landlords, Ricardo analyzed how the relative *income* shares of these three groups—profits, wages, rent on land—vary in the course of the development process.

Capitalists play the key role in the economy. In undertaking production, they rent land from the landlords and provide the laborers with tools and implements of production and advance as wages the food, clothing, and commodities consumed by workers during the production period. They promote development by continually searching for the most profitable investment opportunities, and they reinvest their profits in the accumulation of capital.

Labor is the largest group and is dependent on the capitalists for employment. The wage rate is simply the total amount of funds that capitalists advance to the workers for their maintenance (the "wages fund") divided by the number of workers. There is a certain subsistence real wage, fixed by custom and habit, at which the laborers just perpetuate themselves. If the actual wage rises above this "natural" subsistence real wage, population increases; when going below it, numbers decrease.

As population expands and capital accumulates, the most fertile types of land become more and more scarce. In meeting the higher demand for food, the labor and capital are employed on successively poorer grades of land. This brings about diminishing returns in agricultural output: doubling the inputs of labor, capital, and land will yield less than a doubling of agricultural output. As poorer lands are brought into cultivation, competition among the capitalists for the better grades of land causes a "rent" to be gained by the landlords on the more fertile land. The rent arises when demand exceeds supply, and it is simply a surplus to the landlord. Because land is fixed in amount, the rent cannot induce a larger supply of land: it is a return to the landlord that covers no cost and is merely "that portion of the produce of the earth, which is paid to the landlord for the use of the original and indestructible powers of the soil."

In the classical tradition, Ricardo's analysis assigns overwhelming importance to capital accumulation as the prime force of development. By saving and increasing the wages fund, the capitalists set in motion the forces that increase ouput. Ricardo improves on previous theories, however, by emphasizing how the distribution of income affects the development process, and how the distributional pattern is, in turn, a consequence of development.

As discussed earlier, Ricardo also demonstrates how, under a free trade regime, the pattern of international trade would be based on each country's comparative advantage, with each country specializing in its most efficient production. His celebrated example of Portugal trading wine for cloth from England demonstrates that there are mutual gains from trade for all trading nations if the principles of division of labor and specialization are followed internationally. Each trading country—whether primary producing or industrial—enjoys a higher real income.

The game of trade is not zero sum but of benefit to each trading country. There is a natural harmony of interests under free trade.

Ricardo's analysis is also notable for envisioning the dynamic evolution of the economy, ultimately culminating in the advent of the stationary state. The process takes place in the following manner. Capitalists save a portion of their income and invest it when they recognize profit opportunities. The rate of capital accumulation is governed by the ability to save and the will to save. The ability depends on the amount of the economy's surplus—that is, the difference between the value of all commodities produced minus the value of the commodities needed to just sustain the labor force that produced this output. The larger this surplus or "net income," the greater the means to save. Thus, "out of two loaves I may save one, out of four I may save three." The will to save will be determined by the prospects for profit, and

> while the profits of stock are high, men will have a motive to accumulate. ... The farmer and manufacturer can no more live without profit, than the laborer without wages. Their motive for accumulation will diminish with every diminution of profit, and will cease altogether when their profits are so low as not to afford them an adequate compensation for their trouble and the risk which they must necessarily encounter in employing their capital productively.

As long as capital accumulates, additional workers are hired. If the wage rate is assumed initially to be at its "natural" subsistence level, the addition of the savings to the wages fund, which already exists for the purpose of hiring labor, causes the wage rate to be bid up above its "natural" price. Initially, "it is probable that capital has a tendency to increase faster than mankind." Gradually, however, the Malthusian population demon takes over. There is a greater demand for agricultural commodities that are produced under conditions of diminishing returns. Because the price of food rises, the workers are forced to spend more on food to secure their customary standard of living. The real wage rate returns to its customary, near-subsistence level. But, in money terms, the wage rate is higher because the price of food—the major component of the worker's budget—is higher. This implies that the rate of profit is lower, because profits "depend on high or low wages, and on nothing else." As recourse is had to less fertile land, rents also rise on the superior grades of land. Technological improvements and the opening up of new land overseas may for a time mitigate the downward pressure on the rate of profit. But eventually in a mature economy the redistribution in favor of landowners will cause the rate of profit to fall so low that it does not afford the capitalists adequate compensation for their trouble and risk. The rate of growth in national income then ceases. The economy becomes stationary. Rents are high, the real wage rate is at its minimum subsistence level, the profit rate is near zero, no further capital accumulates, population is at a maximum, and total output remains stationary. Such are the characteristics of Ricardo's stationary state—a marked contrast to Smith's progressive state.

MILL AND ANTIGROWTH THEORY

John Stuart Mill, the last and the most popular of the classical economists, sums up the classical interpretation of growth, but he also anticipates the neoclassical view that the progressive, growing economy loses importance if population can be controlled. Unlike Smith and Ricardo, Mill envisages a stationary state that can actually be quite pleasant.

Before Mill's stationary state could be attained, however, there would first have to be a high level of development. And such development was to be achieved through the classical forces of capital accumulation and technical progress.[8]

Steeped in the classical system, Mill devoted himself in his *Principles of Political Economy* (1848) to an analysis of "the nature of wealth, and the laws of its production and distribution, including, directly or remotely, the operation of all the causes by which the condition of mankind ... is made prosperous or the reverse." Again he emphasized capital accumulation, "without which no productive operations beyond the rude and scanty beginnings of primitive industry are possible."

An increase in the amount of capital formation in a country depends on two circumstances: (1) the magnitude of "the produce of industry," or "the amount of the fund from which saving can be made," and (2) "the strength of the disposition to save," since capital is "the product of saving, that is, of abstinence from present consumption for the sake of the future good." "The strength of the disposition to save" depends, in turn, on the rate of profit or return to be made on savings, and upon "the effective desire of accumulation," which reflects the willingness of individuals to sacrifice "a present, for the sake of a future good."

Mill also recognizes that the law of diminishing returns on land can "be suspended or temporarily controlled by whatever adds to the general power of mankind over nature, and especially by any extension of their knowledge, and their consequent command of the properties and powers of natural agents." Drawing a greater distinction than most classicists would between the laws of production and distribution, Mill says that, while the "laws and conditions of the production of wealth partake of the character of physical truths," the distribution of wealth "is a matter of human institution solely. . . . Society can subject the distribution of wealth to whatever rules it thinks best."

Although Mill was officially associated for 35 years with the India Office, his writings about Indian affairs were confined to routine administrative details, and he showed no general concern with problems of development in non-European countries.

Malthus and Ricardo were pessimists about the course of development, but Mill had no reason to look on the future of the masses "as otherwise than hopeful." This was only because he believed mankind was heeding the Malthusian lesson and voluntary birth control would allow capital to win the race against population. Although he too envisioned the emergence of a stationary state, he had none of the misgivings of Ricardo because he had eliminated the specter of overpopulation. To Mill, if population can be controlled, there is no need for the economy to go on expanding in order that wages should be above the subsistence level. If labor is fixed in amount, some of the surplus production can then go to wages. Mill's stationary state represented a state in which a high level of development had been achieved by technical progress and capital accumulation, held at that level by a stationary population. As such, it would actually be an agreeable state—the very objective toward which policy should be aiming.

MARX ON COLONIALISM

The last of the classical economists, Karl Marx worked with classical tools of analysis to lay bare the "laws of motion" of modern society—but after settling in the British Museum Library for some 20 years, he reached conclusions that were completely contrary to the classical tradition.[9] Marx initiated a divergent line of thought, emphasizing the conflict of interests among classes within a country and among nations in the international economy, in contrast with the classical emphasis on harmony of interests within a country and mutual gains from trade in the world economy.

Although based on elements of classical economics, the Marxian theory involves other psychological and sociological assumptions and implies deep structural changes in the evolution of an economy that were not recognized by Marx's predecessors.

Marx argues that capitalism is the most brutalizing and dehumanizing system history has known, but capitalism is still a necessary stage toward final salvation, because only capitalism can create the economic and technological infrastructure that will enable society eventually to liberate its members: "What the bourgeoisie, therefore, produces is, above all, its own grave-diggers." Within a capitalist economy, Marx envisages progressive impoverishment, increasing severity of economic crises, intensification of class war, and the final expropriation of the expropriators and the advent of full communism.

Like other classical economists, Marx's system of thought was also directed essentially to the European world. But he did write about Asia and the implications of colonialism. Marx maintained that the ultimate victory of socialism rested on the prior universalization of capitalism. European colonial expansion must therefore be endorsed as a brutal but necessary step toward this victory. If the horrors of industrialization are dialectically necessary for the triumph of communism in Europe, so too

are the horrors of colonialism dialectically necessary for the world revolution of the proletariat, since without them the colonies will not be
able to emancipate themselves from their stagnant backwardness.
Through the impact of Western bourgeois society, non-European nations
are drawn into the orbit of universal capitalism.

> The need for a constantly expanding market for its products chases the
> bourgeoisie over the whole surface of the globe. It must nestle everywhere,
> settle everywhere, establish connexions everywhere.

> The bourgeoisie has through its exploitation of the world-market given a
> cosmopolitan character to production and consumption in every country.
> . . . All old-established national industries have been destroyed or are daily
> being destroyed. They are dislodged by new industries, whose introduction
> becomes a life and death question for all civilized nations, by industries
> that no longer work indigenous raw material, but raw material drawn from
> the remotest zones; industries whose products are consumed, not only at
> home, but in every quarter of the globe. In place of the old wants, satisfied
> by the products of the country, we find new wants, requiring for their
> satisfaction the products of distant lands and climes. In place of the old
> local and national seclusion and self-sufficiency, we have intercourse in
> every direction, universal interdependence of nations. And as in material,
> so also in intellectual production. The intellectual creations of individual
> nations become common property. National one-sidedness and narrow-
> mindedness become more and more impossible, and from the numerous
> national and local literatures there arises a world literature.

> The bourgeoisie, by the rapid development of all instruments of produc-
> tion, by the immensely facilitated means of communications, draws all,
> even the most barbarian, nations into civilization. The cheap prices of its
> commodities are the heavy artillery with which it batters down all Chinese
> walls, with which it forces the barbarians' intensely obstinate hatred to
> foreigners to capitulate. It compels all nations, on pain of extinction, to
> adopt the bourgeois mode of production; it compels them to introduce
> what it calls civilisation into their midst, i.e., to become bourgeois them-
> selves. In one word, it creates a world after its own image.

> The bourgeoisie has subjected the country to the rule of the towns. It has
> created enormous cities, has greatly increased the urban population as
> compared with the rural, and has thus rescued a considerable part of the
> population from the idiocy of rural life. Just as it has made the country
> dependent on the towns, so it has made barbarian and semi-barbarian
> countries dependent on the civilised ones, nations of peasants on nations
> of bourgeois, the East on the West. (Marx 1848, ch. 1)

The costs of colonialism were to be endured because they paved the
way to eventual emancipation. The introduction of private property and
of industrial production were to be welcomed as the foundations for the
transition to communism. Imperialism is, according to Marx, the highest
stage of capitalism. Not, however, as Lenin maintained, because it must

lead to a world war that will ultimately destroy capitalism and lead victors and vanquished alike into socialism, but because there is no chance for socialism to emerge unless its foundations are first laid down by capitalism itself.

> England it is true, in causing a revolution in Hindustan, was actuated only by the vilest interests, and was stupid in her manner of enforcing them. But that is not the question. The question is: can mankind fulfill its destiny without a fundamental revolution in the social state of Asia? If not, whatever may have been the crimes of England, she was the unconscious tool of history in bringing about that revolution.

> The bourgeois period of history has to create the material basis of the new world—on the one hand the universal intercourse founded upon the mutual dependence of mankind, and the means of that intercourse; on the other hand the development of the productive powers of man and the transformation of material production into a scientific domination of natural agencies. Bourgeois industry and commerce create these material conditions of a new world in the same way as geological revolutions have created the surface of the earth.[10]

Considering Britain and India, Marx maintained that Britain had a "mission" to perform. The British mission was twofold: "the annihilation of old Asiatic society, and the laying of the material foundations of Western society in Asia." In pursuing this mission, Englishmen were the unwitting instruments of history. The "moneyocracy" shut out India's finished textiles from British markets, and the "millocracy" flooded India with products of Britain's power looms. "British steam and science uprooted, over the whole surface of Hindustan, the union between agriculture and manufacturing industry." But there was no turning back to the misconceived idealism of traditional village life. Ultimately, Britain's intervention in India would sow the seeds of its own destruction.

Later the followers of Marx departed from his unusual view of colonialism. Lenin (1916) in particular saw imperialism as capitalism in that state of development in which the dominance of monopolies and finance capital has established itself; in which the division of the world among the international trusts has begun; and in which the division of all territories of the globe among the great capitalist powers has been completed.

The Marxists argue that, at this point in the development of mature capitalist countries, the forces of stagnation become more acute in the form of a low rate of profit and chronic overproduction. The older industrial countries therefore turn increasingly to stimulation of the foreign trade sector to postpone their final destruction. The export of capital to emerging areas overseas, where the rate of profit is higher, becomes significant in the attempt to offset the tendency toward stagnation. This also becomes a means for encouraging the export of commodities that relieves the pressures of overproduction at home.

According to the Marxist view, further domination of the poorer countries by the advanced capitalist countries accompanies the export of capital. There are resistances to be overcome within these areas if foreigners are to find profitable outlets and to exploit the people. Each capitalist power also desires to exclude competition from other capitalist nations. The governments of the great powers therefore intervene and forcibly create conditions favorable to the process of exploitation. In all this, the people of the poorer regions do not benefit. On the contrary, traditional habits and customs are destroyed; handicraft industries are wiped out by cheap manufacturing imports; and the masses are stripped of their means of production. In short, "finance capital and the trusts are increasing instead of diminishing the differences in the rate of development of the various parts of world economy" (Lenin 1916: 194).

THE STATIC PERIOD

In the 1870s, there was a definite shift in the main current of economic thought—away from the classical economist's vision of an evolving economy, which was thought to progress in a dynamic fashion as a result of cumulative forces, to the neoclassical economist's preoccupation with the static allocation of given resources at a given period of time. This shift was primarily the result of the successful realization of growth: with real wages considerably above the subsistence level and rising, the rate of profit high, and technological and resource discoveries continuing to outstrip population growth, there was no fear of the advent of a stationary state. Short-run problems came to the fore.

W. S. Jevons, Carl Menger, and Leon Walras supported the marginal revolution. By 1871, in his *Theory of Political Economy*, Jevons could dismiss "the doctrine of population" because "it forms no part of the direct problem of Economics." Instead, he defined the "great problem of Economy" as follows: "Given, a certain population, with various needs and powers of production, in possession of certain lands and other sources of material: required, the mode of employing labour which will maximize the utility of the produce" (1879: 289).

Focusing on the search for the conditions of efficiency in utilizing existing resources in the economy, economists totally ignored economic growth as a policy objective for several decades, from about 1870 to the 1930s. The theory of value and resource allocation dominated economic thought. Economic action became the exercise of the logic of choice. Price became the coefficient of choice par excellence, showing the rate at which one commodity could be exchanged for another. In maximizing the satisfaction from consumer choice, or minimizing the cost of the producer's choice, the economist became the guardian of rationality. Economic analysis concentrated on the conditions that would make possible various optima rather than on the conditions that would allow an economy to achieve ever-changing optima of ever-increasing range. Not the movement of aggregate output in the entire economy, but the movement of particular lines of production toward an "equilibrium" position became the neoclassicist's concern. To tighten up the economy and avoid inefficiency was the neoclassicist's objective. Rigorous analysis of individual markets and of price formation was the neoclassicist's hallmark.

One price, however, brought the neoclassicist close to growth problems—the rate of interest. The return to loanable funds is a price that connects the present with the future. It becomes relevant in dealing with the choice between consumption and investment, between present consumption and future consumption, or the willingness to sacrifice present satisfactions for future satisfactions. Because the rate of interest determines the rate of saving and also the rate of investment, it is for the neoclassical economist the key price in the subject of capital accumulation.

For the most part, however, neoclassical writers shortened their time horizon as they considered interrelationships among the various sectors of the economy at a particular moment of time, the determination of prices, the operation of markets, and the distribution of income. In the static world of the neoclassicist, history drops out, time becomes irrelevant, past and future are identical. The subject is the static allocation of resources, not the dynamic growth of an entire economy.

This static interlude of neoclassical economics continued for about seven or eight decades until the end of World War II. During that period, neoclassical economics was in too narrow a groove to incorporate the problems of development.

A minor stream of writing, however, did exhibit some interest in the less developed countries during the neoclassical interlude—the writing on colonial economics. But these writings were only too often little more than descriptive travelogues, without the analytical span of the earlier growth economists. Also influenced by the neoclassicists, many of the books on colonial economics and the multitude of official reports on colonial policy were devoted to fragmentary topics on economic organization, the workings of markets, and the formation of prices. Although cultural anthropologists and sociologists were more at home in their study of colonial societies, their noneconomic observations were not blended into the works of the economists. No indigenous economics arose during the colonial period.

Another feature of much writing on colonial policy was what the Nobel laureate Gunnar Myrdal called "the colonial theory"—apologetic writing attempting to absolve the colonial regimes from responsibility for the state of underdevelopment. Tropical climate, population pressure, lack of resources, or values and institutions that made the people unresponsive to opportunities for improving their incomes and living standards were all frequent excuses for the lack of development in colonial economies.

The static approach and "the colonial theory" were both to end as decolonization occurred after World War II. Nationalist demands of the infamous period were fulfilled in the postwar period, and imperialism and colonialism were in full retreat.

Areas that had been considered "rude and barbarous" in the eighteenth century, "backward" in the nineteenth century, and "underdeveloped" in the prewar period now became the "less developed countries" or the "poor countries" also the "emergent countries" and "developing economies." The international community, national governments, and finally academic institutions all rose to the challenges of promoting development.

3

Early Development Institutions

The institutional context for development activities began to be established soon after the end of World War II. Political motives were mixed, but the core economic objective was to improve living standards in the less developed countries.

The problems of development were thrust upon these institutions by the breakup of colonial empires in Asia and Africa. In the brief span of five years after the war, India, Pakistan, Ceylon, Burma, the Philippines, Indonesia, Jordan, Syria, Lebanon, and Israel all became independent. Colonialism was on the way out far more speedily than had first seemed possible at the end of the war, and many more colonies soon emerged as nations. With the "revolution of rising expectations," leaders of the new nations insisted that international attention be given to their development problems.

BRETTON WOODS ORDER

During the war, President Franklin D. Roosevelt had proclaimed the "Four Freedoms," including "freedom from want . . . everywhere in the world," as postwar objectives of the Western allies. Winston Churchill and Roosevelt also promulgated the Atlantic Charter, which promised the "assurance that all men in all the lands might live out their lives in freedom from fear and want." The United Nations Charter pointed to the goal of colonial emancipation and emphasized among its objectives the promotion of "higher standards of living, full employment, and conditions of economic and social progress and development."

The most important institutional progress came in 1944 when Roosevelt invited delegates from 44 member countries of the United Nations to "a quiet meeting place" in Bretton Woods, New Hampshire, where they were to spend three weeks establishing the most significant international economic institutions of the postwar period—the International Monetary Fund and the International Bank for Reconstruction and Development (World Bank). The Fund was designed to mitigate balance-of-payments problems and provide stability in international monetary affairs. The World Bank was to support investment in productive projects in countries recovering from the war and in need of development support.

It seems clear from the membership that the Bretton Woods conference was called primarily to establish the IMF; the World Bank was a distinctly secondary issue. Only relatively few LDCs, mainly independent nations of Latin America, were invited. The political power lay with the United States and Britain, and from the outset it was apparent that issues of development were not to be on the Bretton Woods agenda.

Of the countries invited to Bretton Woods, Lord Keynes (1980) could write in a dispatch to the British Treasury:

> Twenty-one countries have been invited which clearly have nothing to contribute and will merely encumber the ground, namely, Colombia, Costa Rica, Dominica, Ecuador, Salvador, Guatemala, Haiti, Honduras, Liberia, Nicaragua, Panama, Paraguay, Philippines, Venezuela, Peru, Uruguay, Ethiopia, Iceland, Iran, Iraq, Luxemburg. The most monstrous monkey-house assembled for years. To this might perhaps be added: Egypt, Chile and (in present circumstance) Yugoslavia.

At Bretton Woods, the developing countries tended to view themselves more as new, raw-material-producing nations and less as countries with general development problems. Comprehensive strategies of development and policies to accelerate national development were yet to be identified. The Brazilian, Colombian, Cuban, and Bolivian delegations expressed concerns about "fluctuations in the prices of primary products. ... orderly marketing of staple commodities ... and implementation of international commodity agreements."

By the end of the Bretton Woods Conference, however, Keynes told the British public on the BBC evening news:

> There has never been such a far-reaching proposal [as that of the Bank] on so great a scale to provide employment in the present and increase productivity in the future. We have been working quietly away in the cool woods and mountains of New Hampshire and I doubt if the world yet understands how big a thing we are bringing to birth.

The Bank was to begin operation with capital subscribed by its member countries, subsequently financing its lending operations primarily from its own borrowings in the world capital markets. The Bank's charter stated that it must lend only for productive purposes and must stimulate economic growth in the countries where it lends. It must pay due regard to the prospects of repayment. Each loan is to be made to a government or must be guaranteed by the government concerned. The use of loans cannot be tied to purchases in any particular member country. Moreover, the Bank's decisions to lend must be based on only economic considerations.

To stabilize international monetary conditions, the articles of the IMF charter provided that member states are subject to a core of obligations that the Fund administers with respect to foreign exchange rates and currency arrangements. The Fund was also to receive subscriptions of members in their own currencies and gold, and these resources were to be made available to other members to assist them to meet short-term, balance-of-payments difficulties while observing the code of obligations. But initially the promotion of development was not a direct purpose of the Fund. Indeed, a fundamental principle of the Fund was its uniformity principle—namely, all countries would be treated the same with no special and differential treatment for less developed countries.

A third international institution was envisaged to complement the Fund and the Bank—the International Trade Organization (ITO), which was discussed by representatives of 53 nations in Havana, Cuba, in 1947. As proposed in the Havana Charter, the ITO was to govern trade barriers, but in addition it contained a chapter on "economic development and reconstruction," covering private foreign investment, infant industries, and other issues of concern to primary producing countries. Another chapter dealt with intergovernmental commodity agreements, and another focused on restrictive business practices.

Political delays had made the ITO subordinate to consideration of the Fund and Bank. The ITO also proved more controversial in content because it covered in detail a whole range of commercial policies that went beyond mere tariff reductions. At Havana, the LDCs differed with the more developed countries on provisions for international commodity agreements, state trading, cartels, and restrictive business practices.

The General Agreement on Tariffs and Trade (GATT) was originally designed to serve as a temporary expedient until ratification of the Havana Charter. But the ITO met congressional opposition in America and was never born. The GATT became the narrower substitute, becoming permanent in 1955. When the ITO did not absorb the GATT, the "economic development and reconstruction" chapter of the Havana Charter became moot. In its initial provisions, the GATT did relieve less developed countries of some obligations. The Agreement referred specifically to the type of country "the economy of which can only support low standards of living and is in the early stages of development." Such a country was offered the privileges of withdrawing a tariff concession, increasing tariff rates to permit protection of an infant industry, and invoking quota restrictions on imports "in order to safeguard its external financial position and to insure a level of reserves adequate for the implementation of its program of economic development." Under the latter provision, the developing countries were able to follow import substitution programs and to protect their domestic industries through quotas imposed under the guise of balance-of-payments support.

The GATT did not allow, however, as much special treatment for developing countries as they had sought through the Havana charter. The controversial issue of allowing different trade rules for countries according to their different stages of development has persisted. The request for special and differential treatment for less developed countries again became prominent in the U.N.'s call for a New International Economic Order during the 1970s, the succession of the World Trade Organization (WTO) to the GATT, and in current debates over the impact of globalization, as will be discussed in chapter 10.

Together, the IMF, the World Bank, and the GATT formed the outlines of a rudimentary international public sector. Purposive action was to be taken to attain the multiple objectives of full employment, freer and expanding world trade, and stable exchange rates. But of what direct benefit were these postwar institutions to be for the newly developing countries?

The formation of the United Nations in 1945 added the demand for economic independence to the newly found political independence of former colonies. The emergent nations in the U.N. became aspiring nations that sought to move the world quickly toward both political and economic equality among nations. Their aspirations were now to meld with the aspirations of the new international institutions and the efforts of the international development community.

The U.N. not only passed resolutions relating to development but also established the UNDP for aid activities and the United Nations Conference on Trade and Development (UNCTAD) for proposals on foreign trade and foreign investment. The specialized agencies of the U.N. and the regional economic commissions also became increasingly active in promoting programs of development. Most prominent was the Economic Commission for Latin America (ECLA), organized in 1948. The ECLA turned to intensive studies of Latin American economies with the aim of "programming their future development."[1]

EARLY U.N. REPORTS

During the period 1949–51, three important reports were issued by groups of experts under United Nations auspices. The first—*National and International Measures for Full Employment* (1949)—stemmed mainly from the desire to prevent a recurrence of the Great Depression of the 1930s. Nonetheless, it was also a force for economic development since it advocated international investment for development purposes and urged an extension of activities of the IMF and the World Bank.

The second report—*Measures for the Economic Development of Under-Developed Countries* (1951)—addressed squarely the special problems of the developing world and considered what obstacles had to be overcome and what "missing components" had to be supplied in order to promote development.[2] The report emphasized the accumulation of physical capital, stating:

> It is a commonplace that economic progress is a function, among other things, of the rate of new capital formation. In most countries where rapid economic progress is occurring, net capital formation at home is at least 10% of the national income, and in some it is substantially higher. By contrast, in most underdeveloped countries, net capital formation is not as high as 5% of the national income, even when foreign investment is included. In many of these countries, the savings have been sufficient only to keep up with population growth, so that only a negligible amount of new capital, if any, has actually become available for increasing the average standard of living. How to increase the rate of capital formation is therefore a question of great urgency. (U.N. Dept. of Economic Affairs 1951: 35)

Considering various domestic measures for mobilizing resources for capital formation, the report recognized the existence of surplus labor. "In many underdeveloped areas, the population on the land is so great that large numbers could be withdrawn from agriculture without any fall in agricultural output and with very little change of capital techniques. If this labor were employed on public works, capital would be created without any fall in other output, or in total consumption" (U.N. Dept. of Economic Affairs 1951: 41).[3]

The third report—*Measures for International Economic Stability* (1951)—called attention to "the special difficulties of the poorer underdeveloped countries" (13). It advocated international action to reduce the vulnerability of underdeveloped economies to fluctuations in the volume of trade, to promote a larger flow of international capital, to maintain steady development programs, and to reduce fluctuations in the prices of primary products.[4]

NATIONAL GOVERNMENTS

The United Nations group of experts recommended as early as 1951 that the "government of an underdeveloped country should establish a central economic unit with the functions of surveying the economy, making development programs, advising on the measures necessary for carrying out such programs, and reporting on them periodically. The development programs should contain a capital budget showing the requirements of capital and how much of this is expected from domestic and from foreign sources" (U.N. Dept. of Economic Affairs 1951: 93).

Development programs, national planning boards, and industrial development corporations soon proliferated. Interrelated with the Bretton Woods institutions and aid agencies was the early practice of national development planning. Beginning with India's creation of a central planning commission in 1950, many other developing countries followed suit, desiring the prestige of having a development plan.

Criticizing reliance on the price system, desiring social reform along with development, and stressing the pervasiveness of the obstacles to development, the governments of poorer countries became more attracted to central planning than had ever been the case in the historical experience of the now advanced Western nations. Governments of emergent nations commonly turned to national planning as if this were itself a precondition for development. In Thailand, an official considered "economic planning a matter of necessity rather than choice." And the prime minister of Trinidad claimed from his long experience that "even if a politician in a developing country came into office without intending to plan, he would soon have to invent planning or something very similar."

Planning was also stimulated by the desire to receive external assistance from public international lending agencies. Many plans were prepared with the assumption that a certain percentage of the proposed investment in the plan would be financed from abroad, and requests for aid were presented accordingly. Calculations of the amount of external assistance needed were frequently presented in terms of the necessity of overcoming the shortage in domestic resources to achieve targets of a development plan. Some donors also attempted to promote better planning to coordinate investment activities. Some aid programs, such as the Alliance for Progress in Latin America, during the 1960s, stressed the desirability of national economic planning as an important means of devising self-help measures.

The economist's tool kit also provided some modern techniques that could support the formulation of a development plan—especially input-output analysis, dynamic programming, and simulation of growth models. These techniques provided tests for the consistency, balance, and feasibility of plans. Frequently, visiting missions and foreign advisors cooperated with local planning agencies in producing analyses and policy recommendations underlying development plans. It was not uncommon for groups of "eminent experts" to demonstrate the potential of the economist's techniques for planning. For instance, the U.N. Economic Commission for Asia and the Far East convened a group of experts headed by the Nobel laureate Jan Tinbergen, who recommended in 1959 that even countries like Nepal, Afghanistan, Burma, and Thailand should try to plan through comprehensive growth models.

So too did the Economic Commission for Latin America vigorously advocate detailed planning. During the 1950s, the ECLA engaged a number of Latin American governments in the techniques of programming as it emphasized "programmed" industrialization and "healthy" protectionism, adequate controls over the use of foreign exchange, and the programming of import substitution.

THE WORLD BANK

After its initial attention to European reconstruction, the World Bank turned in the 1950s to developing counties.[5] The Bank's early emphasis was on financing projects for physical infrastructure. Under a set of loan-processing procedures known as the "project cycle," the Bank undertook phases of identification, preparation, appraisal, and supervision.[6] This was a rather mechanistic approach, dominated by engineers and financial analysts. In the early years, technical and commercial criteria prevailed.

After the mid-1970s, attention was given to sector loans—agriculture and social sectors. In the 1980s institutional focus shifted to "structural adjustment lending"—loans for macro policy reforms.[7] This brought the Bank into stronger policy dialogues with client countries and allowed it to apply some of the macro thinking by development economists (as will be discussed in chapter 4). Before that, however, the Bank was noted for its project lending—not any intellectual contribution to the subject of development.

Indeed, not until the presidency of Robert McNamara (1968–1979) did research receive due attention. His appointment of Hollis Chenery as head of the economics department was a turning point. Chenery was followed by Krueger (1982) to head the Economics Research Staff, and afterward Stanley Fischer, as vice-president of development economics and the bank's chief economist (1988), Lawrence Summers (1991), Joseph Stiglitz (1997), and Nicholas Stern (2000). In their respective periods, each of these brought to the Bank the ideas that dominated development thought (as will be discussed in subsequent chapters).

Chenery's research supported McNamara's emphasis on growth and alleviation of poverty. Two books (Chenery 1979; Chenery, Robinson, and Syrquin 1986) were important studies on cross-country analyses of growth. While the former book focused on country regressions, the later work emphasized structural analysis in contrast with the neoclassical interpretation of the sources of growth. (More on this in chapter 4.)

The book *Redistribution with Growth* (Chenery et al. 1974) followed McNamara's 1973 speech in Nairobi to the Bank's governors. McNamara called world attention to the basic human needs of those in "absolute poverty." He said that although there may always be "relative poverty" in the sense of income differentials, the Bank should focus on those in "absolute poverty" who suffer "a condition of life so degraded by disease, illiteracy, malnutrition, and squalor as to deny its victims basic human necessities." Those in absolute poverty were identified as roughly the lowest 40 percent of individuals living in the LDCs—at that time, about 900 million with an average annual per capita income of less than $100. In trying to reconcile growth with equity, *Redistribution with Growth* emphasized rural development and policies directed to the target poverty groups of small-farm proprietors, their laborers, and tenants, as well as the urban poor.

With the formation of a development economics research unit, Bank economists began to interpret development in a wider dynamic context. The Bank's contribution to the understanding of the economics of development, however, came mainly from its application of new ideas and from its expanding comparative knowledge of policies in practice. Over time, the accumulation of data and empirical studies became most valuable for interpreting the experience of development interspatially and intertemporally.

The research department has brought outside thinking to the operational divisions of the Bank, and has also been instrumental in disseminating knowledge of comparative policy making to the general development community. Although the Bank is not noted for original ideas, "once the Bank gets hold of an idea, financial clout ensures that the idea will gain wide currency" (Gavin and Rodrik 1955: 333).

In its institutional evolution, the Bank has outgrown its initial narrow banking approach and has increasingly taken on the objectives of a "development agency" (under McNamara) and a "knowledge bank" (under the presidency of James Wolfensohn). This has been reflected not only in the Bank's research output but also in the activities of its Economic Development Institute (EDI) (now the World Development Institute) and the annual publication of the World Development Reports (WDRs).

Through its courses and seminars, the EDI became instrumental in disseminating advances in development thought to policy makers in the LDCs. World Development Reports have also focused on prominent issues. Especially notable have been the WDR of 1981 on structural adjustment and the WDRs of 1990 and 2000/2001 on "attacking poverty."

In summarizing his assessment of the Bank's research contribution to the understanding of development, Stern and Ferreira (1997: 609) write:

> The Bank's major intellectual contribution may be regarded as in the application of ideas. This is in large part what the operations side of the Bank tries to do and it exercises considerable intellectual influence in its dialogue on policy as a whole and on projects. . . . In concluding our discussion of the intellectual role of the Bank, or the Bank as an intellectual actor, we must recognize that the Bank has rarely seen itself as primarily an intellectual or academic institution. It sees its job as promoting development. It can use and disseminate ideas and encourage an analytical approach in carrying out its task, but the generation of research ideas is not, in itself, its first priority. We have suggested, however, that it cannot put responsibility for the development of ideas entirely outside its boundaries. It should discharge responsibility for the development of ideas in a direct and creative way. This it has often tried to do, with some success, but after more than twenty years with a research establishment its role as an intellectual creator has been a modest one.

IMF RESOURCES

Although Bank activities have been clearly directed to the development objectives of its members, the IMF was not designed to give any special attention to developing countries and only acquired a development role in the course of its evolution. Originally designed to use its resources only "for monetary stabilization operations," the Fund has come to recognize the interdependence between monetary stabilization and development. The LDCs benefit indirectly if the Fund supports the more developed countries and thereby forestalls balance-of-payments restrictions on imports from LDCs or restrictions on capital exports to developing nations. More directly, in some of its policies on the use of its resources, the Fund has managed to give special consideration to the problems of its less developed member countries by creating special facilities to be used by LDCs.

In 1963, for instance, the Fund established the Compensatory Financing Facility to offer financing for fluctuations in the export proceeds of primary producing countries. Members having a balance-of-payments problem may draw on the Fund under this facility if the Fund is satisfied that the problem that caused the shortfall is a short-term one, that it is largely attributable to circumstances beyond the country's control, and that the country will cooperate with the Fund in an effort to solve its balance-of-payments difficulties.

The Fund also provides the Buffer Stock Facility, which assists in the financing of members' contributions to international buffer stocks of primary products when members with balance-of-payments difficulties participate in these commodity stabilization agreements (tin, cocoa, sugar). Again, the member is expected to cooperate with the Fund in an effort to find appropriate solutions for its balance-of-payments problem.

In addition, the Fund established in 1974 the Extended Fund Facility for countries experiencing slow growth and a weak balance of payments that prevents an active development policy; in 1986 the Structural Adjustment Facility, which was replaced in 1999 by the Poverty Reduction and Growth Facility, designed to integrate poverty reduction with macroeconomic policies; and in 1997, the Supplemental Reserve Facility, after the Mexican and Asian financial crises.

By approving standby arrangements or extended arrangements for the drawing of other countries' currencies from the Fund, the Fund allows a developing country to secure temporarily the foreign exchange it needs while it gains time to deal with its balance-of-payments problems, without having to sacrifice its rate of development. The Fund's approval of a standby or extended arrangement provides not only periodic installments of needed foreign exchange to the member country but also encourages other potential lenders to extend additional resources to the country, as the installments from the Fund are made conditional on a specified performance by the drawing country.

Although India failed in its attempt at the Bretton Woods conference to include a clause that would single out assistance for "the fuller utilization of the resources of economically underdeveloped countries," it is ironic that the Fund's loan of $5.75 billion in 1981 to India was then its largest to date—and for essentially development purposes that would improve the country's balance of payments. It is also noteworthy that in recent years most of the loan commitments by the Fund have been to developing countries.

Although the Fund has adapted its activities to meet unforeseen problems that have arisen in developing countries, many of the LDCs remain disappointed. Greater voting power in the IMF organization, more financial assistance, less onerous conditions for access to Fund resources—these have been persistent demands of the developing countries. Since the 1960s, the Fund has been especially active with respect to the external debt servicing problem of LDCs. Controversy, however, surrounds the policy prescriptions and conditionality that the Fund imposes. As more of the developing countries experienced conditionality, the Fund came to be viewed as excessively orthodox, conservative, and monetarist in its terms. They have found the Fund's stabilization programs to be excessively onerous, often requiring unreasonably heavy deflation or massive devaluation, and insensitive to the income distribution and internal social and political effects that the stabilization policies produce.

Many developing countries would still like to respond to the Arusha Initiative—a call issued by a conference in Tanzania in 1980 for a United Nations conference on international money and finance that "will provide a universal, democratic and legitimate forum for the negotiation of a new monetary system." Although less political and ideological in tone, statements by the Group of 24, a group of ministers from developing countries, also call for international monetary reform. After the Asian financial crisis of the 1990s, there has been more discussion of reform in the international financial architecture. Like the World Bank, the Fund has increasingly recognized its role as catalyst. As the problems of developing countries change, so too must the policies of the Bank and Fund adjust to the changing circumstances. More than through the actual provision of resources, the Fund's effectiveness is determined by the quality of its policy advice and the appropriateness of the adjustment policies that it supports in developing countries. The policy action supported by the Fund determines the future mobilization of domestic resources and encourages other sources of external financing for development. Reliance on the Fund's standby arrangements is of considerable importance in reducing the risk of commercial bank lending to developing countries. From a larger perspective, the role of the Fund in promoting order in international monetary affairs is crucial in enabling developing countries to benefit from more stable growth in world trade and investment. (More on this in chapter 9.)

Further, as has been true for the World Bank, the Fund's experience, undertaking of empirical studies, and practice of problem solving have enhanced the understanding of development—particularly on macroeconomic issues of an open developing economy.

The Fund's research publications and its Staff Papers have contributed to a more extensive knowledge of intercountry policies for stabilization and balance of payments support. The IMF institute has also been effective in providing techniques of analysis and guidance on policy making to many governmental participants from developing countries.

Much more legalistic than the Bank, the articles of the Fund were hailed by the Fund's general counsel as one of the great law-making chapters of the postwar world, with the strength and suppleness to adapt to a world of change.

In comparison with the Bank, the IMF is highly concentrated on its central focus of balance-of-payments adjustment and macroeconomic stabilization, while the Bank's activities are much more varied and complex. The Fund has refined its central mission, while the Bank has extended its concerns to structural adjustment, the environment, gender, and governance. Although somewhat exaggerated, there is some point to Arnold Harberger's observation that "while [the image] of the Fund is like a commercial bank in that there is a single corporate line in dealing with the outside world," that of the Bank "is something like a traveling seminar" (Gilbert and Vines 2000: 72).

ACADEMIC INSTITUTIONS

Beginning early in the postwar period, the most intensive thinking about development has occurred in Universities and research institutes. In the 1950s and 1960s, development thought was fashioned less as a formal theoretical discipline than as a response to the needs of policy makers to advise governments on what could and should be done to allow their countries to emerge from chronic poverty. Development economists went beyond their classical and neoclassical predecessors to consider the kinds of policies that an active state and international institutions could adopt to accelerate growth and reduce poverty. In so doing, their thinking quickly incorporated more economic theory and policy analysis than had that of their predecessors, who had observed colonial economies more through the lens of public administration, anthropology, or history than economics. The earlier study of colonial economics would no longer suffice. Previous courses in colonial economics catered mainly to those working in, or hoping to enter, the colonial service. But World War II disrupted the colonial system and introduced new objectives for emerging countries. In the 1950s, universities began to respond with the introduction of courses in economic development. At the University of Oxford, the change from "colonial studies" to "commonwealth studies" and then to "development studies" provides a microcosm of what was happening generally.[8]

Although his title was initially "lecturer in colonial economics," Hla Myint began lecturing at Oxford on economic development in 1951. His lectures in 1951–52 on the "economics of underdeveloped countries" already showed a quantum leap in the subject beyond colonial economics.

Arthur Lewis was appointed reader in colonial economics at the London School of Economics (LSE) in 1947 and in 1948 went to Manchester University, where he began lecturing systematically on development economics from about 1950.

An informative conference on problems of teaching development economics was held at Manchester University in 1964 (Martin and Knapp 1967). The sessions on the "state of knowledge" indicate early views on research, especially in relation to "Anglo-Saxon economic theories" and the need to incorporate noneconomic variables (administrative, social, political) into development models.

The bibliography compiled by Hazelwood (1954) is indicative of how rapidly the subject of development economics had already gown by 1954. This bibliography covered some 600 books, articles and official publications. A second edition in 1958 grew to 1,027 items, and an additional bibliography confined to English-language publications of the period 1958–62 contained 732 listings.

The number of journals devoted to economic development also expanded rapidly. The Ceylon Economist began publication in 1950; *Economic Development and Cultural Change*, 1952; *Pakistan Economic and Social Review*, 1952; *Indian Economic Review*, 1952; *Indian Economic Journal*, 1953; *Social and Economic Studies* (University of West Indies), 1953; *East African Economic Review*, 1954; *Middle East Economic Papers*, 1954; *Malayan Economic Review*, 1956; and *Nigerian Journal of Economic and Social Studies*, 1959. The number of articles in development theory and development policy as reported in the Index of Economic Articles tripled in the decade between 1950–54 and 1960–64.

An increasing number of centers for research in development problems were founded during the 1950s and 1960s—at MIT, Duke, Stanford, Harvard, Sussex, and other universities.

From the universities and postwar international economic institutions came the first generation of development economists. The next chapter presents the highlights in their thinking about development.

4

Early Development Economics 1: Analytics

When Paul Samuelson first published his leading textbook *Economics* in 1948, it had only three brief—almost parenthetical—allusions to matters of development.[1] Shortly thereafter, the first generation of development economists began to analyze some of the leading issues in the subject of development and to establish the subject's policy orientation. Their studies during the 1950s and 1960s gave rise to development as a special subdiscipline of economics.

LIMITS OF NEOCLASSICAL AND KEYNESIAN ANALYSES

The principles and techniques of economic analysis were not abandoned, but it soon became evident that development economists must frequently depart from traditional assumptions and must alter the premises of accepted economic theory to make their analysis relevant to countries that have social systems and economic structures that differ from those to which Western economists are accustomed. Although a completely new set of tools was not needed, and completely different principles of analysis were not necessary, it was essential to acquire a sense of the different assumptions that are appropriate to analyzing a problem within the context of a poor country. Special care was necessary to identify different institutional relations, to assess the different quantitative importance of some variables, and to allow some elements that are usually taken as "given" in traditional economics to become strategic variables that are determined within the development process itself.

The early development economists could appreciate the heritage of classical growth economics with its emphasis on the variables of capital accumulation, population, and technology. But they questioned the relevance of both the market price system of neoclassical economics and Keynesian economics.

The price system in the less developed country existed in only a rudimentary form: markets were fragmented and localized; market imperfections were pervasive; and there was little range for the sophisticated exercise of the logic of choice as in a well—defined price system. Moreover, large changes in the economy were the very essence of development—not the incremental or marginal changes of neoclassical economics. Substantial transformation in the structure of the economy was needed. A widening of the economy was required—not simply the tightening up of the economy through the application of neoclassical principles of resource allocation. For economists concerned with the larger issues of development, the neoclassical analysis was believed silent.

Even though the University of Chicago's economics department was the stronghold of neoclassical economics, its chairman, Theodore Schultz (1956:372), observed:

> In most poor countries there is not much economic growth to be had by merely taking up whatever slack may exist in the way the available resources are being utilized. To achieve economic growth of major importance in such countries, it is necessary to allocate effort and capital to do three things: increase the quantity of reproducible goods; improve the quality of the people as productive agents; and raise the *level* of the productive arts.

The early development economics also found the Keynesian analysis of national income determination wanting in relevance, since Keynes had been concerned with the unemployment of labor and the underutilization of capital during depressions in advanced industrial countries as a result of oversaving. The cyclical type of unemployment that worried Keynes was not the type of unemployment that pervaded the poor countries. Theirs was a chronic surplus of labor, indicated by not only persistent unemployment but also widespread underemployment, disguised unemployment, and employment with low productivity. Many of the underemployed would be willing to work longer hours if jobs were available. Some in disguised unemployment appeared employed but were actually adding nothing or very little to total output. Many were among the "working poor," laboring long hours but at low-productivity tasks, yielding incomes below a poverty level. The unemployment problem was related to a deficiency of capital—not to too much savings, as in the Keynesian diagnosis of an advanced capitalist economy suffering from a short-run cyclical depression. The Keynesian remedy of increasing aggregate demand was not the remedy for poor countries; their task was to mobilize more savings and increase investment. They were not deficient in investment outlets but in savings—that is, in the availability of real resources.

Moreover, Keynesian analysis was limited to the short period of time. Its assumptions of static conditions violated the very nature of the development process. That process was scarcely Keynes's concern when he said: "We take as given the existing skill and quantity of available labor, the existing quality and quantity of available equipment, the existing technique, the degree of competition, the tastes and habits of the consumer, the disutility of different intensities of labor and the activities of supervision and organization, as well as the social structures."

Keynesian analysis thereby paralyzed from the outset many of the essential variables of the development process. Rejecting neoclassical price analysis and Keynesian income analysis, the development economist sought to establish more relevant principles. The founding director of the Institute of Development Studies at the University of Sussex, Dudley Seers, criticized the dominance of Anglo-Saxon economics with its "special case" of the developed, industrial, private-enterprise economy. To analyze the problems of nonindustrial economies, he thought a major revolution in economic doctrine was essential.

So too did the Nobel laureate Gunnar Myrdal (1957) call on the underdeveloped countries to produce a new generation of economists who might create a body of thought more realistic and relevant for the problems of their countries:

> In this epoch of the Great Awakening it would be pathetic if the young economists in the underdeveloped countries got caught in the predilections of the economic thinking in the advanced countries, which are hampering the scholars there in their efforts to be rational but would be almost deadening to the intellectual strivings of those in the underdeveloped countries. I would, instead, wish them to have the courage to throw away large structures of meaningless, irrelevant and sometimes blatantly inadequate doctrines and theoretical approaches and to start their thinking afresh from a study of their own needs and problems. (103–104)

The views of Seers and Myrdal were too far-reaching. An entirely new subdiscipline of "development economics" did not appear. Instead, modifications and additions were grafted to classical growth economics. The progress that has been made in development economics has actually been mainly within the framework of traditional economic analysis. Although it is recognized that problems of underdevelopment are different in degree—and, to some extent, even in kind—from those encountered in developed countries, nevertheless it has not been necessary to forge entirely different economic tools and apply completely different principles of analysis. Many traditional tools and principles of accepted economic theory proved directly applicable to the problems of poor countries, and some conceptions and techniques could become more useful with some ready-made modification or extension.

In approaching development problems, the early development economists first thought of what "obstacles" to development had to be overcome, and what "missing components" of the development process had to be supplied. If the underdeveloped economy bore some resemblance to the classical stationary state, then the positive forces that classical economists had emphasized as delaying the advent of the stationary state—namely, capital accumulation and technical progress—could now also be emphasized as forces to accelerate development. From the classical tradition, a major obstacle to be overcome was the capital deficiency. And from the viewpoint of missing components, it was necessary to fill the "savings gap" and to foster technical progress. Supply-side economics is not new to the development economist.

The emphasis was on planned investment in physical capital, utilizing reserves of surplus labor, adopting import-substitution industrialization policies, practicing central planning, and relying on foreign aid. Some of their policy proposals were initially shaped by their prior experience with Soviet planning, national economic management during the Great Depression, wartime mobilization of resources, and the postwar Marshall Plan for the recovery of Western Europe.

Given the newness of the subject and its wide scope, however, there were crosscurrents, a variety of perspectives, and vigorous debate over some leading issues. An editorial in *Economic Development and Cultural Change* (1952: 3) lamented:

> Even a casual glance at the existing literature reveals not only the absence of a satisfactory theory but also the absence of agreement as to which of the many problems apparent to the observer are important for study. The research worker seeking pathways to adequate theory finds no blazed trails, but instead a veritable jungle of vicious circles, obstacles to change, and necessary (but never sufficient) preconditions for economic growth.

DUAL SECTOR MODELS

While features of "dualism"—economic and social—were frequently observed in less developed countries that had both a traditional economic system and modern exchange system, a more incisive analysis began with the Nobel laureate Arthur Lewis's famed article (1954) presenting a dual sector model.[2] As Nicholas Stern (the chief economist of the World Bank) has remarked, "this was perhaps the single most influential article in the history of the economics of development and raised a number of crucial issues in a clear and systematic way" (Stern 1989: 624).

Elements of Lewis's model appeared earlier when the Central Secretariat of the Caribbean Commission commissioned two reports from Lewis on the suitability for development of potential Caribbean industries. In 1949 Lewis wrote the article "Industrial Development in Puerto Rico" and in 1950 the article "The Industrialization of the British West Indies." His thesis was that the case for industrialization rests chiefly on overpopulation, in the sense that population is larger than agriculture can absorb and that there is a need to create new opportunities for employment off the land. Surplus labor is relegated to unproductive jobs, and "the way to increase agricultural productivity per man is to provide the jobs that will take the surplus labor off the land." In his 1954 article

"Economic Development with Unlimited Supplies of Labor," Lewis returned to some assumptions of classical growth economics: "The classics
from Smith to Marx, all assumed, or argued, that an unlimited supply
of labor was available at subsistence wages. They then enquired how
production grows through time. They found the answer in capital accumulation." Similarly, Lewis writes:

> The central problem in the theory of economic development is to under-
> stand the process by which a community which was previously saving and
> investing four or five percent of its national income or less, converts itself
> into an economy where voluntary saving is running at about 12 to 15 per-
> cent of national income or more. This is the central problem because the
> central fact of economic development is rapid capital accumulation (in-
> cluding knowledge and skills with capital). (155)

Through the process of capital accumulation, the surplus labor is absorbed into the more productive capitalist sector, and the low-
productivity traditional sector withers away.

Lewis begins by recognizing that most countries in the early stages of
economic development have not one economy but two—a high-
productivity, high-wage economy (composed of mines, plantations, factories, large-scale transport) and a low-productivity, low-earnings economy (composed of family farms, handicraft workers, domestic servants,
petty traders, casual laborers). The surplus labor is mainly in the low-
earnings sector. This sector is characterized by the family mode of production, which makes little use of reproducible capital or wage employment but, instead, uses traditional techniques of production and relies
on self-employment or income-sharing in an extended or joint family
system. Productivity of labor is very low, but each worker shares in the
consumption of the family output.

In contrast, the high-earnings sector is the capitalist sector, which uses
reproducible capital and pays capitalists for its use. The capitalists hire
the services of labor for a money wage, produce an output for sale on
the market, and sell the product at some profit or surplus above the wage
payments. "Capitalist" is used in the classical sense of an enterprise that
hires labor and resells its output for a profit. The capitalist may be a
private enterprise or a state-owned enterprise. The capitalist sector is an
island (or a number of tiny islands) surrounded by a vast sea of subsistence workers.

The dualism is widespread:

> We find a few industries highly capitalized, such as mining or electric
> power, side by side with the most primitive techniques; a few high-class
> shops, surrounded by masses of old style traders; a few highly capitalized
> plantations, surrounded by a sea of peasants. But we find the same con-
> trasts also outside their economic life. There are one or two modern towns,
> with the finest architecture, water supplies, communications and the like,
> into which people drift from other towns and villages which might almost

belong to another planet. There is the same contrast even between people; between the few highly westernized, trousered, natives, educated in Western universities, speaking Western languages, and glorying in Beethoven, Mill, Marx or Einstein, and the great mass of their countrymen who live in quite other worlds. Capital and new ideas are not thinly diffused throughout the economy; they are highly concentrated at a number of points, from which they spread outwards. (Lewis 1954: 147–148)

A fundamental relationship exists between the capitalist and subsistence sectors—when the capitalist sector expands, it draws on labor from the subsistence sector. For countries that have experienced high rates of population growth and are densely populated, the supply of unskilled labor to the capitalist sector is unlimited, in the sense that the supply is greater than the demand at the existing wage rate. A large component of the unlimited supply of labor is composed of those who are in very low-productivity agricultural activities and in other overmanned occupations such as domestic service, casual odd jobs, or petty retail trading. Additional sources of labor are women who transfer from the household to commercial employment, the growth in the labor force resulting from population increase, and immigration. The large pool of unskilled labor—in Marxist language, the "reserve army of the unemployed"—enables new industries to be created or old industries to expand in the capitalist sector without encountering any shortage of unskilled labor and without having to raise wages.

Lewis proceeds to show how capital accumulation in the capitalist sector will draw surplus laborers away from unemployment and underemployment in the subsistence sector into more productive employment in the higher wage capitalist sector. In this dual sector model, the traditional sector withers away as production grows in the capitalist sector through time, while the investment in the capitalist sector absorbs the surplus labor from the traditional sector. The major conclusion from the model is that the rate at which surplus labor will be absorbed in the capitalist sector depends on the size of the capitalist sector and the ratio of profits in national income: the larger the capitalist sector, and the greater the share of profits in national income, the more rapidly will surplus labor be absorbed.

Some details of Lewis's reasoning can be filled in. Tracing the process of economic expansion, Lewis emphasizes that the key to the process is the use made of the capitalist surplus. The driving force in the system is generated by the reinvestment of the capitalist surplus in creating new capital. As the capitalist sector expands, it draws labor from the subsistence sector into wage employment—but at a constant wage rate.

The wage that the capitalist sector has to pay is determined by what labor earns in the subsistence sector. Peasant farmers will not leave the family farm for wage employment unless the new real wage allows them a standard of living equal to or higher than that in the subsistence sector.

Capitalist wages, as a rule, will have to be somewhat higher than subsistence earnings to compensate labor for the cost of transferring and to induce labor to leave the traditional life of the subsistence sector. According to Lewis (1966: 77–78), "economists have usually expected wage rates in the modern sector to be about 50 percent above the income of subsistence farmers. This brings the modem sector as much labor as it wants, without at the same time attracting much more than it can handle."

The amount of labor hired at this wage rate in the capitalist sector depends on its productivity, but, in being utilized with capital, the labor produces an output of greater value than its wage. The value of the total product in the capitalist sector is divided between wages and the capitalists' surplus or profit. In the classical tradition, capitalists save part of their profits, and the savings are reinvested in the capitalist sector. The investment raises the productivity of labor, and the expanding capitalist sector then demands more labor. But the surplus labor can still be hired at the same wage rate, so that out of a new larger total output, the share of profits in national income rises. This will mean, in turn, that savings rise as a share of national income, and so does investment. And as investment increases, so too does the demand for more labor. Eventually, capital accumulation catches up with the surplus labor. At that point, the subsistence sector, with its original supply of surplus labor, will have been absorbed into the modern capitalist sector. After that point, the capitalist must offer higher wages to induce more employment of labor.

This type of dual economy model was at the center of the early development economics. It had considerable appeal because of its essentially optimistic vision of the development process. Earlier, other countries had proceeded through such a process, and the latecomers to development might now begin to do the same. The model would run its course to a happy end—provided no components were missing (such as a capitalist class or a market for the product of the capitalist sector), and no obstacles arose (such as a premature rise in wages that cut into profits). The emphasis on capital accumulation could also fit nicely with other elements of economic thinking about development, and with the practice of development planning. Moreover, promotion of the capitalist sector could be readily identified with the objective of industrialization via import substitution. As a model of what might be, it was able to synthesize the most significant elements of development thought in the 1950s.

More than any other pioneer in development, Lewis established "development economics" as a special discipline with his 1954 article and his *Theory of Economic Growth* in 1955. While simple in its construction, Lewis's dual sector model was rich in perceptive insights and formed the basis for subsequent refinements and extensions in dual sector models by Jorgenson (1961) and Fei and Ranis (1961).

BIG PUSH AND BALANCED GROWTH

Before Lewis emphasized the need to raise the savings ratio and expand the modern capitalist sector, Paul Rosenstein-Rodan had also focused on the need for industrialization to absorb the agrarian "excess population" who were in total or disguised unemployment in the "international depressed areas."

His seminal article in 1943 was "Problems of Industrialization of Eastern and South-Eastern Europe." Rosenstein-Rodan was then studying problems of postwar reconstruction at the Royal Institute of International Affairs.[3] A few years later he was to be the first assistant director of the Economics Department at the World Bank, and later a member of the panel of experts for the Alliance for Progress in Latin America. Foreseeing that the development of the "international depressed areas" of the world would be the most important task in the making of the peace, Rodan emphasized the need for a "big push" in investment to accelerate development. His analysis began by focusing on the pervasiveness of rural underdevelopment—"agrarian excess population"—in the less developed countries. He summarized the problem this way: "Labor must either be transported toward capital (emigration), or capital must be transported toward labor (industrialization)." Emigration was not feasible, so the task fell to industrialization.

The crucial task of a development plan was to achieve sufficient investment to mobilize the unemployed and underemployed for the purpose of industrialization. To reach an "optimum size" for industrial enterprises, however, the area of industrialization must be sufficiently large. Private profit calculations underestimate for the community at large the actual social benefits from an investment. It was believed that production must be integrated and centrally planned as though it were taking place in a single "trust." Complementarity of different industries argues in favor of "a large-scale planned industrialization." Only then would the risk for a single enterprise be reduced, all the benefits of a single investment be calculated, and profit estimates revised upward. State investment is therefore required on a broad front.

Rosenstein-Rodan (1943) thus argued for a "big push":

> The theory of growth is very largely a theory of investment. . . . A minimum quantum of investment is a necessary condition for successful development. . . . Launching a country into self-sustaining growth is a little like getting an airplane off the ground. There is a critical ground speed which must be passed before the craft can become airborne. . . . A big push seems to be required to jump over the economic obstacles to development. There may be finally a phenomenon of indivisibility in the vigor and drive required for a successful development policy. Isolated and small efforts may not add up to a sufficient impact on growth. An atmosphere of development may only arise with a minimum speed or size of investment.[4]

The analytical case for "a scheme of planned industrialization comprising a simultaneous planning of several complementary industries" rests on the need to take advantage of external economies. (Rosenstein-Rodan 1943: 204). The big push could take advantage of pecuniary external economies, which yielded economies of scale. Also the "planned creation of a complementary system reduces the risk of not being able to sell, and, since risk can be considered as cost, it reduces costs, and is in this sense a special case of external economies (206).

Rosenstein-Rodan also appealed to the earlier article by Allyn Young, "Increasing Returns and Economic Progress" (1928) to claim that through a sufficiently large investment program, external economies will become internal profits. Young was concerned with how industries can increase their output without increasing their costs proportionately and how external economies can be generated. Beyond changes in output, "changes of another order are occurring. New products are appearing, firms are assuming new tasks, and new industries are coming into being. . . . [M]ovements away from equilibrium, departures from previous trends, are characteristic of it" (528). Especially illuminating for explaining increasing returns is Smith's famous theorem that the division of labor depends on the extent of the market. "The enlarging of the market for any one commodity, produced under conditions of increasing returns, generally has the net effect . . . of enlarging the market for other commodities" (537). Moreover, the advocacy of a big push emphasized technological external economies, which are not due to indivisibilities but very largely due to the "inappropriability" of the advantages of training, learning on the job, and the "skilling" of labor.

The essence of the argument for a big push is that various investment decisions are not independent and have high risks because of uncertainty about whether their products will find a market. But if investment occurs on a wide front, then what is not true in the case of a single investment project will become true for the complementary system of many investment projects: the new producers will be each other's customers, and the complementarity of demand will reduce the risk of not finding a market. Simultaneous industrialization of many sectors of the economy could be profitable for them all, even though no sector would be profitable industrializing alone. Government therefore needs to coordinate activities in a broadly based investment program to "jump" over the economic obstacles to development.

As in dual sector models and the prescription of a "big push," the need to maximize the marginal saving from output growth was also recognized by those who emphasized "the vicious circle of poverty." Reinforcing Rosenstein-Rodan's "big push" argument was Ragnar Nurkse's analysis of capital accumulation with its emphasis on "balanced growth." Nurkse (1953) began with the simple concept of "the vicious circle of poverty." In Nurkse's words, it implies a circular constellation of forces tending to act and react upon one another in such a way as to keep a poor country in a state of poverty. Particular instances of such circular constellations are not difficult to imagine. For example, a poor man may not have enough to eat; being underfed, his health may be weak; being physically weak, his work capacity is low, which means that he is poor, which in turn means that he will not have enough to eat; and so on. A situation of this sort, relating to a country as a whole, can be summed up in the trite proposition: "a country is poor because it is poor." (4)

For Nurkse (1953: 5), the vicious circle of poverty was most important in explaining the low level of capital accumulation:

The supply of capital is governed by the ability and willingness to save; the demand for capital is governed by the incentives to invest. A circular relationship exists on both sides of the problem of capital formation in the poverty-ridden areas of the world.

On the supply side, there is the small capacity to save, resulting from the low level of real income. The low real income is a reflection of low productivity, which in its turn is due largely to the lack of capital. The lack of capital is a result of the small capacity to save, and so the circle is complete.

On the demand side, the inducement to investment may be low because of the small buying power of the people, which is due to their small real income, which again is due to low productivity. The low level of productivity, however, is a result of the small amount of capital used in production, which in its turn may be caused at least partly by the small inducement to invest.

If only the "low" investment could be turned into "medium" and then into "high" values, all the other variables in the circle would also become "medium" and then "high." But how could this increase in investment be achieved? According to Nurkse (1953: 10), "economic progress is not a spontaneous or automatic affair. On the contrary, it is evident that there are automatic forces within the system tending to keep it moored to a given level." How then can the deadlock be broken?

Nurkse's answer is "balanced growth," the synchronized application of capital to a wide range of industries. Private investment will not be induced in a single line of production taken by itself as long as the market is narrow. Workers do not buy the product they produce in the single line of production. But if there is an overall enlargement of the market, through investment in many industries at the same time, the range of demand will guarantee success for the several investments: "An increase in production over a wide range of consumables, so proportioned as to correspond with the pattern of consumers' preferences, does create its own demand" (1953). But how does an economy achieve balanced growth?

Nurkse's policy advice explained the workings of balanced growth:

A frontal attack—a wave of capital investments in a number of different industries—can economically succeed while any substantial application of capital by an individual entrepreneur in any particular industry may be blocked or discouraged by the limitations of the pre-existing market. Where any single enterprise might appear quite inauspicious and impracticable, a wide range of projects in different industries may succeed because they will all support each other, in the sense that the people engaged in each project, now working with more real capital per head and with greater efficiency in terms of output per manhour, will provide an enlarged market for the products of the new enterprises in the other industries. In this way the market difficulty, and the drag it imposes on individual incentives to invest, is removed or at any rate alleviated by means of a dynamic expansion of the market through investment carried out in a number of different industries. . . . Through the application of capital over a wide, range of activities, the general level of economic activity is raised and the size of the market enlarged. (1953: 13–15)

Nurkse (1958: 171–172) also emphasized that balanced growth was "a means of getting out of the rut, a means of stepping up the rate of growth when the external forces of advance through trade expansion and foreign capital are sluggish or inoperative." Less developed countries could no longer rely on growth that was induced from the outside through the expansion of world demand for their exports of primary commodities. Under conditions of export pessimism, governments should look for other solutions that would expand production for their own domestic markets. Balanced growth was one way to accelerate growth.

Other economists joined Rosenstein-Rodan and Nurkse in emphasizing capital accumulation. Many viewed the poor economy as a stationary economy that needed a stimulus to get it off dead center, just as Nurkse sought to break the vicious circle. Richard Nelson formalized the situation with an analysis of the "low-level equilibrium trap." And Harvey Leibenstein propounded the "critical minimum effort" thesis. If the backward economy is in a stationary state, or subject to a vicious circle of poverty, or in a low-level equilibrium trap, then to achieve the transition from the state of backwardness to the more developed state where we can expect steady growth, it is a necessary condition that the economy should receive a stimulus to growth that is greater than a certain critical minimum size. This is because growth sets up not only income-raising forces but also income-depressing forces such as population growth, declining saving rate, and diseconomies of scale. A critical minimum effort must, therefore, be exceeded so that the income-raising forces surpass the income depressing forces. Again, a considerable amount of investment became identified with the critical minimum effort.

The big push and balanced growth doctrines had little influence on those neoclassical economists who continued to argue that the market mechanism could coordinate the changes needed for development. But it did provide some argument for development planning in the 1950s and 1960s.

A major dissent from balanced growth and its implication of top-down planning, however, came from Albert Hirschman's book *The Strategy of Economic Development* (1958). Hirschman argued for a strategy of unbalanced growth that would promote a few key sectors with forward and backward linkages that would create disequilibrium and then induce decisions in other sectors to correct the disequilibrium. An industry creates a backward linkage when it demands inputs from an upstream industry. Forward linkages reduce the costs of downstream users of the investment's product and ease their supply.

Hirschman focuses on decision making as the principal scarce resource in an underdeveloped economy. "If a country were ready to apply the doctrine of balanced growth, then it would not be underdeveloped in the first place" (1958: 53). Instead of simply assuming that there is the capacity to make the complex decisions necessary to establish balanced growth, Hirschman emphasized the process by which the necessary decision making can be induced by considering development as a chain of disequilibria. Underdeveloped countries need special "pressure mechanisms" or "pacing devices" to bring forth their potential. "Development depends not so much on finding optimal combinations for given resources and factors of production as on calling forth and enlisting for development purposes resources and abilities that are hidden, scattered, or badly utilized" (1958: 5).

> Our aim must be to keep alive rather than to eliminate the disequilibria of which profits and losses are symptoms in a competitive economy. If the economy is to be kept moving ahead, the task of development policy is to maintain tensions, disproportions, and disequilibria. . . . [T]he sequence that leads away from equilibrium is precisely an ideal pattern of development from our point of view: for each move in the sequence is induced by a previous disequilibrium and in turn creates a new disequilibrium that requires a further move. This is achieved by the fact that the expansion of industry A leads to economies external to A but appropriated by B, while the consequent expansion of B brings with it economies external to B but subsequently internal to A (or C for that matter), and so on. At each step, an industry takes advantage of external economies created by previous expansion, and at the same time creates new external economies to be exploited by other operators. (1958: 70)

> The way in which investment leads to other investment through complementarities and external economies is an invaluable "aid" to development that must be consciously utilized in the course of the development process. It puts special pressure behind a whole group of investment decisions and augments thereby that scarce and non-economizable resource of underdeveloped countries, the ability to make new investment decisions. (1958: 73)

Unlike macro models that imply coordinated policy making for comprehensive national planning, Hirschman (1961: ix) emphasized "the dynamics of the development process in the *small*" with the objective of maximizing induced decision making for a sequence of investments that create disequilibria through their forward or backward linkages. Although the focus is "in the small," increasing returns can result from the interaction between market size and economies of scale.

STRUCTURALISM AND DEPENDENCY

If the concepts of a big push, balanced growth, and unbalanced growth were contrary to the implications of pure competition and equilibrium analysis as then presented in the mainstream of neoclassical economics, the conclusions of structuralism were all the more so.

Unlike neoclassicists, who assume a smoothly working market-price system, the practitioners of the structuralist approach attempted to identify specific rigidities, lags, and other characteristics of the structure of developing economies that affect economic adjustments and the choice of development policy. They identified supply bottlenecks that appeared in certain sectors of the economy through imbalances in the productive structure—particularly the supply shortfalls in the agricultural and export sectors.

A principal proponent of structural analysis was Raúl Prebisch, who was the first director of the United Nations Economic Commission for Latin America. In considering the question of the international dissemination of technology and the distribution of its fruits, Prebisch believed that the empirical evidence revealed considerable inequality between the producers and exporters of manufactured goods and those of primary commodities. Seeking an explanation, he emphasized that countries of Latin America formed part of a system of international economic relations that he named the "center-periphery" system. This system left a large part of the population on the sidelines of development. Outward-oriented development based on primary exports was considered to be incapable of permitting the full development of the peripheral countries and would lead only to a deterioration in the primary producing country's terms of trade. "The great industrial centers not only keep for themselves the benefit of the use of new techniques in their own economy, but are in a favorable position to obtain a share of that deriving from the technical progress of the periphery" (Prebisch 1950a: 14). Instead, a new pattern of development based on industrialization via import substitution was advocated. It was believed that import substitution by protection would help correct the tendency toward a foreign constraint on development resulting from the low income and price elasticities of demand for imports of primary product by the centers, compared with the high income elasticity of demand at the periphery for manufactures from the centers (Prebisch 1950a, 1984).

Joining Prebisch in the belief that a secular deterioration in the terms of trade of the less developed countries limited their development was Hans Singer (1950). The Prebisch-Singer thesis of export pessimism underlay ECLA's proposals for "programmed" industrialization via import substitution based on protectionist policies. During the 1950s, the Latin American model spread to other countries in Asia and Africa. The domestic promotion of manufacturing over agricultural and other types of primary production became a central objective in many development plans.

Gunnar Myrdal (1957) also argued against the neoclassical equilibrium theory of international trade, contending that if left to take its own course, economic development is a process of circular and cumulative causation that tends to award its favors to those who are already well endowed and even to thwart the efforts of those who happen to live in regions that are lagging behind. The backsetting effects of economic expansion in other regions dominate the more powerfully, the poorer a country is." Believing that trade in primary products will produce only a polarization effect that is stronger than the spread effect, Myrdal argued that "economic development has to be brought about by policy interferences" instead of through a dependence on international markets that "strengthen the forces maintaining stagnation or regression."

Moreover, the case for inward-looking policies appealed to theories of dependency.[5] These theories contended that the development problems of the periphery are to be understood in terms of their insertion into the international capitalist system, rather than in terms of domestic considerations. Being heavily represented by sociologists and political scientists, "dependencistas" emphasized that peripheral countries were "dependent" in political, social, and economic ways on advanced capitalist nations, as contrasted with more autonomous countries. "Center-periphery" trade is characterized by "unequal exchange." This may refer not only to deterioration in the peripheral country's terms of trade but also to unequal bargaining power in foreign investment, transfer of technology, taxation, and relations with multinational corporations. Instead of trying to replicate European–North American patterns of development and being dependent on disequalizing world markets, the dependencistas argued for the "delinking" of the undeveloped countries from the developed so that there would not be further underdevelopment of the periphery by the developed.

The ECLA writings also claimed that the causes of Latin American inflation were to be found not in excess demand but in particular structural bottlenecks that emerged during the process of development—especially in the supply shortfalls of the agricultural and export sectors. This was opposed to monetarist explanations such as those advanced by the IMF. To structuralists, the inflation was believed to be inevitable, and orthodox monetary measures could suppress it only by stopping the very process of development. Instead it was thought that the structural inflation could be cured by well-devised development programs.

In a sense, the Latin American structuralists returned to elements of the Marxist tradition by emphasizing the analysis of social structures as a way to understand the behavior of economic agents. "The structural distortions of underdevelopment hinder the movement toward a pattern of social organization propitious to authentic development. . . . And this attempt to extend the conceptual framework to include internal and external factors conditioning the decision making process led to the theory of dependence" (Furtado 1987).

The views of structuralists and dependencistas combined in support of development planning. Contending that the major problems of the underdeveloped countries were surplus labor, foreign exchange constraint, and tendency for deterioration of their terms of trade, they believed that these could be ameliorated through a series of government interventions involving controls on trade and foreign investment and government allocation of domestic investment. In addition, the state was to undertake directly productive activities.

5

Early Development Economics 2: Historical Perspectives

Insofar as the development process is a matter of the long run, and LDCs are latecomers to development, it was natural to look to history for lessons of development. Examination of the growth experience of a variety of countries first concentrated on trends in population and national output. It also incorporates an examination of analytics.

SPECIAL STUDIES

The demographic transition was identified as a prominent feature during the transformation of a society from a traditional to a modernized society. Societies pass from a phase of low population growth in which both birth and death rates are high, through a phase of rapid population growth in which modernization causes decreases in mortality, and then, after a lag, to a mature phase in which both birth and death rates are low and population growth is again moderate (Notestein 1953). The construct of the demographic transition raised questions about the causal relation between industrialization and the decline in mortality and fertility. The causes and timing were subject to various interpretations—with different policy implications for population control.

Supplementing the qualitative discussions of economic growth as a central dimension of development, analysts began to examine growth as a process with basic characteristics that are quantitative. They turned to long-term records of national product and its components for comparative analysis of the general characteristics of growth of nations. A seminal national income work was *Conditions of Economic Progress*, by Colin Clark (1940), who calculated purchasing power (international unit) in less developed countries for only five Latin American countries. Clark's second (1951) and third (1957) editions expounded on the historical comparison of real products over time and across nations. Special attention was given to whether capital accumulation is a necessary condition for economic progress. Clark also began an international comparison of agricultural output per worker. In the 1960s he maintained in *The Economics of Subsistence Agriculture* that improvements in agricultural productivity must also be regarded as another necessary condition for industrial development.[1]

Especially notable was Simon Kuznets's major study (1966) of the levels and variability of rates of modern economic growth in many countries. Kuznets believed that "by establishing the structural characteristics and growth experience of a variety of nations, differing in size, location, and historical heritage, we could find common features and patterns indicative of some common forces at play, and could associate divergences from such patterns with such factors as our hypotheses might suggest and empirical evidence test and confirm" (1959: 164). Limited as the data were for the underdeveloped countries, Kuznets interpreted the data back into the nineteenth century and claimed that "the disparity in per capita income levels between the advanced countries and the 'rest of the world' has been growing apace over the last century" (1956: 23). Although statistics for the emerging countries were scarce, this study served as a model for later studies and allowed the drawing of some worldwide implications.

Another study of the difference in the size distribution of income among families between underdeveloped and developed countries established greater inequality in the former, due mainly to the higher shares of the upper income groups (Kuznets 1963: 19). Regarding the trend of inequality over time, Kuznets suggested that during the process of development income distribution might follow an inverted-U shape, being at first more and then becoming less unequal. The question of the existence of the Kuznets curve generated considerable controversy over its sensitivity to statistical methodology and the data set examined.

Focusing on the implications of the "modern economic epoch" for the newly developing countries, Kuznets (1966) stressed the application of science-based technology to problems of economic production. He forecast the continuing acceleration of technological change, and he also predicted that food supply would expand more rapidly than population.

MORE ANALYTICAL APPROACHES

Beyond the historical national income accounting tradition, Walt W. Rostow (1960) and Alex Gerschenkron (1962) attempted to capture some stylized facts of development through their more analytical approaches to history.

Rostow sought to understand the process of economic growth from the perspectives of increasing returns, the role of noneconomic factors, and the view of society as an organism—"the dynamics of whole societies." He founded this ambitious task on a dynamic theory of production in which major new production functions are generated and diffused. The societal framework in which economic and noneconomic forces were to be woven was characterized by six "propensities"—the propensity to develop fundamental science, the propensity to apply science to economic ends, the propensity to accept innovations, the propensity to seek material advance, the propensity to consume, and the propensity to have children.[2] Unfortunately, but understandably, Rostow appealed to anthropologists, psychologists, sociologists, and other social scientists outside of economics to "disentangle the motives and societal processes which might determine the effective strength and course of change of these variables under various circumstances" (1960: 14).

Disaggregating output to dynamic sectors, Rostow focused on "leading sectors" and change through "five stages" in modern economies: traditional society, the preconditions for takeoff, the takeoff itself, the drive to maturity, and the age of high mass consumption. The stages are meant to reflect the extent to which a society proved capable of absorbing modern technology. Most attention is given to the "takeoff," defined as requiring all three of the following conditions: (1) a rise in the rate of productive investment from, say, 5 percent or less to over 10 percent of national income; (2) the development of one or more substantial manufacturing sectors, with a high rate of growth; (3) the existence or quick emergence of a political, social, and institutional framework that exploits the impulses to expansion in the modern sector and the potential external economy effects of the takeoff and gives to growth an ongoing character. The prospect of the takeoff suggested the possibility that developing nations would eventually move to self-sustained growth, and foreign aid would no longer be required.

Rostow's formulation of a sequence of stages of growth met considerable criticism from fellow historians. Kuznets (1966) questioned empirical evidence for the division of stages and the meaning of "a political, social and institutional framework which exploits the impulses to expansion in the modern sector, etc." H. J. Habbakuk (1961) could not recognize "a dynamic theory of production": the ideas on stages "do not cohere into anything which could reasonably be dignified as a theory of production. The work is essentially an essay in classification." Moreover, there is "stretching of categories and straining of facts." Albert Fishlow (1965) also claimed that the stages were nonexistent. Contrary to Rostow's undifferentiated approach to industrial history, economies do not pass through uniform stages of growth. They were "empty stages" that failed to fit well the actual diverse paths of development.[3]

In many of the emergent nations, however, Rostow's takeoff became almost a new kind of religion. In the early 1960s, it was the underlying theme for an international symposium of economists in Nyasaland (later to become Malawi). Interestingly, the program cover for this symposium highlighted capital accumulation again by reverentially featuring the

Harrod-Domar formula $\Theta = \sigma\alpha$. This formula had been devised by the Oxford don Roy Harrod (1939) and Professor Evsey Domar of MIT (1947) to indicate what rate of growth in income is necessary to maintain a full employment path of growth in advanced industrial countries such as Britain or the United States. Given α—the inverse of the economist's "marginal capital output ratio," or $\Delta K/\Delta Y$ which shows how much additional capital is needed to produce another unit of output—and given σ, the ratio of savings to national income, or S/Y, it follows that the growth rate Θ, or $\Delta Y/Y$, will be $\sigma\alpha$. To raise the growth rate, capital accumulation becomes the strategic variable in growth.

The analysis assumed a fixed coefficient technology between ΔK and ΔY, and established an equilibrium condition between supply and demand within a static Keynesian framework. But these restrictions were ignored. And even though the conditions in Nyasaland were vastly different from those in Britain and America, the formula was simplistically alluring. If only the propensity to save (σ) could be raised, then the growth rate (Θ) would also rise. Such was the early appeal of Rostow's takeoff into self-sustained growth through a rise in the rate of investment to over 10 percent of national income.

Instead of a single set of prerequisites or Rostovian "necessary preconditions" for development, Gerschenkron claimed that the historical development of countries has begun from different levels of economic backwardness. And these differences in points of departure have substituted for alleged prerequisites and shaped the nature of subsequent development. The more backward a country's economy, the more likely was its industrialization to start discontinuously as a sudden great spurt in manufacturing; the more pronounced was the stress in its industrialization on bigness of plant and enterprise, the greater was the stress on producers' goods as against consumer goods; the heavier was the pressure on the levels of consumption of the population; the greater was the part played by special institutional factors designed to increase supply of capital to the nascent industries; the more there was a case for the "big push."

Contrary to Rostow's undifferentiated approach to industrial history, Gerschenkron denied that economies pass through uniform stages of growth. If necessary preconditions are disclaimed, then the essential question posed by Gerschenkron was how and through the use of what devices backward countries substituted for the missing prerequisites. Institutional innovations, the role of the state, and different types of financial systems are indicated (Gerschenkron 1962: 353–359). Gerschenkron's suggestion that the patterns of substitution for alleged necessary preconditions could be best understood as responses to different degrees of economic backwardness had more appeal to economic historians than Rostow's theory of stages,[4] even though it too had its limitations.

PLANNING

More than was ever the case in the historical experience of the now advanced Western nations, there was in the 1950s considerable appeal in strong state action to "catch up." Beginning with India's creation of a central planning commission in 1950, many other developing countries followed suit, believing in the efficacy of a national development plan that would determine priorities, set quantitative targets, and establish public policies to achieve desired objectives. Governments of emergent nations turned to national planning as if this were a precondition for development.

Confidence in planning also came from the background experience of state action in the Great Depression of the interwar period (including import substitution policies in Latin America), the role of foreign aid through the Marshall Plan after World War II, and the demonstration of the Soviet way of planned industrialization. This experience reinforced the early economics of development as an "economics of discontent"— discontent with the old order, discontent with the legacy of colonialism, and discontent with economic dependence. Development economists were called on to advise governments that sought to narrow the gap between rich and poor countries.

A poor country's initial conditions, however, were believed to be inauspicious for reliance on a market-price system. The supply of entrepreneurship was limited. Private investment was inadequate. Markets were missing or only rudimentary. Pervasive market failure characterized the economy. Problems were structural, not amenable to only price and income changes. Planners therefore questioned the relevance of neoclassical economics for the problems of poor countries. They claimed that even a fairly well defined price system is unreliable when the market prices of goods and factors of production do not reflect their social cost. A planning agency should then correct the market price and allocate resources in accordance with the corrected "accounting" or "shadow" prices. Above all, it was believed that the price system must be superseded when the determination of the amount and composition of investment is too important to be left to a multitude of uncoordinated individual investment decisions, and when the tasks of a developing economy entail large structural changes over a long period ahead instead of simply small adjustments in the present period. If there is to be an industrialization program, secondary industries must be created on a large scale and be supported by sufficient overhead capital in the form of public utilities and public facilities that the several industries use in common.

Once investment was to be expanded in the public sector, it was necessary to consider programs to stimulate domestic savings and to secure needed resources from abroad to support the investment targets. Government was to have an increasing role in the accumulation of capital through taxation, the formation of financial institutions, control of consumption imports, and improvement in the country's terms of trade. Government effort had to be directed toward maximizing savings, mobilizing resources for productive investment, and canalizing the savings in the private sector to serve the purposes of a balanced development program.

The visible hand of the state became more prominent as development programs, national planning boards, and industrial development corporations proliferated. Visiting missions and foreign advisors began to cooperate with local planning agencies in producing analyses and policy recommendations underlying development plans. The economist's tool kit also expanded to provide technical support for the activities of state agents. Macroeconomic models, interindustry projections based on input-output matrices, operational research, simulation of growth models, and the techniques of statistical inference and decision analysis—all these allowed sophisticated studies of planning to multiply.[5] Progress in computer technology permitted mathematical and econometric models of programming and planning to become ever more elaborate—and all the more impressive to the uninitiated. The teaching of development economics in Western universities focused increasingly on these modern techniques; more and more, students from the developing countries attended these courses and took the professional techniques of the "expert" back to their governmental agencies.

A development plan commonly aimed at a forced takeoff and high-speed development, with a large amount of public investment and deliberate industrialization at its core, and supplanted the market mechanism with physical planning that involved the government in numerous decisions of a direct, specific character. Following notions of a big push and balanced growth, a development plan was to consist of a comprehensive program for a simultaneous and balanced expansion of all the important sectors in the economy, so that expanding demands are met by equivalent supplies, and investment on a wide scale allows enterprises to realize internal economies of scale and yield external economies. Planning would solve the coordination problem, and through import substitution industrialization and state-owned enterprises, it was believed that surplus labor would be absorbed and the foreign exchange constraint relaxed.

The centerpiece of many of the early development plans was import substitution industrialization (ISI). The case for protective tariffs and quotas on imports to promote import substitution had much appeal. An increasing number of critics denied the validity of the classical view that international trade will transmit development. They argued in favor of protectionism by contending that the free trade conclusions of classical growth economics did not apply to the special conditions of a less developed country. They also maintained that historically the very forces of international trade have actually impeded the development of poor countries. Instead of recognizing Ricardo's mutual gains from trade, the critics contended that trade could be a zero sum game with the poor country losing what the rich country gains. Or, in a milder form, that the gains from trade could be unequally distributed, with the rich country gaining the larger share.

In theory, there are logical arguments in support of import substitution: to improve the terms of trade; to protect industry in order to offset high wage rates that exceed social opportunity costs in the importable manufacturing sector when there is disguised unemployment in the rural sector; to attract private investment in "tariff factories"; and to protect an infant industry in which the economy might eventually acquire a comparative advantage through the industry's potential for future expansion and an eventual reduction in costs. The export pessimism of Rosenstein-Rodan, Nurkse, and Prebisch also carried over as an argument for ISI: inelastic import demand tended to outstrip inelastic export earnings. Moreover, the notion of structural inflation claimed that the marginal propensity to import exceeded the marginal propensity to export.

Government policy makers, however, were attracted to ISI for simpler and more popular reasons. The new ideology of national independence, the popular desire to overcome the colonial legacy, the need to react to balance-of-payments crises, and the desire of local business and the urban elite for protection—all these political forces were more influential in supporting protectionist policies than the logically valid arguments of economic theory.

The easiest route to industrialization appeared to be through import substitution. If there were imports, there was obviously a market. If the importation of the final commodity (say, an automobile) was then prohibited by a quota or made prohibitively expensive by a tariff, while intermediate inputs (components to be assembled) could be imported freely or at low duties, there would be a stimulus to produce in the sheltered home market. Industrialization might proceed "from the top down"—from the assembling of the components and the putting of the final touches on the finished automobile to the subsequent home production of the intermediate components and the eventual replacement of all imports with local production.

Furthermore, the emergence of balance-of-payments crises stimulated more protectionist arguments. If a deficit in international payments appeared—and the developing countries were especially prone to balance-of-payment deficits—the easiest policy action was to impose another round of tariffs or quotas to limit imports. Instead of bearing the costs of deflation or devaluation of their foreign exchange rates, governments turned to protectionism. The policy instruments were import tariffs, quotas, multiple exchange rates, and subsidies in import-competing industries.

The GATT condoned the restriction of imports by a country "in order to safeguard its external financial position and its balance of payments" (article 12) and "to implement programs and policies of economic development" a country could pursue tariff protection and apply quantitative restrictions for balance-of-payments purposes (article 18). At the same time, the IMF favored fixed exchange rates and made devaluation more difficult but did allow multiple exchange rates for the "transition period." Given these provisions, the less developed countries pursued protection with impunity.

EXTERNAL AID

If the developing country's government was to play a major role in stimulating development, so too was there emphasis on government-to-government assistance from the more advanced countries. As latecomers to development, the newly emergent countries ought to be able to tap the resources, technology, and skills available in the countries that had already developed to high levels. Indeed, some of the most significant components of the development process that were missing in the less developed country could be obtained from abroad—capital aid, technical assistance, and management.

Economists devised a number of arguments for the transfer of resources from rich to poor countries. As a trustee for the poor, the economist might have first come to advocate foreign aid on moral grounds. But he or she quickly went on to purely economic arguments—perhaps best summarized in the "two-gap model" (Chenery and Bruno 1962). This type of model is based on a structuralist concept of development and incorporates explicit limits on the rate of increase of domestic saving, investment, and exports. The model focuses in particular on the savings and foreign exchange constraints to development. The shortage of domestic savings limits the capital accumulation in the developing country. The shortage of foreign exchange limits the country's capacity to import. If the growth in GNP depends on the importation of goods that cannot be produced at home, then the country's growth rate will be constrained by its access to foreign exchange. These two gaps—the savings gap and the foreign exchange gap—might be filled by foreign aid.

It might be thought that, according to neoclassical analysis, an increase in domestic savings should also relax the foreign exchange constraint through the release of resources for import-substitute industries or for exports. In the two-gap analysis, however, this may not occur for structural reasons: there may not be sufficient domestic substitutes for necessary imports, there may be a fixed coefficient between domestic output and the need for imports, and exports may confront a highly inelastic demand.

The foreign exchange constraint could bite before the savings constraint. The "two-gap" model then became a "financing gap" model that claimed to show the high potential productivity of foreign aid in providing foreign exchange and thereby enabling otherwise redundant domestic savings to be used in investment (Chenery and Bruno 1962; Chenery and Strout 1966).

The gap between required and available savings and between required and available foreign exchanges can be filled by an inflow of foreign loans or grants from governments in the rich countries. The inflow of public foreign capital is equivalent to an inflow of savings from abroad: the rich countries transfer their savings to investment opportunities in the poor countries. By relaxing the savings and foreign exchange constraints, the inflow of foreign capital can yield an increase in national income that is several times the cost of the foreign loan.

Some simple calculations were used to demonstrate the need for public foreign investment. The case of India was illustrative. India's national income in 1950–51 was approximately $18 billion, of which about 5 percent, or $900 million, was saved. This was barely enough to maintain the capital stock intact and to keep up with the annual population increase. Even a doubling of the amount of capital available from domestic sources would not provide a very rapid rate of development in India. The inflow or private foreign investment was also small. To mobilize sufficient resources to fulfill the targets of its first five-year development plan (1952–57), India had to rely on foreign aid.[6]

Economists believed, that along with foreign capital, the borrowing of new technology and the acquisition of knowhow from abroad were desirable in order to absorb the additional capital more rapidly. To utilize the inflow of capital productively, the developing country had to acquire the missing components of technology, skills, and management. But it was thought that these could be imported. And there was little questioning of the worth of the knowledge and technological transfers that could come from the accumulated stocks in the advanced countries. Views differed only on whether the technical assistance program should operate on a bilateral basis (such as in the U.S. program) or be multilateral (as in the Colombo Plan for Southeast Asia or the U.N. program).

At the same time that pessimistic conclusions were reached about the developing countries' capacity to export and the ability to finance sufficient investment from domestic sources, optimistic conclusions were expressed about the capacity to accelerate development through the expansion of the public sector, inward-looking policies, and receipt of foreign aid. This combination of external pessimism and internal optimism dominated early development economics.

With slight caricature, government would give reality to the slogans of the early development economists by breaking out of Nurkse's "vicious circle of poverty," via Rosenstein-Rodan's "big push" and through "balanced growth" that would establish complementarity in demand, achieve Leibenstein's "critical minimum effort," break out of the "low-level equilibrium trap," and fulfill the conditions of Rostow's "takeoff."

Although they were dissenters in the minority, there were some who warned that the analysis of development problems should not be "price-less," that the functions of prices should not be ignored, that the responses to individual incentives should not be overlooked, and that the government should be severely limited in its intervention in the market price system. Such a view against planning was expressed early by Peter Bauer and Basil Yamey (1957). So too did Harry Johnson (1958) make a strong case for the market mechanism as against detailed planning. On issues of trade policy, there were also some prominent critics. Jacob Viner (1953) rejected the Prebisch-Singer doctrine of secular deterioration of the terms of trade and argued against ISI. Gottfried Haberler (1959) emphasized the benefits of international trade and concluded that trade made a tremendous contribution and can be expected to make an equally notable contribution in the future, if it is allowed to proceed freely. John Hicks (1959) related increasing returns and the productivity of investment to the volume of trade, warned against a heavily protected home market for consumer goods, and foresaw the possibility that developing countries could become exporters of manufactured goods. Also significant was the interpretation of the value of foreign trade for development put forward by Hla Myint (1954–55). These dissenters, however, did not influence policy makers in the 1950s.

ASSESSMENT

The pioneers in development established the subject as an analytical and policy-oriented subject.[7] At the outset, it went beyond description, beyond simply a story of what happens next in a developing economy to an attempt at building the plot of the development process—why it happens. The objectives of development were interpreted mainly in Kuznets's elements of self-sustaining growth, structural changes in the pattern of production, and technological upgrading.

The early thinking about development in the 1950s and 1960s can be summarized as being structural, shaped by trade pessimism, emphasizing planned investment in new physical capital, utilizing reserves of surplus labor in a dual economy, adopting import-substituting industrialization policies, embracing central planning, and relying on foreign aid.

Upon reading that summary, some might lament: "Would that we had a critique on why this variety of development economics had such a bad start" (Schultz 1987: 18). This is, of course, hindsight. The explanation was to come in the future as the subject evolved in response to experience and advancement of analytical and quantitative techniques. At the time, however, policy making was heavily influenced by nationalism and the legacy of colonialism.

The "grand issues" were the concern of the pioneer economists (Mallon and Stern 1989: 614–645). Debates quickly arose over balanced growth versus unbalanced growth, industrialization versus agriculture, import substitution versus export promotion, planning versus reliance

on the market price system. The debates on some of these issues were
to continue throughout the life of the subject. In the 1950s, the debates
were illuminated by the formulation of grand aggregate models, an appeal to economic history, and sociological considerations.

Quantitative analysis, however, was initially limited. Experiences with
differing rates of development among countries were too narrow and
short for the first generation of development economists. Not until 1968
did the United Nations begin national accounts; the World Bank's World
Tables began in 1976, and World Development Reports with their Statistical Indicators only became annual after 1978.

Historical data covering early periods became available after the 1950s
and 1960s. I. B. Kravis, A. W. Heston and R. Summers (1978) initiated
the International Comparison Program and used common prices or purchasing power yields for more than 100 countries for which they presented annual data as early as 1950. A new set of international comparisons for 130 countries since 1950 was offered by Summers and Heston
(1988) for the Penn World Tables. Crosscountry comparisons for early
dates from 1820 have also been made by Angus Maddison (2001: 169–
175). Richard A. Easterlin (2000) has also quantified historical change in
the standard of living for less developed areas. Statistics on inequality
over time have also been offered by Gary S. Fields (2000), T. Paul Schultz
(1988), and Francois Bourguignon and Christian Morrisson (2002). A rising number of country case studies also responded to the ideas of the
first generation of development economists. In turn, the lessons in a
country study could induce new ideas for development.

Insofar as the issues in the 1950s and 1960s were so wide ranging,
involving the "magnificent dynamics" of growth and change in an
emerging economy, and empirical evidence and country data were still
extremely limited, much of the thinking was necessarily a priori, and
hypotheses were not tested. The macro models were not formal and rigorous. But they had elements of originality and were both visionary and
provocative.

Many of the early insights were to remain integral to the subject of
development. And advances in general economics and econometrics
were later to refine and extend some of the early insights in a more
formal manner. For example, economists were to return to Rosenstein-
Rodan's argument and interpret it as expounding coordination failure
with a more rigorous theory of complementarities, sources of externalities, analysis of multiple equilibria, and poverty traps. (See chapter 8.)

Although they drew on the legacy of classical growth economics, the
early development economists were most provocative in dismissing the
relevance of neoclassical economics. Lewis's dual sector model held
pride of place. His retrospective assessment of his model is illuminating:

> As I was walking down a road in Bangkok one morning in August 1952,
> it suddenly occurred to me that all one needed to do was to drop the

assumption—then usually made by neoclassical macroeconomists—that the supply of labor was fixed. Assume instead that it was infinitely elastic, add that productivity was increasing in the capitalistic sector, and one got a rising profits share. It also occurred to me that this model would solve another problem that had bothered me since undergraduate days: what determined the relative prices of steel and coffee? I had been taught that marginal utility was the answer to this question, but this answer made no sense to me. If, however, one assumed an infinite elasticity of labor in terms of food to the coffee industry, and an infinite elasticity also in terms of food to the steel industry, then the factoral terms of trade between steel and coffee were fixed, and marginal utility was out the window.

So in three minutes I had solved two of my problems with one change of assumptions. Writing this up would take four articles from me, and further exploration by Fei and Ranis and others. The thing became for a time a growth industry, with a stream of articles expounding, attacking, testing, revising, denouncing, or approving. The upshot seems to be that the model is illuminating in some places at some times, but not in other places or other times. This was said when it was first presented. (1984: 132)

The belief in market failure—in both domestic and international markets—shaped policy making and turned governments to inward-looking policies. The pioneers neglected, however, the problem of implementation and political development. Rather naively, they simply assumed that economic development would lead to political development and that problems of political instability and inefficient governments would be overcome.[8]

Moreover, the psychological and sociological determinants of development received little attention. Bert Hoselitz (1960: 17) said: "In attempting a theory of economic growth, the main problem in relating social and cultural factors to economic variables is to determine how the social structure of a less developed country changes into that of an economically advanced country. In particular, economists may ask whether social change occurs by itself or whether it is related to purely economic changes." Nonetheless, this problem was neglected, although there were perfunctory statements that development must be interpreted as a "total" social process. An exception was the pioneering quantitative study of sources of growth by Irma Adelman and Cynthia Taft Morris (1967), who attempted to link the rate of growth to changes in social, institutional, cultural, and political factors.

The optimism that characterized early development economics may possibly be attributed to the neglect of these other problems. After making out the case for planning in backward countries because their "need is so obviously much greater" an in advanced countries, Lewis (1952: 128) was optimistic that

it is also true that this enables them to carry it through in spite of error and incompetence. For, if the people are on their side, nationalistic, conscious of their backwardness, and anxious to progress, they willingly bear great hardships and tolerate many mistakes, and they throw themselves with enthusiasm into the job of regenerating their country. Popular enthusiasm is both the lubricating oil of planning, and the petrol of economic development—a dynamic force that almost makes all things possible.

Optimism also came from Rostow's takeoff: "in a decade or two changes take place which ensure that henceforth both the basic structure of the economy and the social and political structure of the society are transformed in such a way that a steady rate of growth can be thereafter regularly sustained." And from his historical cases, Rostow (1960) concludes that "in the end, the lesson of all this is that the tricks of growth are not all that difficult."

Given the extensive opening up of the subject and its wide scope, there were, however, crosscurrents and a variety of perspectives over some leading issues. As the following chapters indicate, the debates on some of these issues were to continue. The answers and policy solutions were to change, however, as techniques of analysis, empirical evidence, and political forces were to shape the future evolution of the subject.

6

Orthodox Reaction

Concern about government failure became a landmark turning point in the thinking about development in the 1970s and 1980s. Contrary to the early development economists' advocacy of centralized government interventions to remedy market failures, an orthodox reaction now focused on government failure and its antidote of neoclassical economics.

A second generation of development economists criticized the first generation for having ignored fundamental principles of neoclassical economics. If pervasive market failures had earlier been seen to call for governmental remedies, by the 1970s the neoclassical case for the market-price system called for remedying government failures through policy reform. This "neoclassical resurgence" was based on both criticism of the earlier theories and disillusionment with the failed development strategies based on these theories.[1] The subject of development economics—as known by the first generation—went into decline.

Albert Hirschman (1982) suggested that the early development economics lost influence because of "the two fundamentalist critiques" by the "new dependency of Neo-Marxists" and by neoclassicists who believed in "monoeconomics." They

> attacked development economics from opposite directions and in totally different terms, but they converge in their specific indictments—as they indeed did, particularly in the important arena of industrialization. Since the adherents of neoclassical economics and those of the various neo-Marxist schools of thought live in quite separate worlds, they were not even aware of acting in unison. In general, that strange de facto alliance . . . plays an important role in the evolution of thinking on development. . . . [T]he intended victim was the new development economics which had indeed advocated industrial development and was now charged with intellectual responsibility for whatever had gone wrong. . . . In contrast to the multiple indictment [of industrialization] from the Left, the monoecono-

mists concentrated on a single, simple, but to them capital flaw of these policies: misallocation of resources.

The loss of interest in the early development economics is explained differently by Paul Krugman (1993: 29) on methodological grounds. He observes that the development theorists of the 1950s were "at first unable, and later unwilling to codify [their insights] in clear, internally consistent models. At the same time the expected standard of rigor in economic thinking was steadily rising. The result was that development economics as a distinctive field was crowded out of the mainstream of economics. Indeed, the ideas of 'high development theory' (of the 1950s) came to seem not so much wrong as incomprehensible." The informal, nonmathematical style of the early development economists lost appeal to the next generation devoted to formal mathematical models.

Recognition of the undesirable results of development policies was even more influential in supporting the orthodox reaction than was criticism of the analytical basis of interventionist policies. By the 1970s, deficiencies in state-led development had become acute. Contrary to the optimism of the earlier generation and despite the deliberate efforts of governments to accelerate development, it became clearly evident that in many countries the numbers in absolute poverty were increasing, inequality was not diminishing, and more people were unemployed or underemployed. To explain these disappointments, a growing number of development economists attributed policy-induced distortions and nonmarket failure to over planning and inappropriate public policies. Above all, they focused on the neglect of markets and prices—on the need to return to the fundamental principles of orthodox mainstream economics.

Although the early warnings by Peter Bauer (1957: 27, 92) had been ignored, their rereading now supported a criticism of development planning and a return to neoclassical economics.

> Much of the current discussion on underdeveloped countries is vitiated by treating supply and demand as physical quantities unaffected by price, and, perhaps more generally, by regarding quantities as fixed or given, and not as variables. This widespread practice strikes at the root of economics as a distinct discipline and threatens to transform it into a branch of production engineering. . . . [P]olicy cannot be framed rationally unless the effects and implications of prices, including price changes and differentials, are considered.

Against the background of a development record that revealed both successes and failures, the focus of development economics became increasingly directed to the heterogeneity of developing countries and to an explanation of differential rates of development performance, emphasizing the policies of the success stories. Instead of the earlier grand theories and aggregate growth models, more emphasis was being placed on applied research that was country specific. It had become evident that economic rationality characterizes agents in Africa or Asia as well as in the more developed countries (Lipton 1968; Schultz 1964). On this basis, disaggregated microstudies of production units and households, rather than the previously aggregative models, were becoming popular. The "grand theories" and general development strategies of the first generation were now not deemed to be as useful for offering policy advice as were the microstudies based on data that allowed specific policy implications, such as a change in tariffs or agricultural subsidies.

The general ideology of the Reagan-Thatcher administrations also carried over to developing countries. Reagan's "magic of the market" and Thatcher's minimization of government provided a congenial intellectual environment for the neoclassical resurgence. At the institutional level of the World Bank, this also had some reflection in the chief economist's position, as Anne Krueger, who was a strong neoclassicist, succeeded Hollis Chenery, who had propounded structural analysis and programming.

Instead of pursuing the grand theories and general strategies of the first generation of development economists, the second generation was now almost moralistic, dedicated to virtuous policies based on neoclassical economics. Arnold Harberger and other neoclassicists could say to governments of developing countries: "Good economics is good for people."[2] And by "good economics" they meant the logic of the neoclassical market-price system with a minimalist government. At the University of Chicago, the work of Theodore Schultz in agricultural economics and human capital became highly important and influenced Harberger and Chicago development economists (Nerlove 1999). Chicago economics had a growing impact in developing countries, especially in Latin America. William J. Barber (1995) summarizes the illuminating case study of Chicago School economics in Chile.

Emphasizing the role of prices—not only for resource allocation but also for mobilization of resources—the development analyst became ever more the guardian of rationality. Nonmarket failure was especially prevalent in policy-induced price distortions. Given surplus labor and the need to adopt more labor-intensive techniques of production, wage rates for unskilled labor were too high. Given the shortage of capital, interest rates were too low. Given the foreign exchange shortage, exchange rates were overvalued. An increasing number of economists therefore maintained that the policy challenge was to "get prices right." As C. Peter Timmer (1973) expressed it, "getting prices right" does not guarantee economic development, but "getting prices wrong" frequently is the end of development.

ANTIPLANNING

Development planning experienced continued failures. Former supporters of comprehensive planning or even industrial programming began to lament the "crisis in planning" (Faber and Seers 1972; Streeten and Lipton 1969). Critics now pointed to government failures in the formulation and implementation of overambitious plans that were derived from inappropriately specified macromodels, lacked adequate data, were subject to unanticipated dislocations, faced administrative limitations, and became politicized. In many countries, plans were big on paper but not effectively implemented, and objectives remained more rhetorical than realized. The actual behavior of governments was far from the economist's conception of optimal planning.

When the state becomes overextended in an underdeveloped economy, government may ironically lose control of the economy. Inflation, the rise of parallel markets, the breakdown of a price system, rent-seeking, and corruption may then eventually force policy reform for the government to regain a grip on the economy. Actual experience with the adverse consequences of inappropriate policies may be more influential in bringing about policy reform than any prescriptions by economists. Jagdish Bhagwati observes: "As many developing countries learned [the policy lessons] the hard way . . . [P]erhaps learning by other's doing and one's own undoing is the most common form of education!" (1988: 41).

India's experience with comprehensive planning is illustrative. The first Five-Year Plan (1951–56) and the Second Plan (1956–61) emphasized deliberate industrialization through import subsidization and public sector production in heavy industry. But the massive investment relative to resource availability led to a macroeconomic and balance-of-payments crisis. An elaborate system of controls followed—industrial licensing, exchange controls, price controls, nationalizations. "A chaotic incentive structure, and the unlashing of rapacious rent-seeking and political corruption, were the inevitable outcomes of the control system. Indeed the system, instituted in the name of planning for national development, instead became a cancer in the body politic" (Srinivasan 2002: 15).

Ian M. D. Little's critical evaluation of planning (1982: 58, 126) noted that the early proponents of planning started from the negative proposition that laissez-faire policies and the price mechanism were faulty. But they got no further than that.

> They did not take much notice of the fact that governments were not all-powerful monoliths, even if not democratic, and that therefore planning would have to come to terms with political realities. The basic political assumption was that the LDC governments—indeed, all governments—were strong, wise and undivided, and that their sole objective was the welfare of their people. This did not turn out to be true. . . . Planning was, by and large a failure, and sometimes a disaster.

Critics reacted against the undesirable results of a number of specific policies and began to advocate policy reforms that would be more attuned with mainstream orthodox economics. They became most concerned about the effects of import substitution, the lag in agriculture, investment allocation, and problems of macroeconomic stabilization. They now advised: "Get all policies right."

TRADE POLICY

While the Newly Industrial Countries (NICs) of East Asia enjoyed increasing returns and "learned by doing" in their successful export-led development, other countries "learned by their undoing" through the pursuit of a strategy of import substitution industrialization (Bhagwati 1988). The influential study of seven countries by Ian M. D. Little, Tibor Scitovsky, and Maurice Scott (1970) showed how costly import substitution had been. Not only was the domestic resource cost of import substitution greater than free trade cost of imports, but also the subsidization of the urban import-substituting sector entailed perverse effects of an implicit tax on the rural sector and exports. An extensive National Bureau of Economic Research project also documented the undesirable results, especially through the use of tariffs and quantitative restrictions in an attempt to replace imports (Bhagwati and Krueger 1973). Any number of empirical studies followed, demonstrating that the import substitution strategy had been extremely costly to the economy in real terms (Bhagwati and Krueger 1973; Bruno 1972; Bruton 1970).

Especially disturbing was the realization that after a period of import substitution industrialization, the problems of inequality and unemployment had actually become more serious. The use of subsidies, overvalued exchange rates, rationing of underpriced import licenses, high levels of protection, and loans at negative real interest rates had induced the production of import substitutes by capital-intensive, labor-saving methods. This had resulted in industrial profits in the sheltered sector and higher industrial wages for a labor elite, thereby aggravating inequalities in income distribution. Employment creation in the urban import-replacement industrial sector had not kept pace with the rural-urban migration, and the unemployment problem intensified through the transfer of the rural underemployed into open unemployment in the urban sector. After two decades of an import-substitution strategy, many developing countries were left with the major problems of contending with greater numbers in absolute poverty, more unemployment and underemployment, and wider inequality.

The dismal experience with the shortcomings of import-substitution policies together with empirical research and the policy implications of new theoretical insights pointed to reform of trade policy. Advances in theory—and in the capacity to measure the effects of protectionist policies—demonstrated just how dismal the experience was. Especially telling were empirical research studies showing the costs of rent-seeking, high and erratic effective rates of protection, the import bias in effect exchange rates (Krueger 1997: 8–9). Rent-seeking activity had no social value; it used time and resources even when legal, and some methods involved corruption, smuggling, and black markets. High effective rates of protection through the escalation of tariff rates on the degree of processing actually resulted in some cases in negative value added. Although the protected production of import substitutes was profitable in local currency, the value of inputs at world prices exceeded the value of the final product at world prices. The process of import substitution was socially inefficient.

At the same time, dynamic theories of comparative advantage were formulated, and studies of the benefits of dynamic gains from trade were establishing export promotion as the superior trade strategy. More and better data and the increasing use of measurement tools intensified the analytical case for a change to export promotion.

The contrasting experience of the East Asian countries was a major influence in stimulating the change in thinking about trade policy. The orthodox reaction to ISI called for policy reform to promote an outward-looking orientation of export promotion (EP) as in the East Asian countries. Essentially, the strategy was to bring domestic prices into a close relation with world prices (border prices in project appraisal terminology), thereby removing the discrimination against tradeables and establishing a neutral trade regime. Because policies that subsidized imports also constituted implicit taxation on exports, they had to be eliminated. Liberalization of trade policy was essential: quotas (a quantitative instrument) should be replaced by low tariffs (a price instrument) and then by free trade so as to reduce the cost of inputs for exports. Moreover, a competitive real exchange rate should be established through devaluation and macroeconomic stabilization. Positive incentives of a market-friendly character in financial and labor markets should also encourage exporters. Given the prior bias against exports, these reform measures were now unlikely to oversubsidize exports.

A reaction also set in against the overemphasis of industrialization at the expense of agriculture. Agricultural output had in general increased only a little faster than population in the developing counties. In Latin America, food production per head had been at a standstill in the 1970s, and South Asia had changed from a surplus to a deficit region in food. In a number of countries agricultural output per head was even lower in the 1980s than it had been a decade or two earlier.

The weak performance of the agricultural sector called for a revision of policies affecting agriculture. It was common to summarize in four ways how greater agricultural productivity and output could contribute to an economy's development: (1) by supplying foodstuffs and raw materials to other expanding sectors of the economy; (2) by providing an "investable surplus" of savings and taxes to support investment in another expanding sector; (3) by selling for cash a "marketable surplus" that will raise the demand of the rural population for products of other expanding sectors; and (4) by relaxing the foreign exchange constraint through exports or import substitution.

Kuznets (1966) had summarized these contributions as the "market contribution" and the "factor contribution." Little (1982: 105), however, observed that "the role of agriculture in development was discussed in this [early] period independently of the determinants of agricultural performance or policy. It was treated more as a black box from which people, and goods to feed them, and perhaps capital would be released. . . . Most of the discussion was a priori."

By the 1970s, however, evidence supported the growing criticisms of the benign neglect of agriculture—or even discrimination against agriculture—that had been based on the view that the agricultural sector was a reservoir to be squeezed during the structural transformation of the economy. In his review of development experience as a means for testing and improving development theory, Lloyd Reynolds (1985: 52, 121) stressed the importance of the agricultural sector:

> the race between technical progress in agriculture and population growth, which poses some of the most difficult problems in development policy, should also be the main axis of development theory. It is fallacious to suppose that an expanding industrial sector can be fueled for more than a short time by resource transfers from a static agricultural sector. The requirements for the mobilization of the economic potential of agriculture lie at the core of development theory and policy.

Not only was a lagging agricultural sector impeding industrialization, but also the widening urban-rural wage gap was inducing rural-urban migration that resulted in more unemployment and sociopolitical problems associated with rapid urbanization. Reformers believed that attention should now be focused directly on raising agricultural output, fostering rural development, and reducing the poverty of small farmers and landless laborers.

In this redirection of policy, markets and prices were to be emphasized. Schultz (1964) had changed the view of farmers in traditional agriculture by claiming that they were finely attuned to marginal costs and returns. Moreover, new technology and knowledge and new opportunities for investment could transform agriculture from traditional to modern.

A five-volume research project, *The Political Economy of Agricultural Pricing Policy* (1991–92), sponsored by the World Bank, examined the experience of 18 developing countries from the 1960s to the 1980s. It concluded (4: 139):

> Discrimination against agriculture in developing countries has been pronounced. It has been more extreme the more ideologically committed those influencing policy have been to the notions of modernization through industrialization and import substitution; it has been more extreme where agricultural production consists predominantly of traditional exportable commodities; and it has been more extreme when agricultural interests have not been part of the governing coalition.

Noting that indirect discrimination against agriculture though trade regime and exchange rate policies is generally of greater importance than direct discrimination, the report submitted the following findings:

The indirect tax on agriculture from industrial protection and macroeconomic policies was about 22 percent on average for the 18 countries over 1960 to 1985—nearly three times the direct tax from agricultural pricing policies. Industrial protection policies taxed agriculture more than did real overevaluation of the exchange rate. High taxation of agriculture was associated with low growth in agriculture—and low growth in the economy (World Bank 1991–92: vol. 4, pp. 199–200).

The case for reducing price controls on agricultural commodities and the other forms of discrimination associated with protection of importables and an overvalued exchange rate was bolstered by a number of empirical studies offering evidence on the positive supply elasticity of agricultural production in response to price incentives (Askari and Cummings 1976; Schultz 1978).

More recognition was also given to the earlier Schultz volume (1964) on incentives and to studies that demonstrated the efficiency of farmer decision making in allocating resources (Lipton 1968). New attention to contractual choice models also provided a more inclusive analysis of agricultural problems by considering the markets for land, labor, and credit as interlocking factor markets (Binswanger and Rosenzweig 1984; Braverman and Stiglitz 1982). These studies pointed to a reduction in interventions and to a new emphasis on the rationality of markets, incentives, and nondiscriminatory pricing in agriculture.

A reaction against governmental policies that involved public investment in large agricultural projects and that favored large farmers at the expense of small farmers also led to more consideration of market-supporting institutions based on research and education leading to innovations, as Schultz (1964) had earlier envisaged. It was now recognized that special emphasis should be on smallholder agriculture because the smallholders and tenant farmers constitute the bulk of the rural poor and provide the best potential for efficient agricultural development. The task became one of removing the "urban bias" of the past (Bates 1981; Lipton 1977, 1984) and providing positive pricing and taxation policies. The inappropriate policies that had impeded rather than induced appropriate technical and institutional innovations had to be replaced (Hayami and Ruttan 1985).

As C. Peter Timmer (1988: 328) concluded, "the factors needed for inducing the rural information—to 'get agriculture moving'—involves a complex mix of appropriate new chronology, flexible rural institutions, and a market orientation that offers farmers material rewards for the physical effort they expend in their field and households and for the risks they face from both nature and markets."

PROJECT APPRAISAL

The increasing number of public sector projects and private sector projects that required governmental approval also led development economists to question how governments were allocating scarce capital resources. With their neoclassical logic, economists criticized the practice of choosing projects simply by quantitative engineering considerations or by evaluations that used distorted prices. Such crude methods did not lead to efficient allocation or to the fulfillment of national objectives associated with the society's welfare. Analysts therefore began to propose during the 1970s a rational approach to project evaluation based on social benefit-cost analysis.

Social benefits and costs may differ from private benefits and costs. For example, externalities or public goods may have no market price. Some market prices may be less than ideal, such as for education or health. Many market prices may also be distorted through government policies affecting wages, foreign exchange rates, and interest rates, and through the divergences caused by taxes, subsidies, tariffs, quotas, and price controls. The development practitioner was in a "second-best world," but more rational analysis could allow avoidance of the third-best investment choice.

To choose among alternative investment options, the United Nations Development Organization (UNIDO 1972) and Ian M. D. Little and J. A. Mirrlees (1969, 1974) proposed the use of "accounting prices" or "shadow prices" that would better reflect marginal social value and marginal social costs. The practice of project appraisal was then to use a cost-benefit analysis based on measuring the values of outputs (benefits) and inputs (costs) with shadow prices instead of relying on the market prices used in calculating private financial profitability. "National economic profitability" was sought, and the calculation of a project's rate of return should go beyond the internal rate of financial return to the internal rate of "economic" return. The task was to calculate the shadow prices of output, inputs, factors of production, and the social rate of discount for future streams of social benefits and social costs so as to yield the present value of the net social benefit of the project. If the net present value of discounted benefits exceeds the sum of the discounted costs, the project proposal should be accepted.

Shadow prices for exchange rates, wage rates, and interest rates claimed the most attention. They were to correct for government interventions that created divergences between market prices and the opportunity costs to the economy of resources. The purpose was to go beyond financial values to true economic values. In so doing, project appraisal supported reforms in markets for foreign exchange, labor, and capital in order to bring the official prices closer to their true economic values.

Although much of the analysis became too complicated for widespread implementation by the World Bank and many developing countries (see Little and Mirrlees 1990), academic refinements in the analysis have continued to the present time (Curry and Weiss 2000).

MACROECONOMIC STABILIZATION

It is common for an LDC to suffer a balance of payments problem—a deficit in its current account that has to be covered by a loss of foreign exchange reserves and/or an inflow of foreign capital. A pervasive cause of such a deficit is an excess of government expenditure over government revenue. The excess demand financed by monetization of the government's debt spills over into the balance of payments. The demand for imports will also increase when private investment exceeds private savings. When the total demand from government expenditure and private investment exceeds the supply of resources being released by taxes (public savings) and private savings, there will be a resource gap that is filled by imports being greater than exports. This, however, constitutes a foreign exchange gap or balance-of-payments problem that calls for remedial action. When the country has limited foreign exchange reserves it must resort to the remedial actions of deflation, devaluation, and/or direct controls on imports.

Normally a developing country has low private savings and negative government savings. The practice of planning entailed a large governmental budgetary deficit that put pressure on the balance of payments. In the 1970s, inflation, especially in Latin America, together with the shock of rising oil prices, and then the Mexican debt crisis in 1982 and the capital flights from developing countries, intensified concern over balance-of-payment problems. Direct controls on imports were to be avoided. A call for macroeconomic stabilization based on disinflation through tight fiscal and monetary policies became the orthodox reaction. Devaluation of the exchange rates was also advocated.

The influence of monetarist theory supported the orthodox reaction. The Chicago school of economics emphasized monetarism—the view that the quantity of money has the major influence on economic activity and the price level. The growing prominence of monetarism extended the "monetary theory of the balance of payments" to open economies (Kreinin and Officer 1978). The supply of and demand for money affected exchange rates, the balance of payments, and a change in international reserves.

Little (1982: 80–81) summarizes how the monetarists underscored the orthodox reaction.

> First, they insisted that stability could not be achieved without a reduction in the rate of increase of the money supply. Second, they held that stability would be good for long-run growth, for only with reasonable stability could free operation of the price mechanism achieve the efficiency required. Third, many of the inelasticities that the structuralists pointed to were the result of inflation itself or misguided policies that needed to be corrected.

The monetarist remedies went far beyond a simple reliance on reducing the rate of increase of the money supply. Measures intended to make the price mechanism work, and work better, were always included—notably, unification of exchange rates, devaluation, and liberalization of imports.

The World Bank joined the orthodox reaction through its "structural adjustment lending" program in the 1980s. Program loans were now to induce the needed policy reforms that would stabilize the economy, increase its efficiency and flexibility, and achieve an outward-looking economy. The Bank's new president (the commercial banker A. W. Clausen) and the departure of several of the lieutenants (in particular, Hollis Chenery) of the former president (Robert McNamara) changed the operations of the Bank. Given the new wave of neoclassical orthodoxy that surrounded the Bank, Chenery's replacement by Anne Krueger was especially significant. A history of the Bank (Kapur, Lewis, and Webb 1997: 511–512) observes that "Krueger, a distinguished representative of the neoclassical school of development and trade policy, would place a heavy pro-markets, anti-interventionist imprint on the Bank's research and policy-analysis programs. She reshuffled the central economics staffs into closer conformity with her own views and quickly became an articulate and unyielding spokesperson for the new policy prioritie.

The need to remedy balance of payments deficits shaped the agenda of early structural adjustment loans (SALs). As policy-based lending, there was some overlap with the IMF's conditional financing, and early in the 1980s the international debt crisis intensified action by both the Bank and the Fund. Macro views were revised during the 1980s, giving more attention to government failures and favoring policies that liberalized markets and reduced government interventions. Greater emphasis was given to export expansion; nationalizations were discouraged and a shift to private ownership supported; deficit countries were encouraged to devalue; fiscal and monetary policies were advocated to achieve internal and external balance.

PRIVATIZATION

Policy reformers, devoted to the market-price system, wanted more goods and services to be produced and distributed by competitive market criteria. Many a state-owned enterprise, however, operated inefficiently as a state-guaranteed monopoly. The state covered deficits with soft budgets and government influence over easy bank loans. Operations were commonly politicized and violated market criteria. Recommendations for privatization therefore arose.

For neoclassicists, the objective was to achieve higher productivity. The privatizers believed that new owners would respond rationally to incentives. Privatization was to complement the market. It was also thought that privatization would help to depoliticize the economy and create an ownership structure that would enhance efficiency. The priva-

tization movement often became a means of redistributing power between the bureaucrats and private enterprises.

THE "WASHINGTON CONSENSUS"

By the end of the 1980s, the orthodox reaction had become so pervasive
that John Williamson (1990) could label the present set of remedial policies the "Washington Consensus"—endorsed by the U.S. Treasury and
the Washington-based international institutions (the IMF, World Bank,
and Inter-American Development Bank). Policies of liberalization, stabilization, and privatization were to be the principal means of promoting
sustainable growth in developing economics and making their economies
more efficient and competitive. Ten particular reform policies made up
the Washington Consensus (Williamson 1990): (1) fiscal discipline, (2)
public expenditure priorities, (3) tax reform, (4) liberalization of financial
markets, (5) competitive exchange rate, (6) liberalization of trade policy,
(7) foreign direct investment, (8) privatization, (9) deregulation, and (10)
property rights.

Some reinterpreted the "consensus" as "neoliberal" policies in Latin
America or as "market fundamentalism." The influence of policy reform
in Latin America in the 1990s is instructive. Monetary prudence reduced
inflation. Fiscal discipline lowered the average budget deficit from 5 percent of GDP to about 2 percent—and reduced public external debt from
about 50 percent of GDP to less than 20 percent. Tariffs fell from an
average of more than 40 percent to nearly 10 percent. Financial liberalization eliminated direct credit controls, interest rates were deregulated,
foreign direct investment was encouraged, and foreign exchange and
capital account controls were removed. More than eight hundred public
enterprises were privatized between 1988 and 1997 (Birdsall 2002: 6). The
extent of the economic reforms was historical. But in economic growth,
poverty reduction, income distribution, and social conditions the results
were discouraging. Real GDP growth in the region was low in the
1990s—a modest 3 percent a year for a decade, just 1.5 percent per capita.
This was not much higher than the preceding "lost decade" of the 1980s
and substantially below the rates of 5 percent or more in the 1960s and
1970s. Unemployment rose, and poverty remained widespread. Social
development indicators were only slightly better. At the end of the 1990s,
Latin America still had the most unequal distribution of income and
assets of any region in the world (Birdsall 2002: 7).

A REACTION TOO FAR

By the 1990s, a number of economists were questioning whether the
orthodox reaction had gone too far. Tony Killick (1990) and others argued
that the essential question is not how large the public sector should be
or how much government intervention there should be but rather what

kind of intervention. What can government do best? In the use of what types of policy instruments does government have a comparative advantage? This approach does not point to the minimalist state of the neoliberals or market fundamentalists but rather to a broader and more active shift from ineffective planning to governmental policies that can work through markets. Governments were to be both active and market friendly. The problem should be restated: not "too much government" but too much of government doing the wrong things. "The task is to dismantle the disabling state . . . [and] establish the enabling state" (Colclough and Manor 1991: 276). The realistic conclusion on policy reform followed.

> Making markets work is a much more complex process than slogans such as "getting the prices right," "privatization" or "getting rid of controls" would imply. Making markets work involves fundamental changes in enterprise behavior in most cases and substantial changes in the way government itself carries on its functions. Finally, most developing nations are never going to be willing to turn as much over to the market as, say, Hong Kong. Nonmarket controls or hierarchical commands will continue to play a major role in many sectors of most economies. Reform, therefore, is not just a matter of getting rid of such commands. A high growth economy must learn to make both the market and the bureaucracy perform efficiently.

Elements of counterreaction were also derived from what was called "reform fatigue." In Latin America, for example, "public opinion surveys in the late 1990s indicated that Latin Americans thought their economies were not doing well, that their quality of life was lower than that of previous generations, and that poverty was higher than ever." Disagreement with privatization was also widespread and growing (Birdsall and Nellis 2002). Many therefore looked beyond the Washington Consensus. Indeed, at their summit meetings in 1994 and 1998, Latin American heads of state broadened their development objectives beyond the emphasis on adjustment and growth as in the Washington Consensus to the broader goals of poverty reduction, education, and good governance. To the extent that "poverty reduction and equity have come to dominate the development agenda" it displaced the high priority of growth (9). Social objectives and considerations of equity went far beyond the domain of the orthodox reaction.

In reviewing "the decline and rise of development economics," Paul Krugman (1994) advocated a reconsideration of high development theory (early development economics) to reinforce government activism as a way of breaking out of country's low-level poverty trap. Krugman maintained that the early development economics had gone into decline because it was out of character with the formal model building of mainstream economics, thereby allowing the orthodox reaction. But he later recognized that new modeling techniques actually supported a return to earlier insights that gave a more positive role to government. "A constant-returns, perfect competition view of reality had taken over the development literature, and eventually via the World Bank and other institutions much of real-world development policy as well. Good ideas [of early development economics] were left to gather dust in the economics attic for more than a generation" (52, 57).

But in the 1990s "mainstream economics eventually did find a place for high development theory" (such as Rosenstein-Rodan's big push). Kevin Murphy, Andrei Shleifer, and Robert W. Vishny (1989) presented a rigorous model that was not restricted to constant returns and perfect competition but could instead "legitimize the role of increasing returns and circular causation with a neat model that had not been available 35 years earlier."

If the early development economics had gone into decline, allowing the orthodox reaction, the later return to some of the insights of the early development economics—but now with appealing rigorous models—could resurrect development economics and allow economists to look at high development theory.

As interest returned to the broader challenge of reducing poverty and overcoming inequity, there was also a reaction against the narrowness of the Washington consensus. The World Bank's *World Development Report* of 1990 returned to the emphasis of an earlier *Report* in 1980 on poverty, and the *Report* of 2000/2001 reemphasized that "public action must be driven by commitment to poverty reduction." The orthodox reaction had been essentially a neoclassical interpretation of growth, with merely an implicit belief that growth could reduce poverty. Missing was explicit attention to propoor policies that would directly benefit the poor. Nor was there treatment of the negative effect of inequality on growth. Moreover, there was concern about social and political factors and institutional foundations that were not appreciated in the orthodox reaction. As such, the Washington Consensus needed reconsideration.

Looking forward, as in the following chapters, there was clearly much to gain from development thinking and policy making.

7

Modern Growth Theory

New growth issues now go beyond dual sector models (as discussed previously in chapter 4) to quantitative accounting for the sources of growth, emphasis on total factor productivity (TFP), and introduction of the new growth theory. These issues expand the relationship between capital and development to incorporate a more generalized interpretation of capital that recognizes not only physical capital but also the importance of human capital, knowledge capital, and social capital. Correspondingly, there are new public policy implications for development.

SOURCES OF GROWTH

The central issues of growth theory are to explain not only the existence of growth in national income but also what is the relative importance of the various sources of growth, and what determine the intercountry and intertemporal variations in growth. To analyze these issues, the basis of growth theory is an aggregate production function that measures the quantity of output Y for a given quantity of input X:

$$Y = F(X) \tag{1}$$

Over time (t), the production function can change, so that a dynamic relationship between output and inputs can be denoted as:

$$Y = F(X, t) \tag{2}$$

"Technical progress" occurs between two time periods, 0 and 1, if more output can be produced with the same measured inputs, or the same output with fewer measured inputs. If the production function is known, the growth of output between periods 0 and 1 can be decomposed into

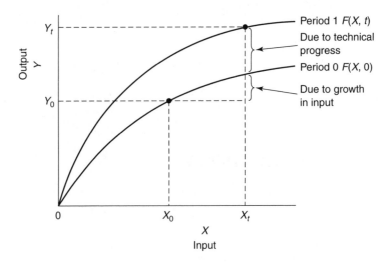

Figure 7.1 Decomposition of the sources of economic growth

two components: (1) the growth of output due to the growth of input, that is, movement along a production function, and (2) technical progress, that is, a shift in the production function. Figure 7.1 illustrates this decomposition between the two periods of time 0 and 1 (Lau 1999: 48).

The serious effort to measure why growth rates in output differ among countries began with neoclassical analysis of the aggregate production function by Robert Solow of MIT (1956, 1957). His seminal analysis of the relative contributions of growth in inputs and growth in efficiency spawned hundreds of journal articles and books—and gained Solow the Nobel Prize in economics in 1987.

Solow's decomposition of growth into factor contributions and a residual was based on a differentiation of a production function, $Y = F(K, L, t)$, where Y is output, K capital, L labor, and t time, to form

$$\frac{\dot{Y}}{Y} = \left(\frac{F_K K}{Y}\right)\frac{\dot{K}}{K} + \left(\frac{F_L L}{Y}\right)\frac{\dot{L}}{L} + \frac{F_t}{Y} \tag{3}$$

(Subscripts denote partial derivatives).

The contribution of capital accumulation to growth is measured by $(\dot{K}/K)$ multiplied by the share of capital in national income (Stern 1991a: 257–258). Labor's contribution to growth is measured by $(\dot{L}/L)$ multiplied by the share of labor in national income.

To measure the inputs of L and K over time (t), Solow relied on perfect competition in order to use observed factor prices as indicators of current marginal productivities. From long-run time series, he then estimated the sources of growth in GDP in the U.S. economy between 1909 and 1949.

Of the average annual growth rate of 2.9 percent, Solow attributed 0.32 percentage points to capital accumulation, 1.09 percent to labor input, and 1.49 percent to a residual that Solow called "technical change in the broadest sense." The Solow residual of "technical change" is termed "total factor productivity" (TFP)—equal to the rate of growth of output minus the weighted average of the input growth rate. Abramovitz (1956: 11) labeled this a challenging "measure of our ignorance" of the causes of growth in output that cannot be explained by simply the increase in inputs.[1]

Solow left the unexplained residual of TFP as an exogenous variable of technical change: technology was left to be explained by causes that lie outside the model. But it is technical progress that is most significant in forestalling diminishing returns from the tendency for the marginal product of capital to fall. In the long run, growth depends on the rate of technical progress—on an exogenous shift in the production function. While higher saving and investment in physical capital yield a higher level of income, it is the TFP growth rate that determines the long-term growth rate in income.

Subsequently, many analysts have proceeded to unpack Solow's "technical change in the broadest sense" into a number of constituent elements. Most commonly, the possible constituents are claimed to be: economies of scale, improvements in the quality of labor, greater technical efficiency of old capital, new technology, better functioning of markets, improved organization of firms and improvements in management, movement of labor and reallocation of capital from low-productivity activities to higher productivity activities, and learning by doing that enables productivity to increase as a function of cumulative investment or output.

In the old growth theory of Solow, TFP is to be interpreted as an exogenous shift in the production function. Let $Y_t = A_t(FK_t, L_t)$ (4), where A represents the level of technology, and $A_t + Y(FK_t, L_t)$. The latter equation represents a trend shift in TFP as a result of technical progress, as depicted in figure 7.1. In equation (4), A is (Hicks-neutral) technological progress, with K and L increasing in the same proportion. $Y + F(K, A(L))$ (5) can represent labor-augmenting technological progress, and $Y = F(AK, L)$(6) can represent capital-augmenting technological progress.

Solow's objective was to estimate in a supply-side model the evolution of potential output—in particular, the conditions for a steady state of growth. The steady-state level of income depends on the rates of saving and population growth. Solow's model was based on perfect competition, diminishing marginal product of capital when other inputs are held constant, and exogenous technology as a public good. Although his model established the importance of growth accounting, it referred to advanced industrial economies, not the less developed. It has, however, much value in raising the central question when examining the growth record of a country: "How much of the growth is due to an increased use of inputs or an increase in TFP?" Understanding the reasons for differences in technical efficiency and TFP growth rates became the main task for growth analysts. If the growth relies only or mainly on additions of labor and capital, its growth is an intensive type that can reach a limit. Improvement in TFP, however, allows an extensive type of growth that can provide continual growth.

Most significant in the residual of TFP are the "production" of human capital and improvements in the level of technology. These considerations lead to the "new growth theory" that attempts to study the endogenous accumulation of human capital and endogenous technological progress. The new growth theory examines production functions that show increasing returns because of an expanding stock of human capital and specialization and investment in "knowledge capital."[2]

Until the 1980s, research on the theory of growth was minimal. Going beyond Solow's growth theory, Chicago's Nobel laureate Robert Lucas (1988) then modeled the accumulation of human capital as an economically motivated activity. He wanted his model to allow "us to think about individual decisions to acquire knowledge, and about the consequences of these decisions for productivity." The result in Lucas's model is that the labor time and other resources used in the "production" of human capital yield external economies and are not subject to diminishing returns. The acquisition of skills by a worker not only increases that individual's productivity but, by increasing the average level of skills in the economy as a whole, has a spillover effect on the productivity of all the workers.

In endogenizing technological progress, Paul Romer (1986, 1990) also focuses on production functions that yield increasing returns to scale by technical change and by positive externalities to capital accumulation. In contrast to Solow's model, Romer's analysis postulates imperfect competition, endogenous technological progress based on ideas and innovations that come from private provision, differences in technology across countries, a possible increase in the marginal product of capital through external effects, and increasing returns to scale at the level of the economy.

Romer wants to recognize two features of growth that are not endogenized in the Solow analysis: (1) "the aggregate rate of technological advance is determined by things that people do," and (2) "many individuals and firms have market power and earn monopoly rents on discoveries" (1994: 12–13). Endogeous technical change in Romer's analysis takes the form of R&D-yielding innovations by imperfectly competitive firms that result in new products, new processes, and a greater variety of capital goods.

> Long run growth is driven primarily by the accumulation of knowledge by forward-looking, profit-maximizing agents. . . . Moreover, the creation of new knowledge by one firm is assumed to have a positive external effect on the production possibilities of other firms . . . [so that] production of

consumption goods as a function of the stock of knowledge exhibits increasing returns; more precisely, knowledge may have an increasing marginal product. (Romer 1986: 1002)

According to Romer (1996: 5, 6), whereas a Solow-type growth theory explains growth in terms of two basic types of factors—technology and conventional inputs—"new growth theory . . . divides the world into two fundamentally different types of productive inputs that we can call 'ideas' and 'things.' Ideas are nonrival goods. . . . Things are rival goods. . . . Ideas are goods that are produced and distributed just as other goods are." Ideas may be expensive to develop, but as public goods they are inexpensive to use.

Ideas are thus the primary source of growth. Knowledge-producing activities are central to growth theory. Knowledge or information, once obtained, can be used repeatedly with no additional cost. Because the new production processes and products create spillover benefits to other firms and various complementarities, aggregate investment in the public stock of knowledge exhibits increasing returns to scale, persists indefinitely, and sustains long-run growth in per capita income.

"Learning by doing" (Arrow 1962) and "learning by watching others doing" (King and Robson 1989) are also knowledge-producing activities. For developing countries, the implication of the new growth theory is to place more emphasis on human capital (including learning)—even more than on physical capital—and also to emphasize the benefit from the international exchange of ideas that comes with an open economy integrated into the world economy. The new growth theory is also relevant for the question of convergence—that is, whether poor countries grow faster than rich countries.[3] Convergence occurs through "catchup" when the "technology gap" and "idea gaps" among countries are overcome. Free mobility of capital among countries will speed this convergence as the rate of diffusion of knowledge increases.

Knowledge capital thus becomes as important as—or more important than—physical capital. Knowledge is the most important scarce factor, but it is also the source of increasing returns. At the beginning of the twentieth century, Marshall had recognized that "although nature is subject to diminishing returns, man is subject to increasing returns. . . . Knowledge is the most powerful engine of production; it enables us to subdue nature and satisfy our wants." Again, in an earlier period, J. M. Clark (1923: 120) observed that "knowledge is the only instrument of production that is not subject to diminishing returns." Now this view is reiterated in the new (or newly rediscovered) growth theory.

The incentives and opportunities for the production of knowledge capital depend on the organization of firms, the degree of market competition, physical infrastructure, financial institutions, political institutions, and the openness of the economy. A rigorous formulation of these complex relations and their empirical testing are, however, still wanting.

The economics of ideas and knowledge require extension. Central policy questions remain to be answered by endogenous innovation models. Knowledge is a public good, but it is highly specific. Innovations depend on incentives, they must be diffused, and there must be absorptive capacity. Can empirical work spell out the attributes of ideas and "idea gaps" as precisely as for economic goods? If deliberate technical progress is to be achieved, what is the institutional design that will motivate behavior for the creation of knowledge? What is the search mechanism for the discovery of the most productivity-enhancing ideas? Can the sectors or locations be identified where the spillover effects may be large? Can governments encourage the production and use of new knowledge? And with globalization, what are the extensions of endogenous growth theory to international trade, international capital flows, and the international diffusion of ideas?

Given their increasing openness, the developing economies will be most affected by the international aspects of the new growth theory. What are the best institutional arrangements for gaining access to the knowledge that already exists in the world? More extensive analysis will have to be given to the nonconvexities involved in the process of diffusion and adoption of new goods and techniques in a developing economy. All of this will have to be integrated with theories of imperfect competition and a country's social absorption capacity for innovations.

Given the special nature of ideas and information that lead to increasing returns to scale in the economy, Kenneth J. Arrow (1995: 18) maintains that

> the development and diffusion of technically useful information depends to a major extent on social institutions of a type quite different from those usually characterized as economic. . . . Each growing nation, developed or not, has to face the issue of creating new technical information and, perhaps more important, of transmitting it to the point where it is used. What is most important to transmit will depend on the economic stage of the country. For some, knowledge for agricultural production is the most critical; for others technical information at different levels of manufacturing sophistication or trade channels. In all these, the abilities to communicate and to receive communication are of the highest importance, and these in turn are derived from educational policy and from attitudes to change and mobility.
>
> The formation of policy for the encouragement of the acquisition and diffusion of productive information is one of the key issues of economic growth. The standard tools of economic theory have only a marginal contribution to make here.

At the theoretical level, the new growth theory is significant for its attempt to interrelate physical investment, technical change, and human capital formation. So far, however, the empirical application has been less for the developing economies than for the advanced industrial nations. One reason is that only after physical capital accumulation has proceeded to a sufficiently high level can investment in human capital be productive, and still later for investment in R & D to be so (Lau 1999: 62). Moreover, if knowledge is a public good that is nonrival and nonexcludable, it becomes available to all countries, and an explanation of the variation in crosscountry growth experiences on the basis of differences in knowledge capital is then ruled out. The externality would have to be geographically limited if it is to help explain differences across countries.

Understanding the determinants of technical change is complicated and still inadequately explained. The appeal to R & D may be part of the answer in more developed countries, but this activity has little relevance for the less developed. Although attempts have been made to model the endogenous component of technological progress (see Aghion and Howitt 1992; Grossman and Helpman 1991; Romer 1990), exogenous elements still remain in the R&D process, innovations, and productivity-increasing improvements at the micro level. Most significantly, growth is produced through productive enterprises, but how the micro economic factors determining innovations at the level of firms are to be connected with an aggregate production function remains vague.

Instead of the more formal models of the new growth theory, reliance on historical and empirical studies may offer fuller understanding of the process of technology diffusion to the LDCs. While a "technology gap" exists between the more developed and less developed countries, the scope for "catchup" varies among countries according to their assimilation of foreign technology, investment, education, institutional change, incentives to innovate, removal of financial market imperfections, and openness to foreign ideas.

Long ago, Ricardo recognized the value of trade in ideas as well as in goods, and Myint (1971) emphasized the "educative effect" of international competition in improving productivity and assimilating new technology. Especially relevant for developing countries are "assimilation" theories of technology that stress the centrality of learning in the identification, adaptation, and operation of new and superior imported technologies (Nelson and Pack 1999). "Assimilation" theories go beyond mere accumulation of capital through savings to focus on entrepreneurship, innovation, and learning that facilitate absorption of new technologies. Instead of movement along a production function, the emphasis is on shifts in the production function. Appropriate institutions, market incentives, and supportive government policies are necessary to induce sufficient entrepreneurial incentive to adopt new methods from abroad. Because the new technology is not costless (Pack and Westphal 1986), the rate of assimilation depends on the institutions, property rights regime, and pricing structure that determine the private profitability of acquiring knowledge. At the level of the firm, absorption depends on successful entrepreneurial efforts to learn about new opportunities, improve organization, and undertake minor but cumulatively significant changes in the production process (Nelson and Pack 1999: 431).

Beyond the initial emphasis on physical capital, and then later human capital and knowledge capital, some economists would now add "social capital" to the sources of growth.

Paul Collier (1998) characterizes "social capital" as the internal social and cultural coherence of society, the norms and values that govern interactions among people, and the institutions in which they are embedded. Social capital has an economic payoff when it is a social interaction that yields externalities and facilitates collective action for mutual benefit outside the market.

Trust, reciprocity, interpersonal networks, cooperation, coordination can be viewed as "civil social capital" that conditions the interaction of agents and yields externalities.[4]

"Government social capital" can incorporate the benefits of law, order, property rights, education, health, and "good government." To the extent that social capital reduces transaction costs and information costs, and makes physical capital and human capital more productive, it can be said to have an economic payoff and be a source of TFP. It can then be viewed more as an A-type shift factor in the aggregate production function than a private input.

Is social capital measurable as a source of growth? (Dasgupta 2000; Solow 1994, 2000). Does it have the attributes of "capital"? What is it a stock of that can be measured? Is it empirically an important contribution to the residual in the decomposition of the aggregate production function? Are there operational guidelines for the accumulation of "social capital"? Who should provide the social capital?

These concerns are somewhat reminiscent of the issue of "absorption capacity" for physical capital in the early development economics. If, however, it is difficult to define and measure activities that create human capital and knowledge capital, this is all the more difficult for "social capital." There is no gainsaying that economic behavior is, of course, socially conditioned. But aside from the technical language, is the appeal to "social capital" anything more than an appeal to consider culture and institutions?

Nonetheless, although we may not expect studies to quantify the residual of "social capital" in a Solow-growth model,[5] we can still explore behavioral patterns qualitatively and distinguish institutional characteristics. More specific and disciplined analysis can be devoted to issues of an efficient administrative system, clear property rights, a reliable legal system, contract enforcement, avoidance of corruption, improvements in corporate governance, the regime of economic incentives, social cohesion, and state capability and credibility in policy making and conflict resolution. Some of this wider analysis may come by establishing stronger linkages among development economics, the new institutional economics, and the new economic sociology.[6]

The emphasis on social capital—or culture, institutions, and social capability—should move the explanation of the process of change into a multidisciplinary endeavor. As Douglass North (1990, 1997) contends, cultural beliefs are a basic determinant of institutional structure. Not economics but psychology, sociology, political science, anthropology, law, and history must then provide the answers to what are the origins of cultural beliefs and how they lead to institutional change and the formation of social capital over time. Interdisciplinary research is needed to understand the obstacles to change in the form of values and institutions. Growth may be limited by lack of social capital. But if development occurs it may deepen social capital, and a favorable interactive process can evolve. Only a beginning has been made in understanding such an interactive and cumulative process. Especially relevant will be attempts to undertake more empirical research on incentives, problems of risk and uncertainty, the reduction of information and transaction costs, and the yield of externalities in social interaction.

What remains clear is that TFP is extremely important in explaining intercountry differences in GDP growth rates.[7] An increase in TFP encompasses all kinds of real cost reductions. Insofar as these real cost reductions operate through individual firms, analysis should focus on productive enterprises at the micro level. Behind the growth accounting is the driving search for real cost reductions by managers and entrepreneurs (Harberger 1996: 384). The multitude of real cost reductions at the micro level can then be added up to constitute the GDP of an industry, a sector, or the whole economy.

INTERNATIONAL OPENNESS

Growth in an open economy is heavily influenced by trade in commodities and services, international movements of factors, and the diffusion of technology. Since the time of Ricardo (1817) and the enunciation of the principle of comparative advantage, orthodox economics has seen no conflict between the gains from trade and the gains from growth. The opening of a country to trade provides another production function by which exportables (the inputs) can be transformed into importables (the output). By following its comparative advantage, the cost of indirectly producing the importable through specialization in exports is less than that of producing importables directly at home. Openness minimizes the opportunity cost of acquiring importables. When a country specializes according to its comparative advantage and trades at the international exchange ratio, it gains an increase in real income. This gain is tantamount to an outward shift in the country's production frontier, even if the economy operates under the constraints of fixed amounts of resources and unchanged techniques of production.

This classical view, however, was challenged in the early period of development economics. As we have seen (chapter 4), some development economists claimed that some other pattern of resource allocation, different from that governed by comparative advantage, might lead to an even greater outward shift in the production frontier over time. They asserted that classical trade analysis was static analysis and that although the resource allocation associated with trade might conform to requirements for production efficiency in a single period, it is possible that another allocation—even if it violates comparative advantage—might conform more closely to the multiperiod, not merely single-period, requirements for maximizing output over time. Arguments for import substitution followed.

These arguments, however, overlook the extensive analysis that has been made on the dynamics of basic trade models for growing economies (Helpman and Krugman 1985; Jensen and Wong 1997). And the actual realization of dynamic gains from trade that have accounted for considerable growth in developing countries.

Although it was not central in classical thought, there was nonetheless some recognition of the dynamic and growth-transmitting aspect of trade. The gains from trade were a fundamental part of classical growth economics (recall chapter 2). John Stuart Mill, for one, was exceptionally clear on this. Trade, according to comparative advantage, results in a "more efficient employment of the productive forces of the world," and this may be considered the "direct economical advantage of foreign trade. But," emphasizes Mill, "there are, besides, indirect effects, which must be counted as benefits of a high order" One of the most significant "indirect" dynamic benefits, according to Mill, is "the tendency of every extension of the market to improve the processes of production. A country that produces for a larger market than its own, can introduce a more extended division of labour, can make greater use of machinery, and is more likely to make inventions and improvements in the processes of production" (1848: vol. 2, bk. 2, ch. 17, sec. 5).

Mill also showed his awareness of the special conditions in poor countries by observing that trade benefits the less developed country through

> the introduction of foreign arts, which raise the returns derivable from additional capital to a rate corresponding to the low strength of the desire of accumulation; and the importation of foreign capital which renders the increase of production no longer exclusively dependent on the thrift or providence of the inhabitants themselves, while it places before them a stimulating example, and by instilling new ideas and breaking the chain of habit, if not by improving the actual condition of the population, tends to create in them new wants, increased ambition, and greater thought for the future. (1848: vol. 1, bk. 1, ch. 13, sec. 1)

Considering the classical economists more generally, Hla Myint (1958) distinguished a dynamic "productivity" theory in classical thought. The "productivity" theory links development to international trade by interpreting trade as a dynamic force that widens the extent of the market and the scope of the division of labor, thereby permitting a greater use of machinery, stimulating innovations, overcoming technical indivisibilities, raising the productivity of labor, and generally enabling the trading country to enjoy increasing returns. These gains correspond to a modern reading of Mill's "indirect effects, which must be counted as benefits of a high order."

This conception of the impact of trade emphasizes the supply side of the development process—the opportunity that trade gives a poor country to remove domestic shortages and to overcome the diseconomies of the small size of its domestic market. Of major benefit is the opportunity that trade offers for the exchange of goods with less growth potential for goods with more growth potential, thereby quickening the progress that results from a given effort on the savings side (Hicks 1959: 132). An obvious example is the opportunity to import capital goods and materials required for development purposes.

Moreover, the capacity to save increases as real income rises through the more efficient resource allocation associated with international trade. The stimulus to investment is also strengthened by the realization of increasing returns in the wider markets that overseas trade provides. Further, by allowing economies of large-scale production, the access to foreign markets makes it profitable to adopt more advanced techniques of production that require more capital; the opportunities for the productive investment of capital are then greater than they would be if the market were limited only to the small size of the home markets (Hicks 1959: 183–185).

Perhaps of even more value than the direct importation of material goods is the fundamental "educative effect" of trade. As emphasized in the new growth theory, deficiency of knowledge is a more pervasive handicap to development than is the scarcity of any other factor. Contact with more advanced economies provides an expeditious way of overcoming this deficiency. The importation of technical knowhow, skills, and entrepreneurship are crucial for technological progress. The importation of ideas in general is a potent stimulus to development. This is vital not only for economic change in itself but also for political and sociocultural advances that may be the necessary preconditions of economic progress. By providing the opportunity to learn from the achievements and failures of the more advanced countries, and by facilitating selective borrowing and adaptation, the international openness of a developing country can promote the formation of not only physical capital but also human capital, knowledge capital, and social capital.

For these several reasons, the conclusion of mainstream economics has been that international trade stimulates a country's development. Above and beyond the static gains that result from the more efficient resource allocation with given production functions, international trade also transforms existing production functions and induces outward shifts in the production frontier. The dynamic benefits of trade can be summarized as meaning, in analytical terms, that a movement along the production frontier in accordance with the preexisting comparative cost situation will tend to push the production possibility frontier upward and outward. Thus, when they are properly interpreted in their dynamic sense, the gains from trade do not result merely from a once-over change in resource allocation but are continuously merging with the gains from growth.

If trade increases the capacity for development, then the larger the volume of trade that is based on dynamic comparative advantage, and the greater should be the potential for development. As a country proceeds up the ladder of dynamic comparative advantage, the increasing value of its exports contributes all the more to the economy's growth. Beginning initially with Ricardo-type exports based on "natural" differences in labor productivity or Heckscher-Ohlin-type goods based on historical factor endowments, the value added in exports increases as the country proceeds on to skilled labor-intensive, capital-intensive, and knowledge-intensive exports. In the higher rungs of the ladder, the exports are of Porter- and Krugman-type goods, in which comparative advantage is not simply natural or historical but has been acquired.[8] Michael E. Porter and Krugman stress the creation of comparative advantage in new products through proprietary knowledge, innovations, investment in human capital and physical capital, and the realization of economies of scale in production. Such sources of comparative advantage are dynamic, involving a process of economic transformation and the creation of comparative advantage in differentiated goods through technical capability and learning by doing.

Dynamic comparative advantage is increasingly linked in a rapidly changing technological world to technological diffusion and adoption, the transfer of skills, and knowhow—all the elements that might contribute to accelerating the country's "learning rate." Although growth theory has not yet formalized the determinants of a country's "learning rate," foreign trade has to be allotted a substantial role in promoting dynamic learning scale economies via the competitive stimuli it creates, its cost-reduction effects, its external economies, and its contribution to increasing productivity.

Figure 7.2 illustrates the ladder of comparative advantage with the composition of exports changing over time. It also indicates that as a "leading" country moves up the ladder, "followers" occupy the vacant rungs.

From the development record, we can readily conclude that export promotion has contributed more to raise a developing country's rate of growth in income than has import substitution. This has been mainly because of dynamic gains from trade in practice.

Export expansion has been shown to be positively, and import substitution negatively, correlated with changes in total factor productivity (Nishimizu and Robinson 1984: table 5). Econometric analysis also indicates that marginal factor productivities in export-oriented industries are significantly higher than in the non-export-oriented industries (Feder

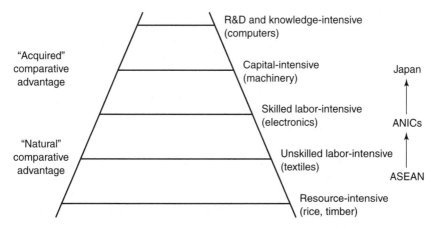

Figure 7.2 Ladder of comparative advantage. The sources of comparative advantage evolve over time, thereby changing a country's composition of trade and its position on the ladder of comparative advantage. At the lower rungs, "natural" comparative advantage is related to Ricardian and Hecksher-Ohlin-type goods that have a cost-based type of advantage. The higher rungs of "acquired" comparative advantage relate to Porter- and Krugman-type goods that have a product-based type of advantage.

1982). The difference seems to derive, in part, from intersectoral beneficial externalities generated by the export sector.

Most important has been a realization of dynamic efficiency in the sense of a fall in the incremental capital/output ratio, the realization of "X efficiency," the extension of informational efficiency, enjoyment of external economies, and realization of Verdoon effects. Considering the latter, there is evidence that the faster export output grows, the faster is the growth in productivity. This is because of economies of scale, higher investment embodying capital of a more productive vintage, and a faster pace of innovation in products and processes (Amsden 1985: 271–284).

More generally, dynamic efficiency may be interpreted as a reduction in what Myint terms "organizational dualism." Myint interprets a developing country as being within its production-possibility curve on a lower curve—its production-feasibility curve. Even if one could remove all the policy-induced distortions, a substratum of "natural" dualism would still exist in factor markets, goods markets, and in the administration and fiscal system because of institutional features and the costs of transactions, transportation, information, and administration. Given the incomplete state of development of its domestic organizational framework, the country is within its production-possibility frontier. The gap between the production-possibility curve and the production-feasibility curve is not uniform but is skewed against an increase in output of the traditional sector. This is because the frictions and the costs of overcoming them are not uniformly distributed. These frictional costs are higher within the unorganized traditional sector and in the transactions between the traditional and the modern sectors and are lower within the modern sector and in the transactions between the modern sector and the outside world.

The incompletely developed organizational framework of a developing country can be improved by appropriate trade policies or repressed by inappropriate policies. By overcoming indivisibilities and filling in the gaps in the organizational framework of the traditional sector, the expansion of exports may be able to shift the production-feasibility curve upward. In moving from a position on the production-feasibility curve to the production-possibility curve, a developing country gains much more than simply a once-over change to comparative advantage. Organizational dualism is reduced in the sense of a reduction in the costs of transactions, transportation, information, and administration.

The improved effectiveness of the domestic economic organization allows the developing country to take advantage of available external economic opportunities in the form of international trade, foreign investment, technological adaptation, and ideas from abroad. There is institutional adaptation to realize the potential comparative advantage in trade. The mutual interaction between economic policies and economic institutions results in improvement of the organization of production, more effective incentives, and a strengthening of markets. Dynamic efficiency is realized as diseconomies of a small economy are overcome, the transformation capacity of the economy widens, and the learning rate of the economy accelerates.

Regarding capital movements, we saw previously that the early development economists were initially concerned with the inflow of foreign capital in the form of international aid. Nurkse (1953: 131), however, also recognized the need for "a theory of capital movements that is concerned with capital as a factor of production" and a theory that

> would direct attention to the unequal proportions in which capital cooperates with labor and land in the different parts of the world; to the technical forms which capital should assume in response to different relative factor endowments; to the relations between capital movements, population growth and migration; and to other such fundamental matters. Only fragments of this type of capital-movement theory exist today [1953], but the great awakening is forcing the attention of economists all over the world to these basic questions—with some benefit, one may hope, not only to the theory of capital formation and development, but to international economics generally.

More attention is now given to private foreign investment than foreign aid. Its positive contribution to the real income of the recipient country is increasingly recognized. An inflow of private capital contributes to the recipient country's development program in two general ways—by helping to reduce the shortage of domestic savings and by increasing the supply of foreign exchange. To this extent, the receipt of private foreign investment permits a more rapid expansion in real income, eases the shortage of foreign exchange, and removes the necessity of resorting to a drive toward self-sufficiency and the deliberate stimulation of import-substitution industries out of deference to foreign exchange considerations.

Beyond this initial contribution, the essence of the case for encouraging foreign investment is that in time, as the investment operates, the general increase in real income resulting from the act of investment is greater than the resultant increase in the income of the foreign investor. There is a national economic benefit if the value added to output by the foreign capital is greater than the amount appropriated by the investor: social returns exceed private returns. As long as foreign investment raises productivity, and this increase is not wholly appropriated by the investor, it follows that the greater product must be shared with others, and there must be some direct benefits to other income groups. These benefits can accrue to domestic labor in the form of higher real wages, consumers by way of lower prices, and the government through expanded revenue. In addition, and of most importance in many cases, there are likely to be indirect gains through the realization of external economies.

The presence of foreign capital may not only raise the productivity of a given amount of labor but may also allow a larger labor force to be employed. This may be especially significant for heavily populated countries where the population pressures are taken out through unemployment or underemployment in the rural sector. If, as is frequently contended, a shortage of capital limits the employment of labor from the rural sector in the industrial sector where wages are higher, an inflow of foreign capital can make possible more employment in the advanced sector. The international movement of capital thus serves as an alternative to the migration of labor from the poor country. When outlets for the emigration of "surplus" labor are restricted, the substitution of domestic migration of labor into the advanced sector becomes the most feasible solution. The social benefit from the foreign investment in the advanced sector is then greater than the profits on this investment, for the wages received by the newly employed exceed their marginal productivity in the rural sector; and this excess should be added as a national gain.

Some benefits from foreign investment may also accrue to consumers. When the investment is cost reducing in a particular industry, there may be a gain not only to the suppliers of factors in this industry through higher factor prices but also to consumers of the product through lower product prices. If the investment is product improving or product innovating, consumers may then enjoy better quality products or new products.

In order that labor and consumers might gain part of the benefit from the higher productivity in foreign enterprises, the overseas withdrawal by the investors must be less than the increase in output. But even if the entire increase in productivity accrues as foreign profits, there will still be a national benefit when the government taxes these profits or receives royalties from concession agreements.

From the standpoint of contributing to the development process, the major benefits from foreign investment are likely to arise in the form of external economies. Besides bringing to the recipient country physical capital, direct foreign investment also includes nonmonetary transfers of other resources—technological knowledge, market information, managerial and supervisory personnel, organizational experience, and innovations in products and production techniques—all of which are in short supply. By being a carrier of technological and organizational change, the foreign investment may be highly significant in providing "private technical assistance" and "demonstration effects" that are of benefit elsewhere in the economy. New techniques accompany the inflow of private capital, and by the example they set, foreign firms promote the diffusion of technical advance in the economy. Technical assistance may also be provided to suppliers and customers of the foreign enterprise. In addition, foreign investment frequently leads to the training of labor in new skills, and the knowledge gained by these workers can be transmitted to other members of the labor force, or the newly trained workers might be employed later by local firms.

Private foreign investment can also stimulate additional domestic investment in the recipient country. If the foreign capital is used to develop the country's infrastructure, it may directly facilitate more investment. Even if the foreign investment is in one industry, it may still encourage domestic investment by reducing costs in other industries; profits may then rise and lead to expansion in the other industries. Since there are so many specific scarcities in a poor country, it is common for investment to be of a cost-saving character by breaking bottlenecks in production. This stimulates expansion by raising profits in all underutilized productive capacity and by allowing the exploitation of economies of scale that had previously been restricted.

There is also considerable scope for the initial foreign investment to create external investment incentives by raising the demand for the output of other industries. The foreign investment in the first industry can give rise to profits in industries that supply inputs to the first industry, or that produce complementary products, or that produce goods bought by the factor-owners who now have higher real incomes as a result of the inflow of foreign capital. A foreign investment that is product improving or product innovating may also have similar effects. A whole series of domestic investments may thus be linked to the foreign investment.

These external effects raise production outside the foreign enterprise, but the foreign investor cannot appropriate this additional output. The spill over goes unpriced and is an uncompensated service. To the extent that the foreign investment yields an external economy, the marginal social net product of the foreign capital is greater than its marginal private net product.

CONVERGENCE

How do the productivity experience and rates of growth compare between the more developed and less developed countries? It will be recalled (chapter 4) that the economic historian Gerschenkron (1962) formulated an "advantage to backwardness" hypothesis that maintained that the backwardness of poor countries offered greater opportunities for fast growth driven by rapid productivity catchup, once a successful institutional response had been created. Modern growth theory has extended this notion into a hypothesis of convergence—namely, that the poor countries, the followers, grow faster than the rich countries, the early leaders. Convergence in levels of per capita income across countries might then be expected (Barro and Sala-I-Martin 1995).

The hypothesis is based on a Solow-type neoclassical growth model that has diminishing returns to capital setting in slowly as an economy develops. The poor country should have a higher growth potential for the following reasons (Abramovitz and David 1996: 22). When tangible capital is replaced in the poor country and new capital is installed, it can embody state-of-the-art technology; on that account, it can realize larger improvements in the average efficiency of its productivity facilities than are available to the more developed economy. The same difference applies to managerial practices. The marginal product of capital also tends to be high in the poor countries when there are low levels of capital per worker. The transfer of surplus labor from low-productivity to higher productivity activities in the modern sector also adds to the growth rate of productivity. The rise in aggregate output in itself encourages technical progress as markets widen.

Given that capital-scarce countries should have a higher rate of return, it is hypothesized that if economies differ only in their initial levels of productivity but otherwise have similar conditions in investment rates, population growth rates, and technology levels, then their per capita growth rates tend to be inversely related to the starting level of output or income per capita. In a Solow-style model of growth, there exists a unique and globally stable growth path to which productivity and per capita output will converge, and along which the rate of advance is fixed exogenously by the rate of technical progress. If poor countries at the lower level of income per capita grow faster than the rich countries, there should then be conditional convergence in levels of per capita income— the dispersion in relative productivity levels of an array of countries should be reduced. Marginal productivities of physical capital and human capital in poor countries should tend to close the technology gap between rich and poor countries. If systematic differences do remain, it must because of a variety of exogenous factors.

The new growth theory is often referred to as neo-Schumpeterian, insofar as Joseph Schumpeter's *Theory of Economic Development* (1911) and *Capitalism, Socialism and Democracy* (1942) emphasized innovations and positive spillovers. According to Peter Howitt (2000: 429), the evidence is actually more supportive of the Schumpeterian version of endogenous growth theory than of neoclassical theory. Per capita income varies across countries not only because of differences in capital stocks per worker but also because of differences in productivity. Modern growth theory should provide an integrated analysis of capital accumulation and endogenous innovation.

Empirical tests of the hypothesis for advanced Organisation for Economic Co-operation and Development (OECD) countries that are fairly homogeneous do show conditional convergence, but global convergence has not occurred for a more heterogeneous set of poor countries (Baumol 1986; Pritchett 1997). Some LDCs have stagnated, while others, equally poor in 1950, have since grown at unprecedented rates (Baumol and Tobin 1989). The lagging countries still lack sufficient savings and are without technological progress. The technological advancement in the more developed countries has not been sufficiently diffused to LDCs. While the inflow of private capital and diffusion of technology into developing countries have increased in recent years, such developments have been concentrated in middle-income rather than low-income countries. Moreover, the potential for large technological leaps based on borrowable technology is not realized if there is not technological congruence because of disparate factor proportions, scale of industry limited by small market size, and scale of industry limited by institutional factors (Abramovitz 1995: 26–27). More generally, deficiencies in social capital or social capability may limit the catching-up process.

Abramovitz and David (1996) summarize their general proposition about convergence:

> [C]ountries' effective potentials for rapid productivity growth by catch-up are not determined solely by the gaps in levels of technology, capital intensity, and efficient allocation that separate them from the productivity leaders. They are restricted also by their access to primary materials and more generally because their market scales, relative factor supplies and income-constrained patterns of demand make their technical capabilities and their product structures incongruent in some degree with those that characterize countries that operate at or near the technological frontiers. And they are limited, finally, by those institutional characteristics that restrict their abilities to finance, organize, and operate the kinds of enterprises that are required to exploit the technologies on the frontiers of science and engineering. Taken together, the foregoing elements determine a country's effective potential for productivity growth.

In refining Gerschenkron's 1952 view of the degree of backwardness and subsequent "catchup" (chapter 4), Abramovitz (1995: 45–46) concludes that

> Having regard to technological backwardness alone leads to the simple hypothesis about catch-up and convergence. . . . Having regard to social capability, however, we expect that the developments anticipated by that hypothesis will be clearly displayed in cross-country comparisons only if countries' social capabilities are about the same. One should say, therefore, that a country's potentiality for rapid growth is strong not when it is backward without qualification, but rather when it is technologically backward but socially advanced.

An empirical study by Lant Pritchett (1997: 15) concludes that a quarter of the 60 countries with initial per capita GDP of less than $1000 in 1960 have had growth rates less than zero, and a third have had growth rates less than .05 percent over the 1960–90 period. There are also forces for "implosive" decline, such as that witnessed in some countries in which the fabric of civic society appears to have disintegrated altogether, a point often ignored or acknowledged offhand as these countries fail to gather plausible economic statistics and thus drop out of our samples altogether. Backwardness seems to carry severe disadvantages. For economists and social scientists, a coherent model of how to overcome these disadvantages is a pressing challenge.

> But this challenge is almost certainly not the same as deriving a single "growth theory." Any theory that seeks to unify the world's experience with economic growth and development must address at least four distinct questions: What accounts for continued per capita growth and technological progress of those leading countries at the frontier? What accounts for the few countries that are able to initiate and sustain periods of rapid growth in which they gain significantly on the leaders? What accounts for why some countries fade and lose the momentum of rapid growth? What accounts for why some countries remain in low growth for very long periods?

It is clear that catchup or convergence is not automatic, and a country requires country-specific favorable conditions to attain its growth potential. In a bold attempt, however, to forecast the course of world income growth and income inequality of the century to come, Robert E. Lucas (2000: 166) predicts that "sooner or later everyone will join the industrial revolution, that all economies will grow at the rate common to the wealthiest economies, and that percentage differences in income levels will disappear. . . . Ideas can be imitated and resources can and do flow to places where they earn the highest return."

REGRESSION ANALYSIS

As a complement to theories of growth, many analysts have undertaken crosscountry regressions that supposedly "explain" the rate of growth. On the left side of the equation, growth in GDP per capita is taken as the dependent variable of a variety of economic forces, economic policy indicators, political variables, and institutional elements on the right side. More than 50 variables have been found to be significantly correlated with growth in at least one regression. Every other week, another regression is run in an attempt to determine the influence on growth of a set of variables on the right side of the cross-sectional regression.[9] Some findings are that growth is influenced positively by macroeconomic stability, increasing share of investment in GDP (especially in equipment), human capital, protection of property rights, quality of bureaucracy, enforceability of contracts, democracy, depth of financial intermediation, openness to trade, and technological progress (Barro 1997; Fagenberg 1994; Hall and Jones 1999; Knack and Keefer 1995; Levine and Renelt 1992).

The statistical results, however, are not robust to the choice of explanatory variables but are fragile to small changes in the information set and to measurement sensitivity (Levine and Renelt 1992). From the standpoint of statistical inference, the regressions commonly suffer from problems of simultaneity in the sense that the righthand variables are jointly determined with the growth rate (what are the exogenous variables?), multicollinearity, bias from omitted variables, limited degrees of freedom, and measurement error (Temple 1999).

Given the limitations of regression analysis, more meaningful explanations of the determinants of growth and a richer interpretation of development experience may come from historical studies of country experiences. If Romer supplements Solow, historical cases can supplement Romer. This would mean a return to some of the first generation's questions posed earlier by Kuznets, Gerschenkron, and Rostow (chapter 4).[10] This return can be aided by recent endogenous growth theories combined with analytical country narratives that are now based on more data and to institutions other than the market that are required for coordination and enforcement.

As the economic historian Avner Greif observes,

> the [neoclassical theorists make the] assumption that secure property rights and large numbers are necessary and sufficient conditions for the emergence of markets and that markets always efficiently provide incentives and coordination renders irrelevant the analysis of market formation and the nonmarket institutions that support, complement, and supplement the market. . . . These assumptions [of neoclassical cliometrics] limited the study of issues that were traditionally the focus of economic historians, such as the nature and role of nonmarket institutions, culture, entrepreneurship, technological and organizational innovation, politics, social factors, distributional conflicts, and the historical process through which economies grew and decline. The importance of examining such issues and the cost of neglecting them, however, [have] become obvious.[11]

From a review of historical perspectives on development, another economic historian, Nicholas Crafts (2001: 326), also concludes that "first, the attempts to force patterns of economic growth and development into the framework of the augmented-Solow neoclassical growth model are seriously misconceived. Second, institutions matter for economic growth, but countries can be expected to diverge significantly and persistently in their institutional arrangements."

More attention to microlevel institutional features of development history together with the conceptual framework of the new development economics (chapter 7) may now offer more policy-relevant predictions than regression analysis can.

DIAGRAMMATIC SUMMARY

Besides figure 7.2, much of growth theory can be summarized in two other diagrams (figures 7.3, 7.4).

The sources of growth are decomposable into the following developments.

1. Initial movement from the poor country's underdeveloped initial position P_0 to its production-possibility frontier (technical efficiency) results from improved allocation of resources and better functioning of markets, even with given resources and techniques of production.
2. Subsequent growth in output—the outward movement of the

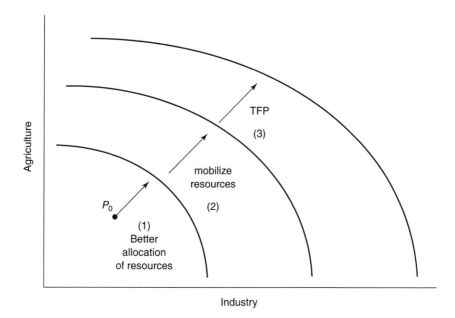

Figure 7.3 Sources of growth

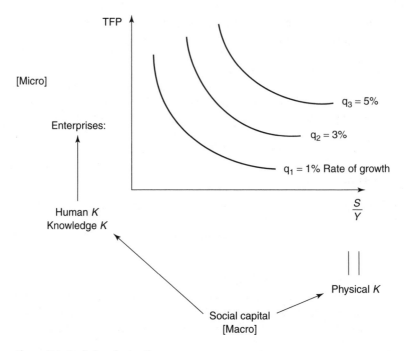

Figure 7.4 Capital and growth

production frontier—as a results from increase in the quantity of inputs plus an improvement in their quality.

3. Further growth in TFP results from the openness of the economy and technical change: human capital, knowledge capital, social capital.

A structural transformation of the economy occurs if the pattern of growth consists of a proportionately greater shift in the industrial output (X) than in the agricultural output (Y). New and improved institutions together with government policy and the better functioning of markets will determine both the rate and pattern of growth.

Aggregate output is a function of savings and TFP. Savings are a function of national income, real interest rates, risk, transaction costs, and rates of return; TFP is a function of human capital, knowledge capital, social capital, and other elements in technical change (the residual). An increase in TFP results in a reduction of real costs within enterprises. Government policy may thus have a positive micro impact by "delivering" a reduction in costs through provision of infrastructure and promotion of human capital and knowledge capital. Government may also enable a fall in costs by controlling inflation, reducing economic distortions, rationalizing, and promoting open trade policies. Protection of property and contract rights in the legal infrastructure are also important components of social capital. Although growth theory is usually expressed in terms of an aggregate production function, the emphasis on TFP means that the process of growth involves real cost reductions in business enterprises (Harberger 2001: 546–549). Government policies that promote real cost reductions are therefore of prime importance.

8

The New Development Economics

Advances in general economic theory during the last two decades introduced marked changes in thinking about development. In both positive and normative analysis, the changed concepts are so different from traditional mainstream neoclassical economics that Joseph Stiglitz (1986) labels them the "new development economics."[1] He maintains that

> market failures, particularly those related to imperfect and costly information, may provide insights into why the LDCs have a lower level of income and why so many find it difficult to maintain existing current differentials, let alone to catch up. What is at stake is more than just differences in endowments of factors, but basic aspects of the organization of the economy, including the functioning of markets. . . . The kinds of market failures with which I have been concerned are markedly different from those that were the focus of attention some two decades ago. (1989: 201)

THE IMPERFECT INFORMATION PARADIGM

In his Nobel lecture, Stiglitz recalls that his first visits to the developing world in 1967, and a more extensive stay in Kenya in 1969, made an indelible impression that turned him "away from the competitive equilibrium model to a concern with the imperfections of information, the absence of markets, and the pervasiveness and persistence of seemingly dysfunctional institutions, such as sharecropping" (2002: 460).

The traditional neoclassical paradigm does allow for some market failures in the form of external diseconomies and public goods. Beyond this, however, the new development economics focuses on more pervasive market failures associated with information and learning, incentives, incomplete markets, missing markets, and imperfect markets. It also departs from the assumptions and implications of the standard neoclassical growth model by considering institutions, historical legacies, distribution of wealth, adverse selection, moral hazard, coordination failures, multiple equilibria, and poverty traps. The contention is that industrial and developing countries are on different production functions and are organized in different ways. What has to be understood is the nature of the equilibrium in developing countries that may hinder development. Failures of collective action or collective rationality can account for coordination failures and low-level equilibria (poverty traps) that are inferior to other possible equilibria.[2]

Central to the modern theory of underdevelopment traps is imperfect information. Imperfections in information are more pervasive in less developed countries and can result in less efficient resource allocation than in more developed countries. In emphasizing the imperfect information paradigm, Stiglitz (1985: 26) maintains:

> Traditional economic theory has ignored the central problems associated with costly information. When due attention is paid to these information theoretic considerations, the basic propositions of neoclassical analysis no longer remain valid: market equilibrium may not exist, even when all the underlying preferences and production sets are "well behaved"; when equilibrium exists, it is, in general, not Pareto efficient; it may not be possible to decentralize efficient resource allocations; the separation between efficiency and equity considerations which characterizes traditional neoclassical theory no longer obtains; market equilibrium may be characterized by an excess demand for credit or an excess supply of labor (that is, the law of supply and demand no longer holds). The theory which has been developed explicitly incorporating information theoretic considerations provides an explanation of phenomena about which traditional theory simply had nothing to say.

ORGANIZATION OF THE RURAL SECTOR

As an illustration of the more general paradigm, Stiglitz (1986: 257–278) reinterprets the organization of the rural sector in a developing economy. He analyzes sharecropping as an institution that represents a response to market failure. It has general significance in being an example of the importance of institutions in explaining economic behavior.

There are five central tenets in the new economics of rural organization.[3]

1. Individuals, including peasants in the rural sector, are rational.
2. Information is costly, and individuals acquire only imperfect information. Thus transactions (buying labor service, extending credit, renting land) that would be desirable in the presence of perfect information may not occur. Similarly, certain contracts (for example, for certain services at a certain standard) may not be feasible, especially if it is costly to ascertain, ex post, whether or how well those services have been performed.
3. Institutions adapt their structure to reflect information costs.

4. The economy is not Pareto efficient (that is, at an equilibrium position where it is impossible to make someone better off without making someone else worse off). With imperfect information and incomplete markets, the economy is constrained Pareto inefficient—that is, a set of taxes and subsidies exists that can make everyone better off.

5. This implies that there is a potential role for the government to effect a Pareto improvement. But informational problems and incentive problems are no less important in the public sector than in the private, and these may limit government actions as remedies for certain observed deficiencies in the market.

The foregoing approach can be applied to an understanding of the system of sharecropping whereby the tenant pays the landlord a portion of output for the use of the land. Alternative contracts could involve rental of the land or wage labor on the land. Earlier views held that sharecropping was an inefficient form of organization, insofar as the worker received less than the value of his or her marginal product and therefore had less incentive to exert effort.

But why then is the system still so prevalent? Part of the explanation is that the peasant workers are more risk averse than landlords and do not want to rent the land from landlords. More pointedly, sharecropping provides an effective incentive system as an alternative to the costly supervision of a worker in a wage system. Since the worker's pay in a sharecropping system depends directly on his or her output, he or she has some incentives to work. In the other alternative of land rental, the landlord would have to bear some of the costs of risk-taking by the tenant when the landlord has limited ability to force the tenant to pay back rents. "Thus, sharecropping can be viewed as an institution, which has developed in response to (a) risk-aversion of the part of workers; (b) the limited ability (or desire) to force the tenant to pay back rents when he is clearly unable to do so; and (c) the limited ability to monitor the actions of the tenant (or the high costs of doing so)" (Stiglitz 1986: 258). When the landlord cannot directly control the effort of the worker, he views sharecropping as providing the additional incentives to work hard.

Interlinkages between land, labor, and credit markets also characterize the rural organizational network. This illustrates situations where there are important moral hazard problems. The landlord as supplier of credit to tenants runs the risk of default, and thus actions of the tenant-borrower will affect the landlord-cum-creditor. Recognizing the externalities between his or her transactions for land and credit, the landlord-cum-creditor adjusts the transactions so as to be as well off as possible. The externalities are internalized, and the interlinkage of markets is motivated by the desire for economic efficiency (Braverman and Stiglitz 1982).

A number of other tenancy models have been formulated (Binswanger and Rosenzweig 1981). In these, costly supervision arises because of imperfect information. Information is asymmetrically distributed between landlord and tenant because only the tenant knows how much effort will be forthcoming. If the government has no more information than the landlord, it cannot improve on the existing allocation. As long as there are underlying constraints on information or land transfer, the share tenancy equilibrium is optimal with respect to these constraints, albeit a second-best optimum.

Over time, workers first become sharecroppers, then fixed-rent tenants, and finally owners of their own land. In a given period, however, the coexistence of different contractual arrangements can be explained by differences in risk aversion, screening of workers of different quality, and market imperfections for inputs other than labor. Different classes of workers will prefer their respective contracts. Contractual choice models identify the causes of the market imperfections that lead to contracts in interlinked markets. Further, the characteristics of land and labor contracts in agrarian economies help to explain why the decentralized system of small-scale family farms continues to be the dominant mode of production (Hayami and Otsuka 1993).

FINANCIAL SYSTEM

The relationship between finance and development was until recently a relatively neglected topic in development. Perhaps the neglect is traceable to an early assertion by Joan Robinson (1952: 86–87) that finance is not a bottleneck in the development process: "It seems to be the case that where enterprise leads, finance follows. The same impulses within an economy which set enterprise on foot make owners of wealth venturesome, and when a strong impulse to invest is fettered by lack of finance, devices are invented to release it . . . and habits and institutions are developed."

Financial markets have more notable characteristics, however, than being simply demand-following and subject to human discretion. It is especially important to achieve a better understanding of the evolution of financial institutions. In connection with the implementation of the new development economics for banks and other credit institutions, Stiglitz observes:

> there seems an almost universal under-appreciation of the importance of the role played by these institutions. . . . Recent work on the economics of information has led us to understand better that what used to be thought of as "capital market imperfections" are simply the reflections of the informational imperfections which are endemic—and which it is the social function of these institutions to address. (1989: 61)

The new development economics thus interprets a country's financial sector as different from other sectors in being characterized by a combination of information asymmetries—namely, providers of funds know less about their ultimate use than do the borrowers, and the giving of credit involves intertemporal exchange of future claims on resources for present ones. There is an inherent element of uncertainty. Information imperfections in credit markets and credit rationing give rise to problems of adverse selection because of hidden information and to problems of moral hazard because of hidden action. High transaction costs may limit trade or prevent the creation of a market. Further, efficient intermediation requires diversification, but many developing countries are too small to make this possible.

To minimize the problems of uncertainty and risk—not to mention deleterious effects of financial crises from external shocks—there is need for supervision and monitoring by both markets and nonmarket supervisory institutions. Given the unique character of finance and the range of market failures to which financial markets are subject, government actions are commonly needed to create new financial institutions and regulate financial market instruments. Government interventions may be especially needed to improve the efficiency of the banking system and secondary markets. Necessary research is now being done on prudential regulation.

When information is imperfect, markets may be thin or missing. More research is being directed to the effects of different institutional arrangements for insuring individuals in developing countries against various types of risk and facilitating their access to credit and investment (for example, through land reform, rural credit markets, micro credit).

Whereas the early development economics emphasized the accumulation of capital, the emphasis now is on the allocation of capital—the determination of what firms receive the loanable funds, the monitoring of the borrower's performance, and the growth effects of the different forms in which capital is accumulated. Research is demonstrating the different consequences of debt and equity for risk and is identifying failures in both the presence of debt and equity rationing (Greenwald, Kohn, and Stiglitz 1990).

The importance of the financial sector is now being seen not in raising savings and the quantity of capital but rather in a better allocation of savings and improvement in the quality of investment. Given the unique character of finance and the range of market failures to which financial markets are subject, government actions are commonly needed to create new financial institutions and to regulate financial market instruments. In terms of social objectives, government actions may provide consumer protection, ensure bank solvency, establish macroeconomic stability, promote competition, stimulate growth, and improve the allocation of resources. Public actions, however, are also subject to constraints and limitations, so that the essential problem of public regulatory policy is to determine when government action improves market performance and when, in contrast, private action can take better advantage of information and incentives within the marketplace (Stiglitz 1994: 36).

COORDINATION FAILURES

Advocacy of a "big push" and "balanced growth" was prominent in the early development economics (recall chapter 3). It was recognized that it was not profitable for the single investor to invest if others did not also do so. Although no sector would generate sufficient demand and be profitable investing alone, the simultaneous industrialization of several sectors can become profitable for all of them through positive spillovers. Strategic complementarities can create demand and yield economies of scale. The market mechanism alone, however, need not succeed in coordinating the activities needed to ensure development (Hoff 2000). Hence government interventions to create a "critical minimum push" (Leibenstein 1957) are believed necessary to break out of a low-level equilibrium trap.

The new development economics recognizes this problem as a "coordination failure," where the inability of individuals to coordinate their choices leads to a state of affairs that is worse for everyone than some alternative state of affairs that is also an equilibrium. Coordination failures and the possibility of underdevelopment traps are now analyzed in rigorous terms based on the formal modeling of diffuse externalities, technological progress, and increasing returns to scale.

Returning to the earlier concepts of Rosenstein-Rodan and Nurkse, an article by Murphy, Shleifer and Vishny (1989) analyzed the "big push" in the context of an imperfectly competitive economy with aggregate demand spillovers and interpreted the big push into industrialization as a move from a bad to a good equilibrium. The article generates formal models of economies with small domestic markets and analyzes how these markets can expand so that a country can get out of a no-industrialization trap. It focuses on the contribution of industrialization of one sector to enlarging the size of the market in other sectors through the demand spillovers from the coordination of investment across sectors. The article associates the big push concept with multiple equilibria of the economy and interprets it as a switch from cottage production equilibrium with constant returns to scale to industrial equilibrium with imperfect competition and increasing returns to scale. The industrialized equilibrium is shown to be an improvement in welfare (Pareto preferred).

The coordination problem is also relevant to Lewis's dual sector model (recall chapter 3). The modern capitalist sector pays a wage premium (some 50 percent in Lewis's model). Although the supply of labor is initially infinitely elastic at this level, the modern firm has to generate enough sales to buyers other than its own workers to be able to afford paying the higher wages. Again, coordinated investment is needed among firms producing different products so that all invest and expand production together. They can all sell their output to each other's workers and so can afford to pay the wage premium and still profit (Murphy et al. 1989: 1011).

In contrast to the previous discussion that relies on coordinated investment in the domestic market for industrialization, it might be thought that the argument does not apply if a country can depend on sufficiently large export markets. Experience shows, however, that in most countries, it is domestic demand that accounts for a sizeable share of the growth in domestic industrial output. Moreover, a substantial rise in exports usually comes only after the domestic industry is well established.

Even in the export-oriented economy of South Korea, solution of the coordination problem was essential—and indeed was a considerable factor in Korea's success. Rodrik (1995) demonstrates how the South Korean and Taiwanese governments got interventions right in managing

> to engineer a significant increase in the private return to capital. They did so not only by removing a number of impediments to investment and establishing a sound investment climate, but also more importantly by alleviating a coordination failure that had blocked economic take-off. The latter required a range of strategic interventions—including investment subsidies, administrative guidance and the use of public enterprise—which went considerably beyond those discussed in the standard account. (57)

> For a number of reasons, the economic take-off could not take place under decentralized market conditions. Chief among these reasons are the imperfect tradability of key inputs (and technologies) associated with modern-sector production, and some increasing returns to scale in these activities. These conditions created a situation of coordination failure. In other words, while the rate of return to coordinated investments was extremely high, the rate of return to individual investments remained low. (78)

Although foreign markets may be available, coordinated investment at home may still be necessary to utilize efficiently a large infrastructure project, such as a railroad or power station that has high fixed costs (Murphy et al. 1989: 1019). In addition, even with foreign markets, the output of exports may require a range of nontradable intermediate inputs that are produced under increasing returns to scale and that depend on coordinated demand for their efficient production (Rodrik 1996).

A prominent feature of the new development economics is that models of coordination can have multiple equilibria—for example, a no-industrialization equilibrium and an industrialization equilibrium, depending on expectations. If firms expect other firms to invest and income to rise, and all firms do invest in anticipation of profits, then industrialization equilibrium can result. The industrialization equilibrium—

based on positive spillovers—is Pareto-preferred to that without industrialization (Murphy et al. 1989: 1013, 1017–1018).

POLICY IMPLICATIONS

Unlike those who attribute disappointments in the development record
to government-induced interventions, proponents of the new development economics see a positive role for government. Many of the policy
implications stem from diffuse externalities that are pervasive in a developing economy, associated with innovations, knowledge, and information. The externalities can often give rise to positive feedback systems.
The role of government is therefore to be determined by answers to the
question of what are the important sources of positive feedback externalities, which cannot be internalized and thus require government intervention. There are not always government failures. The crucial issue
is to determine when and why governments fail and when and why
governments can support development efforts.

Insofar as the modern theory of underdevelopment focuses on information and knowledge, agency theories, and resultant market failures,
there are some general implications for government policies. These call
for measures to improve information flows and reduce information imperfections, produce and disseminate knowledge, and mitigate agency
problems. Whether these measures will be forthcoming and effective in
promoting development will ultimately depend in many cases on the
quality of institutional change and social capital.

To achieve the preferred situation of industrialization via coordinated
investment, a government can act to encourage or subsidize investments
that yield external economies. The obstacle to attaining the better state
of affairs is not a matter of technological opportunity, or resources or
preferences, but only of coordination. The policy implications of the
modern theory of market failures and government failures therefore center on the effort to move the economy from an inferior to a better equilibrium.

The modern theory of underdevelopment traps is based on low innovation and inefficient institutions. As such, it is argued that there is
no tendency of market forces to lead from the worse (low-level equilibrium) to the better (high-level equilibrium) (Hoff 2000). Proper policy
action by the government, however, might do so.

Possible policies are of various types. Dilip Mookherjee and Debraj
Ray (2001) indicate that the policy implications are of two kinds. There
may be policies designed to overcome "inertial self-reinforcement" of
expectations that give a low-level equilibrium, as in coordination problems. The second kind of policies may overcome "historical self-
reinforcement" that stems from ownership structures or distribution of
wealth in the past.

Some government interventions may be only temporary but sufficiently effective to "tip" the situation from an inferior equilibrium to a superior equilibrium by being designed to overcome inertial self-reinforcement. A subsidy, for example, may stimulate the needed investment. The provision of information and policies that lower search costs may provide incentives and change the beliefs of agents so that there can be a shift to a better equilibrium. Other policies may have to be permanent in overcoming historical self-reinforcement. For example, land reform, creation and protection of property rights, or wealth redistribution may accomplish this. The dynamic sequencing of policies can also determine if a better situation is achieved and maintained over time.

This involves the promotion of organizational change. Moreover, in this effort, the government itself is endogenous and is to be explained. If market failure is to be remedied, so too is government failure—in the sense of inferior policy choices—to be avoided.

An entire range of policy choices are available to overcome market failures and move an economy from one equilibrium to another—credit subsidies, tax incentives, administrative guidance, public investment, trade policy, labor training. The objective is to get the private sector to internalize the coordination externalities. Where there are diffuse externalities, policies have to achieve strategic complementarities and coordination by providing the appropriate incentives that will change the beliefs and actions of agents.

Although the modern theory of poverty traps supports a range of government interventions, it does not support comprehensive planning. Rosenstein-Rodan's 1943 proposal of an East European investment trust was based on the belief that "if we create a sufficiently large investment unit by including all the new industries in the region, external economies will become internal profits out of which dividends may be paid easily." This would receive modern endorsement as a move from a bad to a good equilibrium based on knowledge of the sources of externalities and scale economies.

The new development economics, however, does not endorse the centralized planning "from above" recommended by the early development economics in the 1950s. As Karla Hoff (2000: 30) says, "neither governments alone, nor markets alone, can solve it (the problem of coordination). Early writers who correctly pointed out the sources of coordination failures drew the wrong policy lessons when they interpreted coordination failures as a call for 'big push' industrialization centrally controlled by the state."

Although concern with the new market failures gives a more active role to government, there is at the same time recognition that government is not a neutral, omnipotent agent that can readily correct market or organizational failures. Government itself is constrained in its capacity to process information, is itself a group of agents with particular incentives, and may lack the capacity to perform some suggested policies.

Government failure can also stem from informational problems and wrong incentives.[4]

CHANGE IN THINKING

The new development economics is the most important change in thinking about development that has taken place during the past 50 years.[5] It strengthens the microeconomics of development through its emphasis on the economics of information, institutions, and incentives. No longer does the perfectly competitive market environment underlie development analysis. Nor does the neoclassical growth model. Central principles are that one individual can have externality-like effects on others, and that individual rationality need not yield social rationality in collective decision making. The economy may have multiple equilibria, and the particular equilibrium situation may depend in part on history and path dependence. Certain conditions can then be established under which nonmarket interventions may break poverty traps.

There is a shift in focus from neoclassical models that hypothesize that we can explain output, growth, and the differences between industrial and developing countries by focusing on "fundamentals"—resources, technology, and preferences. Instead, the modern theory of market failures focuses on incomplete markets, incomplete contracts, and incomplete information. Development is no longer seen primarily as a process of capital accumulation but rather as a process of organizational change (Hoff and Stiglitz 2001: 389–390). These departures are significant in understanding some development problems and in providing new views on private as well as public failures.

The new development economics is most significant in refining and extending the microeconomics of development. By focusing on incomplete markets, incomplete contracts, and incomplete information, it redirects development analysis from the neoclassical market fundamentalism approach and emphasis on capital accumulation to a concern with collective interdependence in decision making and the allocation of capital.

Further, unlike the usual view that a government intervention and market solutions are substitutes, there is a change in thinking of the state and market as complementary. This is especially important to overcome coordination failures that can be more general than market failures. Moreover, while the range of market failures is extended, so too there is more attention to government failure and the constraints on public policy. Although it is claimed that government needs to be endogenized, this has not yet been done, beyond the usual public choice type of interpretation. A more complex analysis of public policy making remains to be undertaken. This may draw upon the new political economy.

The possibility of multiple equilibria demonstrates that several different outcomes can occur, even when the fundamentals are the same. A range of multiple equilibria models extend from the vicious circle type of low-level equilibrium trap to the virtuous circle type of high-level equilibrium trap. To solve the equilibrium selection problem, analysts have considered evolutionary game theory, history, and path dependence, as well as choice of high-quality economic policies. The determination of beliefs or expectations of economic agents in the solution of a specific equilibrium still needs to be explained.

These changes in thinking make institutions and incentives more prominent in the subject of development. Good institutional arrangements are necessary to reduce transaction costs, provide appropriate incentives, and avoid or resolve conflict so that there can be mutually beneficial collective action. From this perspective, the new development economics connects to my earlier discussion of institutions and social capital.[6]

There are, however, shortcomings from the perspective of a more inclusive approach to the subject of development. With the emphasis on the microeconomics of development and the theory of organization, analysis is partial and reductionist in the sense of going down to particular sectors and to firms and to households. The subject, however, also requires us to focus on development as a dynamic process with attention to the interrelation of its parts. The subject has to be synthetic and integrative so that the relationships of the parts in a wider way can be understood. The early development economics attempted this with large ideas, grand design, and vision (chapter 4). These are missing in the narrower approach of the new development economics. Although particular aspects of development are illuminated (for example, rural credit, labor markets, finance), there is no inclusive theory of development. Trees are illuminated but not the forest. For the more inclusive analysis of structural transformation, attention still has to be given to the process of capital accumulation, the residual, and some fundamentals of neoclassical theory. Fundamentals across societies do matter. Moreover, while there is a concern with institutions and a call for endogenizing government policy, these black boxes of the past have so far been only slightly opened. The main focus has been on resource allocation, but there are other dimensions to development.

Indeed, the new development economics can certainly not claim to be able to settle all questions of development. And it does not so claim. The subject still awaits further evolution with the next generation of development economists. Its biography is scarcely finished.

9

Culture, Social Capital, Institutions

When analyzing why there are crosscountry differential rates of growth, it may be tempting to appeal to national "culture." In the early days of the subject there were studies of the sociocultural and social psychology aspects of development problems and modernization (Hagen 1968; Hoselitz 1967; McClelland 1961). These efforts, however, did not make much of an impression among economists, and mainstream thinking about development did not focus on the social and institutional dimensions of economic development.

CULTURE

Recently there have been two forceful calls for renewed attention to culture. In his book on *The Wealth and Poverty of Nations*, the economic historian David Landes supports Max Weber's early thesis of attributing differences in the economic performance of countries to differences in culture: Weber's "ideal type" of capitalist was rational, ordered, diligent, and productive. Landes (1998: 516–517) concludes:

> If we learn anything from the history of economic development, it is that culture makes all the difference. Here Max Weber was right on. . . . Yet culture, in the sense of inner values and attitudes that guide a population, frightens scholars. It has a sulfuric odor of race and inheritance, an air of immutability. In thoughtful moments, economists and social scientists recognize that this is not true, and indeed salute examples of cultural change for the better while deploring changes for the worse. But applauding or deploring implies the passivity of the viewer—an inability to use knowledge to shape people and things. The technicians would rather change interest and exchange rates, free up trade, alter political institutions, manage. Besides, criticisms of culture cut close to the ego, injure identity and self-esteem. Coming from outsiders, such animadversions, however tactful

and indirect, stink of condescension. Benevolent improvers have learned to steer clear.

So too does V. W. Ruttan (1989: 1385) believe that cultural endowments have a role in constraining or facilitating economic growth, but he recognizes that

> professional opinion has, however, not dealt kindly with the reputations of those development economists who have made serious attempts to incorporate cultural variables into development theory or into the analysis of the development process. But in spite of the failure of research on the economic implications of cultural endowments to find a secure place in economic development literature or thought, the conviction that "culture matters" remains pervasive in the underworld of development thought and practice. . . . In my judgment, it is time for a new generation of development economists to again take stock of the advances in the related social sciences and attempt to assess what they can contribute to our understanding of the development process and to institutional design.

Despite these appeals, many still believe that culture does not have causal priority. From his analysis of the econometric evidence on the sources of economic development, Jeffrey Sachs (2000: 42–43) concludes that political factors and poor economic institutions rather than culture per se lie behind lagging economic development. Cultural explanations should be tested against a framework that allows for geography, politics, and economics to play their role. Controlling for such variables sharply reduces the scope for an important independent role of culture.[1]

The majority of development economists are reluctant to include "culture" on the right side of a growth regression. It is difficult to operationalize a term as broad as "culture." At the worst, the appeal to culture can only too readily degenerate into bias, elitism, paternalism, and amateur notions of psychology and sociology. Moreover, discussions of culture tend to personalize rather than analyze. Too often they assume a homogeneous society and over generalize the value system in a society. Further, if they imply immutability, then "culture" is beyond the policy maker's control and is too readily the end of the story. At the least, we would want demonstration of how a particular cultural trait affected the behavior of a particular unit of analysis at a particular time. Most economists would still rather leave the matter of culture to professional social psychologists, sociologists, and cultural anthropologists.

Assertions about a nation's culture do not conform to the economist's way of thinking. And yet nobody would deny that noneconomic factors and forces do affect economic behavior, that behavioral patterns do differ among countries, and that they do matter for development.

How then can we link up some of the notions of differences in behavioral patterns with the economist's way of thinking about development? Recently an explanatory link has been sought through the concept of "social capital" and an operational link through the recognition that "institutions matter."[2] Reinforced by the new development economics, this approach allows a fresh consideration of issues that were previously related to "culture."

SOCIAL CAPITAL

What is "social capital"? The concept is used differently by sociologists,[3] political scientists, and economists (Woolcock 1998: 189–190). Various types of social capital are relevant for analysis of different situations. The World Bank defines social capital as the social relationships, networks, and norms that shape the quality and quantity of a society's interactions.[4]

The "social" characteristic of social capital is the fact that it embodies associational relationships among individuals. It has attributes of "capital" because it may take time and effort to accumulate and is an asset that has the potential to increase income or a stream of benefits over time.[5] For developing countries, it is useful to divide social capital into "civil social capital" and "government social capital" (Collier and Gunning 1999a).

Civil Social Capital

At the micro level, "civil social capital" includes the interactions of households and firms and relates to their values, beliefs, attitudes, and norms of behavior. These are individual in origin and can be characterized as cognitive. They embody in civil society such attributes as trust, reciprocity, and cooperation. These are externalities that may arise from social interaction in clubs, associations, networks, and hierarchies. Although internal and subjective, civil social capital reflects broader shared meanings within society and has the merit of helping to create and maintain an environment in which mutually beneficial collective action becomes expected and thus more likely (Uphoff 2000a: 220–221). While social capital benefits individuals, it is expected to produce goods that are more collective than just individual. The significance of the relationships formed by social capital is that they lead to mutually beneficial collective action by yielding positive externalities, solving coordination problems, and minimizing conflicts. Market failures are reduced, and the nonmarket relationships of social capital make economic transactions more productive.

There is thus a public good aspect to social capital. Insofar as there are positive externalities, however, an individual receives only part of the benefits. Civil social capital may therefore be undersupplied. The less the civil social capital, the greater is the need for government social capital.

Government Social Capital

At the macro level, "government social capital" relates to rules, procedures, and "good government." It embodies the rule of law, the establishment and protection of property rights, contract enforcement, the absence of corruption, transparency in decision making, an efficient administrative system—in short, state capability and credibility. Government social capital has a more structured form and is relatively external and objectified. As an economy develops, more government social capital tends to be formed and also facilitates mutually beneficial collective action.

Social capital is generally understood as having some combination of mental or attitudinal (cognitive) and role-based or rule-based (structural) origins. These are complementary factors that shape expectations of economic agents, leading to cooperative behavior that produces mutual benefits. Over time, the interrelationships between civil and government social capital vary as a country's development process evolves. Traditional life with reliance on civil social capital gives way to more formal organizations and government social capital. At different phases of development, there are different optimal combinations of civil and government social capital. As Norman Uphoff (1992: 273) says: "paradoxical though it may seem, 'top-down efforts' are usually needed to introduce, sustain, and institutionalize 'bottom up' development. We are commonly constrained to think in 'either-or' terms—the more of one the less of the other—when both are needed in a positive-sum way to achieve our purposes."

Trust

The attribute of "trust" deserves special emphasis. As Arrow (1974: 23, 26) observes,

> trust is an important lubricant of what the economist would call "externalities." They are goods, they are commodities, they have real, practical economic value; they increase the efficiency of the system, enable you to produce more goods or more of whatever values you hold in high esteem. But they are not commodities for which trade on the open market is technically possible or even meaningful.
>
> [A]mong the properties of many societies whose economic development is backward is a lack of mutual trust. Collective undertakings of any kind, not merely governmental, become difficult or impossible not only because A may betray B, but because even if A wants to trust B, he knows that B is unlikely to trust him. And it is clear that lack of social consciousness is in fact a distinct economic loss in a very concrete sense as well, of course, as a loss in the possible well-running of a political system.

Trust can be produced and links up with "reputation" that can be accumulated. It is important in determining expectations among individuals or organizations and between government and civil society. Conditions of trust may make promises among individuals credible. And governmental policies may also be considered credible. On determinants of trust and its relation to the game-theoretical aspects of social capital, see Partha Dasgupta (1999: 329–334).

Insofar as trust yields external economies, it tends to be undersupplied. How trust and other components of social capital can be accumulated, however, is complex with no simple answer. If the sources are not to remain merely exogenous, the mechanisms of accumulation in a developing economy have to be related to institutional change, as discussed hereafter.

In advanced economies, the nonmarket relationships of social capital are taken for granted—such as a clear system of property rights and a regulatory mechanism that curbs fraud, anticompetitive behavior, and moral hazard. There are also institutions that mitigate risk and manage conflicts. These attributes of social capital, however, are absent or weak in many developing countries. Numerous case studies conclude that corruption, bureaucratic delays, suppressed civil liberties, vast inequality, divisive ethnic tensions, and failure to safeguard property rights are major impediments to development (Woolcock and Aryan 2000: 235).

It is striking that social capital tends to be lower where polarization and fractionalization among groups exists. Fractionalization from high levels of ethnolinguistic or religious diversity coupled with denial of political and civil liberties tends to lower growth rates. With low levels of civil social capital, civil wars and tribal conflicts have certainly slowed Africa's growth (Collier and Gunning 1999a). Easterly and Levine 1997) also conclude that high levels of fractionalization in Africa combined with high spillover effects of one country's poor economic policies on its neighbors can explain up to 45 percent of that region's slow growth rates. Conversely, Easterly (2001: 277–281) demonstrates that developing countries that have countered ethnic and class polarization with "good institutions" and have achieved a "middle-class consensus" have enjoyed higher economic growth and development.

Rodrik (1999) also shows that divided societies have more difficulty in recovering from economic shocks. The shocks require the management of conflict among different interests in society, but without the social capital for managing conflict, the risk and loss are intensified.

Most significant, the other forms of capital—physical, human, knowledge—are all tangent with social capital. Social capital is important in influencing the rate of accumulation and quality of these other types of capital. Together they raise total factor productivity. Social capital acts as a shift factor in a Solow-growth model that raises the production function so that greater output is produced with the same amount of inputs. The organization of society can give greater value to output than simply what the value of inputs would indicate.

Because enterprises at the micro level are the means by which the rate and pattern of growth are transformed, social capital is important in affecting managerial capability in both the private sector and public sector. Managerial capability improves when social capital reduces information costs, transaction costs, and risk and helps to avoid moral hazard and adverse selection. Where social capital reduces the extent of information asymmetry and builds deeper markets, management benefits through a reduction in the potential for disputes because of the clear definition of property rights and contract enforcement, and through the support of competition. Quite simply but somewhat paradoxically: the nonmarket relationships embedded in social capital allow more people to play the market game.

Measurement

How to measure social capital? Can it be incorporated in figure 7.3? If it is difficult to define and measure activities that create human capital and knowledge capital, it is all the more difficult for social capital. Solow (1995: 38) points to the need to characterize a stock of social capital as larger or smaller than another such stock; there also needs to be an identifiable process of "investment" that adds to the stock, and possibly a process of "depreciation" that subtracts from it. These conditions are not yet met.

Nonetheless, although we may not expect studies to quantify the residual of social capital in a Solow-growth model, we can still explore behavioral patterns qualitatively and distinguish institutional characteristics that social capital suggests.

Some studies, however, have in fact been undertaken to determine whether some proxies for social capital have had an influence on total factor productivity. A significant number of studies demonstrate the role of social capital in raising productivity in the use of common property natural resources and in participatory irrigation management. For example, the Gal Oya water management project in Sri Lanka illustrates a case in which the investment of social capital produced desirable benefits, whether considered in terms of "social infrastructure" or organizational "software" to make more productive the physical "hardware" of irrigation facilities (Uphoff 2000a: 1884–1885).

A game-theoretic analysis also shows that social capital in the form of water user groups can also yield more effective coordination of activities and avoid opportunistic behavior of economic agents (Ostrom 1995).

OTHER MICRO STUDIES

Other micro studies at the household and community level demonstrate the value of local associations. The oft-studied Gameen Bank in Bangladesh or Compartamos in Mexico indicate that group-based lending schemes work effectively because members have better information on each other than banks do. The information-sharing role of social capital and the peer pressure permit the poor to overcome the constraint on their access to credit.

A study of village life in India by Robert M. Townsend (1994) indicates how local associations and networks enhance the ability of the poor to provide some insurance against hazards. In rural Tanzania, a survey of associational activity by households and individual trust in various institutions and individuals concluded that these components of village-level social capital raise household incomes (Narayan and Pritchett 1997).

Another group of studies, using econometric data in crosscountry analysis, estimates the impact of different components of social capital at the macro level. Examining why output per worker varies enormously across countries, Robert E. Hall and Charles I. Jones (1999) conclude that physical capital and educational attainment can only partially explain the variation and that the primary and fundamental determinant is a country's social infrastructure—that is, the institutions and government policies that provide the incentives for individuals and firms. "Those incentives can encourage productive activities such as the accumulation of skills or the development of new goods and production techniques, or those incentives can encourage predatory behavior such as rent-seeking, corruption, and theft" (95). The proxies for social infrastructure are created from data on political risk and on the openness of the economy. A cross-section analysis of 127 countries results in the highest measured levels of social infrastructure being in Switzerland, the United States, and Canada, and all three are among the countries with the highest levels of output per worker. Two countries that are close to the lowest in social infrastructure are Haiti and Bangladesh, and both have low levels of output per worker (103).

Using indicators of trust and civic norms for a sample of 29 economies, Stephen Knack and Philip Keefer (1997a) find that these components of social capital are stronger in countries with higher and more equal incomes, with institutions that restrain predatory actions of chief executives, and with better educated and ethnically homogeneous populations.

INSTITUTIONS MATTER

Given the importance of social capital, the fundamental question is how more productive social capital can be accumulated. This comes down to the ultimate question of how high-quality institutions can be formed.

By an "institution" we mean an established way of acting. In his Nobel lecture, Douglass C. North observes that institutions are "the humanly devised constraints that structure human interactions." They form the incentive structure of an economy, and the political and economic institutions are the underlying determinants of economic performance. Institutions are made up of informal and formal constraints and their enforcement characteristics (1994: 359–360). An informal institution can be an established custom, a norm, standard, or relationship. The behavior of economic agents is shaped by these self-imposed codes of conduct, norms of behavior, and conventions that yield civil social capital such as trust, reciprocity, or cooperation within a group. Studies based on the transaction cost analysis of the new institutional economics (NIE) illustrate how these informal constraints often substitute for missing markets and help solve coordination problems.

The formal institutions embedded in government social capital establish political, judicial, and economic rules and procedures. Constitutions, laws, and regulations are most important in ensuring property rights, contract enforcement, and absence of corruption.

The informal and formal institutions can be substitutes or complements. As an economy develops and social organization becomes more complex, formal rules tend to replace informal institutions. Complementary, however, can also arise in the sense of mutually supportive relations between public and private actors. More significant, there can be synergy between market exchange and a rule-governed environment. Although various relationships between the informal and formal are possible, positive developmental outcomes are most likely when institutions—public and private—are characterized by both high organizational integrity and synergy (Rauch and Evans 2000). Civic engagement strengthens state institutions, and effective state institutions create, in turn, an environment in which civic engagement is more likely to thrive (Evans 1996: 1034; Nugent 1993).

From the standpoint of development, institutions matter because they shape or embody social capital and provide the constraints and incentive structure for progrowth decisions. They establish the rules of the game in society—the constraints on behavior and the incentives for patterns of behavior (North 1990: 3). North distinguishes clearly institutions from organizations. The players in the game are organizations—firms, political bodies, unions, the central bank. They react to the opportunities and incentives offered by institutions. The institutional matrix defines the opportunity set. Progrowth institutions provide the highest payoffs to productive activities, as in the new growth theory (North 1997: 1–7).

As illustrated in figure 9.1, the interactions between institutions and organizations shape the choices that affect development performance. North maintains: "It has to be the incentive structure imbedded in the institutional/organizational structure of economies that is a key to unraveling the puzzle of uneven and erratic growth." Unlike the earlier emphasis on capital accumulation, "the primary source of economic growth is the institutional/organizational structure that determines incentives"(2000: 493–494). But, North asserts, "Third World countries are poor because the institutional constraints define a set of payoffs to political/ economic activity that do not encourage productive activity" (1990: 110). This theme is again propounded by Easterly (2001: 289), who attributes development failures to "failed incentives. . . . Prosperity happens when all the players in the development game have the right incentives." If the institutions provide proper incentives and encourage productive activity by the organizations, they raise total factor productivity.

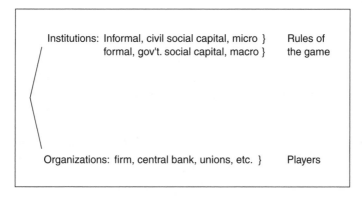

Figure 9.1 **Structure of the economy based on institutions → constraints and incentives → creative choices → performance (TFP)**

To say that incentives matter is to say that institutions matter. Institutions, however, can be good or bad for a country's development. If incentives are the underlying determinants of economic performance, then good institutions shape the right incentives for economic performance. Good institutions promote social capital and thereby facilitate information flows, reduce transaction costs, and avoid or resolve conflict. They provide a good kind of institutional infrastructure for a market economy. For example, the establishment and effectiveness of financial markets will be determined by such institutions as laws, regulations, and customs, including accounting systems, fraud laws, and securities and exchange commissions. But while economists can specify how to create efficient economic markets, it is a more daunting and ambiguous task to determine the conditions for "efficient political markets" that will determine the development of the economic markets.

Regarding governance of the public sector, good institutions should establish high standards and competence for activities by the state. Over time, they should also have the capacity to adapt to changing technology, demographics, and other development problems. This is especially important for an economy that is in transition from a planned economy to a market economy.

With the emphasis on incentives, we can say that along with differences in physical capital, human capital, and knowledge capital, the variation among countries in their social capital and institutions also explains their differences in economic growth.

Empirical studies now demonstrate this. One of these by Dani Rodrik (1997) shows that an index of institutional quality does exceptionally well in rank-ordering East Asian countries according to their growth performance. The institutional quality index relates to quality of the bureaucracy, rule of law, risk of expropriation, and repudiation of contract by government.

A high score on quality of bureaucracy indicates autonomy from political pressure, expertise and efficiency in providing government services, and superior modes of recruitment and training. A high score on rule of law denotes sound, political institutions, strong courts, and orderly succession of political power. A low score on risk of expropriation indicates the possibility of confiscation and forced nationalizations of private investments, repudiation of contracts by government, and risk of modification in contracts with the government. These high and low scores are converted to a scale of 1 to 10, with high values indicating good institutions.

Figure 9.2 shows the variation across East Asian countries in the ranking of their institutions. Japan, Singapore, and Taiwan receive very high grades (above 8). They have the best institutions and the highest growth rates. The Philippines scores particularly low (below 3), and Indonesia also scores low.

Janine Aron (2000) evaluates a number of studies that try to link quantitative measures of institutions with growth of GDP across countries and over time. A review of the evidence suggests a link between the quality of institutions and investment and growth, but the econometric evidence is by no means robust.

The central question now is how high-quality institutions can be formed. We can judge whether an institution is good or bad after the

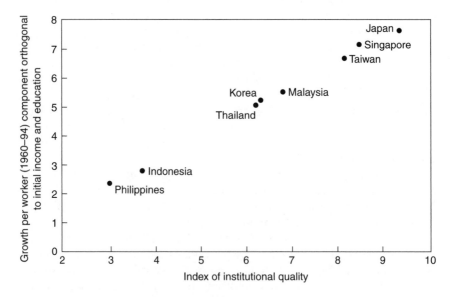

Figure 9.2 Relationship between growth and institutions

fact. Historical narratives do this. But it is still difficult to predict whether a good institution will arise. It remains a complex question as to what policy makers can do to improve institutions. It is complex because the desirable types of institutions differ among countries at different levels of development, even among countries at the same level of development.

Before attempting to determine how to get institutions right, it would be helpful to determine through positive analysis how institutions are formed and how they change. The sources of government social capital can come from transplantation of institutions from other countries, historical evolution, institutional innovations, or response to economic shocks. Formal financial institutions, for example, might be subject to prudential regulation, rule of law, improved administrative procedures—based on copying another country, or learning by doing over time, or a discretionary policy decision. Most difficult is the effort to treat institutional innovation and change as endogenous to the economic system. Theories of property rights and economic regulation attempt this, but until recently most institutions were taken as given or exogenous to economic analysis. A notable exception is the modeling of institutional innovation as induced primarily by changes in relative resource endowments and the growth of demand (Ruttan 1989). The new institutional economics also analyzes institutions, especially in terms of transaction-cost economics in institutions of governance (Williamson 1998; 2000).

North (2000: 495) summarizes the essential characteristics of institutional change as follows.

1. The continuous interaction of institutions and organizations in the economic setting of scarcity, and hence competition, is the key to institutional change.
2. Competition forces organizations continually to invest in skills and knowledge to survive. The kinds of skills and knowledge individuals and their organizations acquire will shape evolving perceptions about opportunities and hence choices that will incrementally alter institutions.
3. The institutional framework dictates the kinds of skills and knowledge perceived to have the maximum payoff.
4. Perceptions are derived from the mental constructs of the players.
5. The economies of scope, complementarities, and network externalities of an institutional matrix make institutional change overwhelmingly incremental and path dependent.

More broadly, economic views of institutions are now being formulated with game-theoretic apparatuses, particularly those borrowed from the theory of evolutionary and repeated games (Aoki 2000; Greif 2000). The approach, labeled historical and comparative institutional analysis (HCIA), studies institutions through equilibrium analysis, viewing institutions as equilibrium constraints that influence social interactions and provide incentives to maintain regularities of behavior. It considers institutions that are outcomes emerging endogenously and that are self-enforcing in the sense that they do not rely on external enforcement. The HCIA's research strategy is an inductive, empirical analysis regarding the relevance of particular institutions based on evaluating and synthesizing microlevel historical and comparative evidence and insights from context-specific, microtheoretical models.

Insofar as HCIA is still only in its early stages, its policy implications are not yet clear. North (1995) claims that "it is the polity that specifies and enforces the economic rules of the game." Unlike this view of the rule-of-the-game theorists that rule making is susceptible to conscious design either by legislators, political entrepreneurs, or mechanism design economists, there is no clear consensus on this issue among the equilibrium-of-the-game theorists (Aoki 2000).

The government itself is a strategic player of the game in the polity domain. The upshot is that if an institution is "the product of long term experiences of a society of bounded rational and retrospective individuals" (Kreps 1990), an equilibrium-theoretic game approach can help explain the emergence and change of institutions. To specify the equilibrium that is actually chosen in a multiple equilibria situation, the use of comparative and historical information and inductive reasoning is also needed.

For developing countries, the major question is how improvement in their institutions can be achieved. Some institutions evolve as corrections for market failure. Arrow (1974: 26), for example, suggests that societies "in their evolution have developed implicit agreements to certain kinds of regard for others, agreements which are essential to the survival of the society or at least contribute greatly to the efficiency of its working." Formal institutions become more prominent as the economy develops and becomes more complex. The capacity to copy relatively productive institutions from other countries is another possibility. The performance characteristics, however, can be very different from the original country because the informal norms and enforcement characteristics will be different (North 1995: 25).

But how to make institutions more efficient? Answers have to be country specific and time specific. Moreover, there is no limit to the full range of potential institutional possibilities that might be adopted in the future (Unger 1998: 24–25). Some general observations, however, can be offered. Quality improvement is more likely to be forthcoming if there are opportunities for widespread political participation, civil liberties, more education, and an open economy. Democracy is thus more conducive to institutional improvement. As Sen notes (1999: 7), democracy has three distinctly positive contributions: it enriches individual lives through more freedom (involving political and civil rights), it provides political incentives to government to respond positively to the needs and demands of the people, and the process of open dialogues and debates that it allows and encourages helps in the formation of values and priorities. Partha Dasgupta and Martin Weale (1992) and Robert J. Barro (1996) also find that political and civil rights are positively and significantly correlated with real national income per head and its growth. But see Dasgupta (2001: 66–75) for ambiguities in answers to the question of whether democracy is associated with economic progress.

Openness in trade and services is now especially significant because of forces of globalization and information technology. These forces should accelerate institutional reform in the developing world. The World Bank's *World Development Report 2001/2002* is relevant in its consideration of the role of institutions in promoting market growth and in allowing all members of society to have access to market opportunities. The *Report* documents how weak institutions—tangled laws, corrupt courts, biased credit systems, overly complex regulations of business—hinder development. Alternative conflict resolution systems, such as those based on social norms, are clearly important. The *Report* argues that market-supporting institutions perform one or more of three functions: they ease or restrict the flow of information; define and enforce property rights and contracts; and increase or decrease competition. These institutions should also be judged on how they increase access for the poor.

In its summary, the *Report* recommends the following four principles to guide policy makers in building more effective institutions.

> *Complement what exists:* The design of any single institution should take into account the nature of the supporting institutions, skills, technology and corruption. Costs of building and maintaining the institution must be commensurate with per capita income levels to ensure access and use.
> *Innovate*: Institutions are not immutable. Be prepared to experiment with new institutional arrangements and to modify or abandon those that fail.
> *Connect*: Connect communities through open information flows and open trade. In particular, the exchange of information through open debate creates demand for institutional change.
> *Promote competition*: Foster competition between jurisdictions, firms, and individuals.

Competition creates demand for new institutions, changes behavior, brings flexibility in markets, and leads to new solutions. (World Bank 2002: ch. 1). Although economics is mainly concerned with the operation of markets, development economics has to be concerned with the prior question of how markets are formed and evolve. As I have emphasized, what matters for economic performance is the incentive structure embedded in institutions that support markets and progrowth policies.

Noting that markets are "embedded" in a set of nonmarket institutions,[6] Rodrik (2000: 5) suggests five types of positive market-supporting

institutions: property rights, regulatory institutions, institutions for market stabilization, institutions for social insurance, and institutions of
conflict management.[7] The latter are important in developing countries
that are characterized by deep cleavages among ethnic or income lines.

From the concern of the new development economics with incomplete
or missing institutions there may also be renewed interest in the dual
sector model of the early development economics. Early on, Myint (1985)
suggested that dualism is preeminently a phenomenon of an underdeveloped organizational framework, characterized by the incomplete development not only of the market network but also of the government's
administrative and fiscal system. This concept of "organizational dualism" moves the policy implications on beyond "getting prices right" to
an examination of what constitutes the development of right institutions.

This movement is reinforced by the new institutional economics.
Oliver Williamson (1994: 172) observes that development economics
and industrial organization have both undergone similar three-stage pro-
gressions. Stage 1 is an aggregative or macroanalytic approach (the Harvard tradition). The neoclassical approach (the Chicago tradition) dom-
inates stage 2. The new institutional economics now shows up as stage
3. Figure 9.3 shows Williamson's progression to the new institutional
economics.

Starting from the objective of economizing transaction costs, the NIE
analyzes how firms and markets establish institutions for governance of

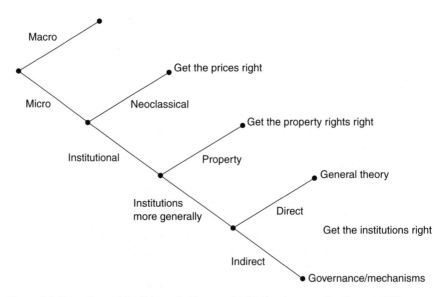

Figure 9.3 From Harvard to Chicago to the new institutional economics. Source: Williamson (1994): 172.

contracts, investment, and private ordering. There are alternative modes of organization: markets, hybrids, hierarchies, and public bureaus. Each mode establishes different incentives and controls that lead to different degrees of competition, credible investment conditions, and credible contracting.

The approach of the NIE is especially relevant for the micro aspects of North's analysis of institutions and for civic social capital. Besides allocative efficiency, however, institutional change also involves a redistributive change (Bardhan 1989: 1391–1393). This raises issues of collective action, bargaining power, state capacity (Evans 1992), and political processes that are related more to government social capital.

While development economists in the 1970s could advise developing countries to "get prices right" and then in the 1980s and 1990s could say "get macro policies right," it is now much more difficult to establish a normative approach to "getting institutions right" and establishing right incentives. But like the new development economics, this chapter's focus on social capital and institutions has presented some new dimensions and mechanisms for policy reform. The next chapter reinforces the need for reforms to overcome the "institution gap" that was neglected in the Washington consensus, or the "orthodox reaction."

10

The Impact of Globalization

What are the effects of economic globalization on poor countries? Since the backlash demonstrations against globalization at the ministerial meetings in Seattle and Genoa in the late 1990s, this question has entered public debate. Neither globalization nor protests, however, are new. Indeed, throughout the history of development economics, attention to the implications of international integration has been of prime interest, especially regarding whether foreign trade and investment reduce or increase inequality. Now international financial "crises" and issues of global economic governance also pervade the debate. This chapter relates the response of development economics to these concerns.[1]

FORCES OF ECONOMIC GLOBALIZATION

For centuries the world economy has become ever more integrated, but in the past half century the pace has accelerated. Before turning to contemporary issues of globalization, we should recognize some lessons of history. As Kevin H. O'Rourke and Jeffrey G. Williamson (1999: 287) say in concluding their study of the evolution of the nineteenth-century Atlantic economy, "the globalization experience of the Atlantic economy prior to the Great War speaks directly and eloquently to globalization debates today. Economists who base their views of globalization, convergence, inequality, and policy solely on the years since 1970 are making a great mistake."

Peter H. Lindert and Williamson (2001) decompose the past five centuries into four distinct globalization epochs: two of which were proglobal (1820 to 1913, and 1950 to 2001) and two antiglobal. Exploring whether the two proglobal epochs made the world more unequal, they conclude that a "lesson of history is that globalization is not a necessary condition for widening world income gaps. It happened with and without it" (7). The interwar period was an antiglobalization period, as barriers against migration, trade, and capital flows intensified, but international income gaps widened in this period, more so than in any other period. Lindert and Williamson write: "Correlation is not causation, but here is more evidence rejecting the view that world globalization means wider gaps between rich and poor countries. We did not see the correlation before 1820, and we do not see it now for 1914–1950" (213). Their general conclusion is that the net impact of globalization has been far too small to explain the long-run rise in world inequality since 1800.

On the convergence debate, O'Rourke and Williamson (1999: 286) believe that their study

> demonstrates the causal link between globalization and convergence in the late-nineteenth-century Atlantic economy. It remains to be seen whether the interwar disintegration of the world economy was responsible for the breakdown of convergence and whether open economy forces have been mainly responsible for the renewed convergence since 1950. Our priors are that open economy forces are still important. . . . We believe that the catching up of poor countries with rich may have as much to do with open economy linkages as with any other force identified by growth theory. . . . [W]here there has been openness, there has been convergence; where there has been autarky, there has been either divergence or cessation of convergence. . . . [I]t was globalization in factor markets that mattered most prior to World War I, especially globalization of labor markets. Thus, one must be cautious in applying lessons of history to the present, where mass migrations are so much more modest. . . . [I]t is not enough to show that openness is correlated with growth. Economists and historians need to examine whether the mechanisms that theory says should have linked the two were actually in operation during a given era, and if so, they need to quantify the impact of these mechanisms on convergence.

Although there was the earlier period of globalization before World War I, some of the forces of globalization in the past half century have differed in kind and intensity. Through telecommunications, the decline in information costs has been greater. Not only has distance been shortened; time has also been compressed. The diffusion of technology and ideas has been more extensive. The integration of capital markets may not be any greater, but the composition of capital flows to developing countries has been different, with foreign aid and short-term capital investments, greater provision of financial services, and a change in foreign direct investment (FDI). A greater share of FDI is in the form of industrial production slicing, as multinationals decompose their production functions around the world according to factor endowments and base more activities in developing countries. Not only have movements of goods, services, and factors increased, but they have also become more responsive, or more elastic, to differences between domestic and foreign variables. Commodities and services flow more rapidly with respect to price differentials among nations, and financial capital moves more rapidly in response to interest rate differentials. The internationalization process also results in a greater stock of foreign factors of production within countries—especially more foreign investment and foreign technology related to the activities of multinational enterprises.

Another feature of the contemporary internationalization process has been the internationalization of institutions. Beyond the nation-state, a number of intergovernmental institutions have arisen—ranging from international organizations, such as the World Bank, the IMF, the WTO, and UNCTAD, to regional groups, such as the European Union (EU), the North American Free Trade Agreement (NAFTA), the Association of Southeast Asian Nations (ASEAN), or the OECD. Interest groups, such as labor unions, employer associations, NGOs, and foundations, have also expanded across national borders. Above all, the population of multinational corporations has increased remarkably, and many more large firms operate an expanding number of foreign subsidiaries around the globe.

Following Rostow (1987: 136–141), some may link the forces of globalization to a new international industrial revolution based on science and technology that are revolutionizing patterns of industrial production and are also transforming agriculture and a wide range of services. As was not the case in previous industrial revolutions that were national in location, the ramifications of the revolution are immediately internationally diffused, and the less developed countries are involved to a greater extent than in any of the historical industrial revolutions.

The growth in world merchandise trade has been considerably faster than growth in world output: from 1950 to 2000, world merchandise output increased over 5 times, but world merchandise trade increased over 14 times. Trade as a share of GDP is higher for more countries. This has become especially true for developing countries (see table 10.1). More countries are now politically independent and are no longer integrated into the world economy in a colonial status. Accordingly, the composition of their trade has also changed: a larger number of developing countries have achieved an increasing share of manufactures in their total exports—from less than a quarter in 1980 to more than 70 percent in 2000. Twenty years ago, 75 percent of LDC exports were primary products, and now only 20 percent are.

More developing countries have followed policies of liberalization and greater openness. Some 24 developing countries—with 3 billion people—have doubled their ratio of trade to income over the past 20 years (World Bank, 2002: 5). In brief, more developing countries have become "proglobalizers." David Dollar and Aart Kraay (2001a) identified a group of developing countries that experienced large increases in trade after 1980, and then ranked them according to their increases in trade as shares of their GDPs and labeled the top third the "post-1980 globalizers."

The East Asian Tigers—Hong Kong, South Korea, Singapore, and Taiwan—had become "globalizers" earlier in the 1960s and 1970s. Globali-

Table 10.1 Openness in the postwar period (in percent)

	1950–59	1960–69	1970–79	1980–89
Industrial Countries	**23.3**	**24.6**	**32.0**	**36.8**
North America	11.2	11.7	17.8	21.9
Western Europe	37.2	38.9	48.7	56.9
Japan	21.8	19.5	22.9	23.9
Developing Countries		**28.0**	**34.4**	**38.4**
Africa		48.2	55.1	54.1
Asia				
East		47.0	69.5	87.2
Other		17.2	19.6	24.0
Middle East		41.5	60.4	46.9
Western Hemisphere	26.3	23.9	24.9	27.9

Note: "Openness" is defined as nominal merchandise exports plus imports as a percent of nominal output.
Source: IMF (1994: 89).

Table 10.2 Post-1980 Globalizers

Argentina	Jordan
Bangladesh	Malaysia
Brazil	Mali
China	Mexico
Columbia	Nepal
Costa Rica	Nicaragua
Côte d'Ivoire	Paraguay
Dominican Republic	Philippines
Haiti	Rwanda
Hungary	Thailand
India	Uruguay
Jamaica	Zimbabwe

Source: Dollar and Kraay (2001b: 16).

zation, however, has not yet included many other poor countries—with about 2 billion people—where trade is actually less than it was 20 years ago (Dollar and Kray 2001a: 2).

GLOBALIZATION AND INEQUALITY

If the alleviation of poverty is a central theme of development economics, a corollary is reduction of inequality—both between rich and poor countries and within a poor country. The forces of economic globalization—especially with respect to trade and foreign investment—are causing development economists to ask again whether international integration is good for growth, and whether growth is good for reducing inequality between and within nations.

Ever since the time of the classical economists, theoretical analysis has maintained that a country's integration into the world economy through trade according to its comparative advantage should raise its level of real income. Modern theorists also maintain that there is potential for growth in real income through the realization of dynamic gains from trade (see chapter 5). In contrast, however, in the early development economics (see chapter 4), there were critics of classical and neoclassical trade theory who questioned this. They asked: Does international trade operate as a mechanism of international inequality, with the gains going to the advanced industrial countries? Would a developing country's growth be better served by import-substitution industrialization instead of comparative advantage? Would delinking from the world economy avoid backwash effects and be a superior development strategy?

During the 1960s, the dependendistas in Latin America and the New World Group in the Caribbean were concerned not with "development economics" but with "dependency economics." They argued that conditions of dependency in world markets of commodities, capital, and labor power are unequal and combine to transfer resources from dependent countries to dominant countries in the international system.

In the 1970s, a United Nations declaration called for a "new international economic order" (NIEO) "based on equity, sovereign equality, interdependence, common interest and cooperation among all states, irrespective of their economic and social systems which shall correct inequalities and redress existing injustices." Several specific policies were called for, including: "just and equitable relationship between the prices of exports and imports with the aim of bringing about sustained improvement in (the developing countries') unsatisfactory terms of trade"; preferential and nonreciprocal tariff treatment; more favorable conditions for the transfer of financial resources; a reformed international monetary system that would promote development and provide an adequate flow of real resources to the developing countries; and more international aid and external debt relief.

Now with the concerns about the effects of globalization, there are echoes of this early discontent. Indeed, Stiglitz's book *Globalization and its Discontents* criticizes bad management of globalization and laments its adverse effects on the poor, environment, and stability. The liberalization of trade and financial and capital markets "pushes a particular ideology—market fundamentalism—that is both bad economics and bad politics. . . . More generally, globalization itself has been governed in ways that are undemocratic and have been disadvantageous to developing countries, especially the poor within these countries" (Stiglitz 2002a: 1). When countries do not make globalization work for them and succumb to outside pressures, they run into problems that are beyond their capacity to manage well. It is claimed that adverse effects come from liberalization of international trade and capital movements. Echoing earlier critics, Stiglitz contends that the IMF "exhibits a certain paternalism, a new form of the old colonial mentality" (2002a: 3). Moreover, "the trade liberalization agenda has been set by the North. . . . Consequently, a disproportionate part of the gains has accrued to the advanced industrial nations, and in some cases the less developed countries have actually been worse off" (2002a: 6; 2002b: 7). Serious reforms in governance are needed to remove the "inequities of the global economic architecture." Reminiscent of the earlier periods of dependency and the NIEO, there is the argument that globalization is essentially a manifestation of Western imperialism in ideas and policies. The essential issue now is whether globalization is well managed so that the potential benefits of globalization can be realized by rich and poor countries alike and by the poor within a developing country.

In an earlier article, similarly entitled "Globalization and Its Discontent," Sen (2000: 7) concludes:

> The difficult issue that globalization requires us to address is not the efficiency of markets, nor the importance of modern technology, which are well established. The debate, rather, is about inequality: between nations and within nations, in economic affluence as well as in social opportunity and political rights. What is needed is neither the rubbishing of globalization, nor treating it in isolation, as an automatic solution to world poverty. Doubts about globalization can be put to constructive use, but we have to be determined to do just that.

It is now important to recognize that a number of empirical studies focus on whether globalization is good for growth and whether growth is good for reducing inequality between and within nations. The empirical evidence considers two central questions: Do trade and foreign investment lead to growth so that the "proglobalizers" grow more rapidly? Does the more rapid growth, in turn, diminish poverty and reduce the inequality within the "proglobalizer"?

Most studies of convergence (recall chapter 4) have focused on closed economies with little or no role for trade and foreign investment. Recently more studies have examined whether trade liberalization and openness have led to higher rates of growth.[2] These studies have included country cases and, in an attempt to be more general, crosscountry regressions.

In analyzing the performance of nearly 120 countries between 1970 and 1989, Jeffrey D. Sachs and Andrew Warner (1995) concluded that open developing countries grew nearly three percentage points faster than closed ones.[3] The fastest-growing developing countries were those that succeeded in generating new export growth, especially in manufactured goods (Sachs 1998: 101). Examining a group of open economies, they found evidence for conditional convergence of the poorer countries with the richer ones but no evidence of convergence for the closed economies.

It is also evident that the smaller a country, the larger the benefits of trade openness and economic integration are larger (Alesina, Spolaore, and Wacziarg 2002: 15). Openness can substitute for a large domestic market and give positive scale effects. Many empirical studies show positive effects of trade on productivity and growth. Examining data for 93 countries, Edwards (1998) concluded that more open countries experienced faster productivity growth.

To the extent that studies have relied on crosscountry regressions, however, they are subject to criticisms of choice of data, measurement, and endogeneity, (recall the discussion of regression analysis in chapter 4). Indeed, Francisco Rodriguez and Dani Rodrik (2000: 7) criticize the methodology of various studies (listed in note 2) and conclude: "Once simple corrections are made for such [statistical] problems, one rarely finds a statistically significant relationship between the level of tariff and non-tariff barriers and economic growth across countries." Moreover, Rodrik (1999: 13–14) also has said: "First, openness by itself is not a reliable mechanism to generate sustained economic growth. Second, openness will likely exert pressures that widen income and wealth disparities within countries."[4] Nonetheless, Rodrik (2000: 7–8) does write:

> No country has developed successfully by turning its back on international trade and long-term capital flows. . . . But it is equally true that no country has developed simply by opening itself up to foreign trade and investment. The trick in the successful cases has been to combine the opportunities offered by world markets with a domestic investment and institution-building strategy to stimulate the animal spirits of domestic entrepreneurs. There is no evidence from the last 50 years that trade protection is systematically associated with higher growth. The point is simply that the benefits of trade openness should not be oversold. When other worthwhile policy objectives compete for scarce administrative resources and political capital, deep trade liberalization often does not deserve the high priority it typically receives in development strategies. This is a lesson that is of particular importance to countries (such as those in Africa) that are in the early stages of reform.

After reviewing the empirical studies, Rodriguez and Rodrik (2000: 62–63) conclude:

> We do not want to leave the reader with the impression that we think protection is good for economic growth. We know of no credible evidence—at least for the post-1945 period—that suggests that trade restrictions are systematically associated with higher growth rates. What we would like the reader to take away from this paper is some caution and humility in interpreting the existing cross-national evidence of the relationship between trade policy and economic growth. . . .
>
> Our concern is that priority afforded to trade policy has generated expectations that are unlikely to be met, and it may have crowded out other

institutional reforms with potentially greater payoffs. . . . The effects of trade liberalization may be on balance beneficial on standard comparative advantage grounds; the evidence provides no strong reason to dispute this. What we dispute is the view, increasingly common, that integration in the world economy is such a potent force for economic growth that it can effectively substitute for a development strategy.

Although crosscountry regressions yield ambiguous conclusions, country case studies provide more credible evidence that trade liberalization and integration into the global economy support higher rates of growth. As Cooper (2001) notes, "the key policy issue is whether for each country, starting where it is, some liberalization of trade (or foreign investment) would improve its economic performance. The answer to that question cannot be found in cross-section country regressions, however carefully they are specified, but rather in detailed analysis of the country under study."

T. N. Srinivasan and Jagdish Bhagwati (1999: 6) argue that nuanced, in-depth analyses of country experiences in major OECD, NBER, and IBRD studies have shown plausibly, taking into account numerous country-specific factors, that trade does seem to create, even sustain, higher growth. From country studies, we can conclude that the success stories of the East Asian countries in the 1960s and 1970s have been followed by other proglobalizers in the 1980s and 1990s.

The contribution of foreign investment to growth is more ambiguous than that of trade. It is very much a matter of what type of foreign investment occurs and its country-specific context. Much of the criticism of globalized capital movements is rightly directed to volatile short-term capital flows. The volatility of short-term capital inflows has had perverse effects, as discussed hereafter.

More favorable assessments can be made of foreign aid and foreign direct investment. Country experiences demonstrate that foreign aid can raise a country's investment and growth rate, provided appropriate complementary policies are undertaken. Paul Collier and D. Dollar (2001) present a model of efficient aid in which aid increases the benefits from good policy, while at the same time good policy increases the impact of aid. The combination of good policy and aid produces especially good results in terms of growth and poverty reduction.

Foreign direct investment—particularly the post-1980 type of investment in process manufacturing—has contributed more to the growth of developing countries than has portfolio investment. This is because the inflow of capital is accompanied by improved management, technological absorption, new skills, access to foreign markets, and spillovers to domestic firms. In their study of FDI and growth in 69 developing countries over the period 1970–89, Borensztein (1998) concludes that FDI makes a positive contribution to growth. The increase in FDI in the 1990s and its more productive character would probably show even more positive results.

Subject to some criticism of regression studies and some country study exceptions, the general conclusion among development economists is that trade liberalization and openness have led to growth.[5] A major reason for this outcome lies in the classical belief concerning the stimulating educative effect of an open economy—receptive to new ideas, new wants, new techniques of production and methods of economic organization from abroad (Myint 1971; Ng 1971: 176). The concern with knowledge capital in modern growth theory also emphasizes that the "notion of an idea gap directs attention to the patterns of interaction and communication between a developing country and the rest of the world" (Romer 1993). It is striking that the recent globalizers have experienced an acceleration of their average growth rates from 1 percent per year in the 1960s to 3 percent in the 1970s, 4 percent in the 1980s, and 5 percent in the 1990s. In contrast, the developing countries not in the "globalizing" group had a decline in the average growth rate from 3.3 percent per year in the 1970s to 0.8 percent in the 1980s and 1.4 percent in the 1990s (Dollar 2001: 13).

But has the growth reduced poverty and inequality within globalizing countries? An unambiguous answer was given by the chief economist of the World Bank (Stern 2000: 7):

> One of the most common claims today is that globalization typically leads to growing income inequality within countries, so that its benefits go primarily to the rich. This claim is simply not true. In fact, it is one of the big myths of the anti-globalization movement. Certainly there are important examples, notably China, where opening has gone hand-in-hand with rising inequality, but that has not been a general pattern. In many developing countries, integrating with the international market has coincided with stable inequality or declines in inequality. Examples would be Ghana, Uganda, and Vietnam. Further, in China's case the rise in inequality has more to do with the establishment of market-oriented incentives in a previously centrally planned economy than it does with China's opening to international markets. When trade liberalization goes hand-in-hand with stable or declining inequality, the benefits for the poor are quite powerful. In Vietnam, per capita income of the poor has been rising at about 5 percent per year since the country's opening up began in the early 1990s.

Marked declines in absolute poverty have also been experienced in other countries that have experienced rapid growth through greater openness, such as India, Thailand, and Malaysia.

The view that "growth is good for the poor" receives empirical support from an econometric study by Dollar and Kraay (2001a), who document an empirical regularity between average income in the lowest quintile and mean national income in a large sample of 92 countries spanning four decades. The evidence shows that growth in average per capita income (PPP basis) can be expected to raise average income in the poorest quintile roughly in proportion. Further, there is little evidence of a systematic tendency for inequality in the distribution of income (based on Gini coefficients) to either increase or decrease with increased trade. From such evidence, one can conclude that when globalization leads to growth, it is good for the poor in reducing their poverty and in maintaining their position in the income distribution. Growth-enhancing policies benefit the poorest fifth and everyone else in society proportionately.[6] The basic proportional relationship between incomes of the poor and average incomes holds regardless of level of development, time period, or crisis situations.[7] Evidence cited by Ravallion (2001), however, shows that there are large differences among countries in how much poor people share in growth, and there are diverse impacts among the poor in a given country. Many country studies show that the income of the poorest tends to grow one-for-one with average income. In some countries at some times, however, the poor do better than average, and sometimes they do worse.[8]

Most development analysts would now conclude that the balance of the evidence shows that economic globalization can yield benefits of growth,[9] contributing to rising incomes, reducing the gap between the richer countries and the post-1980 globalizers, and also being good for the poorest of society. In contrast, many of the countries that have not benefited from growth and falling poverty are those that have not been able to become integrated with the global economy. Or the countries themselves have not had appropriate institutional development and policies to take advantage of the global forces.

The challenge for the future is to have globalization be more development friendly for more countries and also to become more "propoor." In meeting this challenge, the international community will have to solve problems of international financial crises, trade policy, and global governance.

CAPITAL FLOWS AND FINANCIAL CRISES

International financial crises (Mexico, 1994; Asia, 1997–98; Argentina, 2002; Brazil, 2002) raise a number of questions regarding the development effects of the liberalization of capital flows and the surge of capital into emerging markets. What have been the causes of the crises? How can financial crises be prevented? How can responses to crises be improved? Does the "global financial architecture" need reforming? These questions call for more attention to both the macroeconomics and microeconomics of an open developing economy.

Over the last five decades, different types of capital flows have been successively dominant. The immediate postwar period was one of official capital flows through foreign aid. This was followed in the 1970s and 1980s by crossborder lending from multinational banks to governments. Foreign direct investment then increased. And in the 1990s, private sector portfolio flows and commercial bank lending became prominent. Volatile types of short-term capital flows that involve debt instruments became associated with international currency crises—for example, government tesobonos in the case of Mexico, interbank loans in the case of Korea.

The traditional textbook causes of balance-of-payments crises identify excessively easy money and fiscal policies that allow private investment to be greater than private savings and government expenditure to exceed revenue. Failures in domestic macroeconomic policies, however, were not the causes of the Mexican and Asian crises. Mexico's consolidated budget deficit for 1994 was no more than 2 percent of GDP. Thailand's budget was actually in surplus in the years preceding the crisis. Nonetheless, in both crises, the current account deficit was large—some 8 percent of GDP.

The earlier financial liberalization had led to a rapid expansion of the domestic financial sectors and the exceptional rise in offshore borrowing and domestic lending. Foreign financing was allowing private investment to exceed private savings, by short-term portfolio capital flows in Mexico and international banking loans to Thailand. Attracted by the success stories of Asian countries, the financing to domestic banks in Thailand was being lent on to domestic borrowers engaged in speculative investments, especially in real estate and finance. A portfolio mismatch occurred between the short-term capital inflows and long-term local loans and into nontradable assets. Most important, the exchange rate remained pegged (in Mexico, within a well-defined band against the U.S. dollar; and in Thailand's case, the U.S. dollar had the most weight in the basket peg). During 1994 when Mexico's current account deficit rose, Mexico's international reserves declined about two-thirds. Devaluation failed to stabilize the peso, and the government was forced to let the peso float freely. The exchange value of the peso plummeted, reserves flowed out, and Mexico had to receive an extraordinary package of external support from the IMF and the United States.

In Thailand, as the dollar appreciated relative to the yen and European currencies, Thailand's competitiveness deteriorated. By June 1997, Thailand's short-term debt to international banks was one and a half times its foreign reserves. The reserves fell markedly with international bank outflows and capital flight. Contagion then spread from Thailand to Malaysia, Indonesia, Philippines, and South Korea, where devaluations also had to occur.

In a few months in 1997, foreign banks and investment companies reduced new loans and investments to the five most troubled Asian countries by $100 billion, equivalent to two-thirds of the capital inflow to these countries in the previous year. The reversal of capital flows was sudden and extensive. Withdrawals of short-term lines of credit, an outflow of portfolio capital, and offshore flight by domestic investors in the Asian countries turned the capital flow around from an inflow of $97 billion in 1996 to an outflow of $12 billion in the last half of 1997 (Institute of International Finance 1998).

Bank claims on the private sector rose markedly; but without efficient monitoring in undersupervised financial systems, nonperforming loans rose, and insolvency spread in the private sector. The deterioration in bank balance sheets and the decline in stock markets worsened the adverse selection and moral hazard problems in the domestic financial system. The short duration of debt contracts and their denomination in unhedged foreign currencies helped turn the currency crises into financial crises, as balance sheets deteriorated for both financial and nonfinancial enterprises. Bankruptcies rose, lending contracted, and national output declined (1999).

In providing financial assistance, the IMF initially imposed its usual program of conditionality—namely, a stabilization package of tight monetary and fiscal policies and price liberalization. A prominent feature of the IMF programs in Thailand, Indonesia, and South Korea was a large increase in interest rates as well as a decline in governmental expenditure. After the countries suffered severe recessions and an increase in bankruptcies and domestic debt defaults occurred in the private sector, the IMF eased the fiscal and monetary targets.

Despite the imbalances and weaknesses in the Asian countries, it may be argued that a combination of financial panic on the part of the international investment community, policy mistakes at the outset of the crisis by Asian governments, and poorly designed international rescue programs led to a much deeper fall in otherwise viable output than was either necessary or inevitable (Sachs and Radelet 1998; Sachs and Woo 2000).

INTERNATIONAL FINANCIAL ARCHITECTURE

Beyond the particular cases of Mexico and Asian countries, the general problem is whether the globalization of capital markets contributes to global financial instability with resultant hardships for developing countries. In the wider perspective, what are the causes of and remedies for global financial instability?

The imperfections in financial markets and the "instability bias" in the financial system are not present in most other markets (Crockett 1997). Economists identify five main types of financial crises (Radelet and Sachs 2000: 107–111):

1. *Macroeconomic policy-induced crisis:* Domestic credit expansion is inconsistent with the country's pegged exchange rate. Foreign exchange reserves fall, and the economy is forced to allow a floating rate.

2. *Financial panic:* Short-term debts exceed short-term assets; no single private-market creditor is large enough to supply all the credits necessary to pay off existing short-term debts; and there is no lender of last resort. Lacking coordination and in a herd effect, short-term creditors withdraw their loans from borrowers

in a sudden but essentially unnecessary withdrawal of credits from viable economic activities.

3. *Bubble collapse:* Speculators purchase assets at prices above their fundamental value in the expectation of a subsequent capital gain, but the bubble eventually collapses.
4. *Moral hazard crisis:* May occur when banks are able to borrow international funds on the basis of implicit or explicit public guarantees of bank liabilities. If banks are undercapitalized or underregulated, they may use these funds in overly risky ventures.
5. *Disorderly workout:* If there is a "debt overhang," a disorderly workout may occur when markets operate without the benefit of creditor coordination via bankruptcy law.

Analytical models of currency crises have evolved parallel to the occurrence of different crises. A first-generation model by Krugman (1979) demonstrated that because exchange rate policy is incompatible with the country's underlying monetary and fiscal policies, the rundown of a finite stock of foreign reserves is inevitable.

In second-generation models (Obstfeld 1996), there is a self-fulfilling speculative attack on the currency, and the fixed exchange rate must be abandoned in order to pursue an expansionary monetary policy.

After the Asian financial crisis, third-generation models of currency and financial crises focused on financial sector crisis—bank lending and asset bubbles—unlike the preceding models that emphasized fiscal deficits or speculation (Sarno and Taylor 1999).

Related to all these models is the widely recognized problem of the "impossible trinity" or the "open economy policy trilemma" (figure 10.1). The problem is that a country cannot simultaneously maintain an open

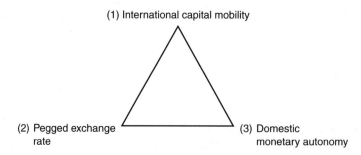

Figure 10.1 Open economy policy trilemma. With the free flow of capital, only two of the three objectives can be attained simultaneously (1 and 2 or 1 and 3). In the current international monetary systems, any two objectives can only be achieved at the expense of the third. An independent monetary policy of domestic stabilization must be sacrificed if the policy objectives of an open capital account and a fixed exchange rate are desired.

capital account, fixed exchange rate, and independent monetary policy. Only two of the three objectives can be attained simultaneously. If the exchange rate is pegged and capital can flow in freely, the government has to give up its independent stabilizing role for domestic monetary policy as it intervenes to hold the rate. If capital mobility and monetary autonomy is wanted, then the country needs floating rates. If a fixed exchange rate with monetary autonomy are wanted, then capital flows have to be controlled. The trilemma may be solved by maintaining either a hard peg (through intervention with sufficient reserves) or a floating exchange rate regime or dollarization.[10]

Although distinctions can be made among the various types of crises, they are frequently intertwined. A set of remedial policies may then be necessary—ranging from capital controls to stabilization policies, a new exchange rate regime, and action by a lender of last resort. The need for remedial policies raises the question of designing a new international financial architecture. Reform of the IMF is necessary to improve the trade-off between financial liberalization and financial stability.

In considering measures for a new international financial architecture, Eichengreen and Hausmann (1999: 2–6) make six basic assumptions: (1) Liberalized financial markets have compelling benefits. (2) International financial liberalization and growing international capital flows are largely inevitable and irreversible. (3) Capital markets are characterized by information asymmetries that can give rise to overshooting, sharp corrections, and, in the extreme, financial crises. (4) The instability provides a compelling argument for erecting a financial safety net despite the moral hazard that may result. (5) Information and transaction costs can create coordination problems and can prevent decentralized markets from quickly and efficiently resolving financial problems. (6) Economic policy is framed in a politicized environment. These assumptions are valid for a discussion of expanded roles for the IMF as crisis lender and crisis manager.

A number of policies are now recommended to prevent the recurrence of international financial crises that cause real costs to the economy.[11] If the general objective is to minimize the risk involved with short-term capital flows, it is necessary to have a proper perception of the risk and adequate pricing of the risk. Proper perception of the risks, however, is difficult because of imperfect information, incomplete markets, bounded rationality, and the destabilizing dynamics of cumulative speculation, with the resultant external costs to the economy. The social risk is therefore greater than the private risk, and there is a case for public policy intervention. Self-fulfilling runs on currencies, self-fulfilling runs on banks, the presence of multiple equilibria—these argue for more policy intervention.

To help prevent a crisis in the first place, the IMF should continue to strengthen its surveillance process of policies and performance in developing countries, increase the transparency of policy making, and improve the conditions for the prequalification of loans (Fischer 2002: 18–26). Since the Asian crisis, this has involved greater transparency of programs and policies adopted by the IMF itself; steps to institute standards of good behavior, including data provision, transparency in the conduct of fiscal, monetary, and financial policies, and reserve and debt management practices for emerging markets; and experimentation with ways to improve the assessment of compliance with various international standards by developing member countries (Citrin and Fischer 2000: 1134).

Now, for a better sense of timing and more effective practice of conditionality, the IMF has established the Contingent Credit Line (CCL) facility. Rather than delaying in its crisis management, the IMF provides countries in advance with the insurance of a line of credit—provided the country prequalifies through the pursuit of good macroeconomic policies and a strong financial sector and is meeting international standards in various areas. By prequalifying countries, the CCL now enables the IMF to use its financing in a preventive way and to support good performers, thereby seeking to prevent crises beforehand by providing a financial incentive for appropriate policies and needed reforms ahead of time (Citrin and Fischer 2000: 1140).

Also contributing to crisis prevention are proper exchange rate policies (Fischer 2002: 3–7). A pegged exchange rate has been crisis prone in recent cases. Developing countries should not allow a pegged exchange rate to become overvalued. Flexible exchange rates are now preferable. But the effects of sound macro fundamentals on exchange rate movement need more attention—especially the role of an inflation targeting approach to monetary policy and fiscal policy. The full range of freely floating exchange rates may be avoided while managed flexibility will entail intermediate regimes, such as arrangements for a basket, band, or crawl.

Whether capital controls are required is debatable. Capital flows provide the valuable function of international financial intermediation whereby savings from rich countries are transferred to poor countries, risk is shared, and intertemporal trade facilitated. When, however, the short-term capital flows are volatile, information is incomplete, and financial markets are distorted, there is a case for preventing a potential crisis by limiting the inflow. Both China and India had capital controls and avoided the Asian crisis. Short-term policies to control precipitous flows might include sterilization of "excess" inflows, raising reserve requirements for banks on foreign transactions, taxes on short-term foreign borrowing, and limitations on open foreign exchange positions of financial institutions. As much as is feasible, the restrictions should be market based rather than subject to discretionary administrative controls.

Or if a crisis is imminent, capital outflow from the developing economy may be limited by standstill mechanisms.[12] A government may prefer such emergency action to the alternatives of a rise in interest rates or devaluation. Controls on an outflow, however, scare off investors and are an invitation to corruption (Rogoff 1999: 34–35). They are also subject to politicization, as various creditors may be affected differently.

Again, in sequencing a general liberalization program, the liberalizing of domestic banking transactions and portfolio markets should be delayed until the requisite regulatory institutions are in place in the domestic financial system (McKinnon 1993). When the World Bank *Development Report* of 1989 supported financial liberalization,[13] it maintained:

> Reform should start by getting the fiscal deficit under control and establishing macroeconomic stability. The government should then scale down its directed credit programs and adjust the level and pattern of interest rates to bring them into line with inflation and other market forces. In the initial stage of reform the government should also try to improve the foundations of finance—that is, the accounting and legal systems, procedures for the enforcement of contracts, disclosure requirements, and the structure of prudential regulation and supervision. It should encourage managerial autonomy in financial institutions. If institutional insolvency is widespread, the government may need to restructure some financial institutions in the early stages of reform. (127)

Unfortunately, these recommendations were not implemented.

All the IMF financial facilities are limited in amount. Indeed, while the Fund's resources have grown through a series of increases in countries' quotas, the Fund's capacity has diminished relative to the globalization in trade that has occurred since Bretton Woods. Insofar as private capital flows were very small in the 1940s, the Fund's resources relative to capital flows have declined even more than relative to trade flows. And yet if the Fund is to act more effectively in financial crisis management, and avoid the alternative crisis actions that result in an overshooting of the desired adjustment, it will need to act as a lender of last resort. This in turn is likely to call for an increase in the amount of liquidity created by the IMF. Just as there is a question of what is the "right" exchange rate, so too is there a question of what is the "right" amount of liquidity—and how it should be created and for whom. Given the large flows of capital, one may argue that there is no shortage of liquidity. If creditworthy, countries can engage in sovereign borrowing from international capital markets. The issue, however, is the adequacy of a country's "owned reserves," without recourse to debt, and the need for official international liquidity in a financial crisis. "Owned reserves," unlike "borrowed reserves," do not need to be periodically financed; they avoid the higher cost of acquiring reserves through borrowing; and they are not subject to abrupt withdrawal.

If the special drawing right (SDR) is ever to become "the principal reserve asset" of the international monetary system, as specified in the IMF's articles of agreement, an increase in SDRs will be necessary. To support development and improve crisis management, a case might be made for a special SDR allocation to the developing countries. Indeed,

Cooper (2002: 10–11) has also advocated the issuance of SDRs to allow "the IMF to play a surrogate lender of last resort for international financial crises, something it cannot assure today because of potential shortage of funds. . . . The conditions for temporary issuance world have to be tightly drawn, and any SDRs actually issued would subsequently be withdrawn when the emergency had passed."

At present, however, with insufficient public funding, the IMF should also involve the private sector in the resolution of financial crises. If the public sector takes upon itself the full responsibility for financing countries from which the private sector is withdrawing, the problem of moral hazard arises. Foreign investors may believe that governments in emerging markets will not allow banks to fail and that together with the IMF there will be lenders of last resort to protect crossborder interbank funding. It would be desirable to eliminate the moral hazard of a "bailout" and have the individual investor exercise due diligence. Irrational private risk must be priced sufficiently high. There should be higher interest rates to firms with uncovered foreign exchange exposures and very high debt-to-equity ratios. Capital adequacy standards for banks should be raised and capital adequacy geared to the riskiness of bank assets. It should also be known that if a crisis occurs, there will be a standstill on capital outflows and a workout procedure of burden sharing that will bail in private investors.

Related to this is the proposal that the IMF should establish a new sovereign debt restructuring mechanism (SDRM, modeled on bankruptcy law) that would allow countries to suspend payments temporarily and seek legal protection from their creditors while they negotiate a restructuring or rescheduling (IMF 2002).[14] An orderly and predictable framework is desired to overcome coordination and collusive action problems among creditors. As Fischer (2002: 37) asks,

> what criteria need to be considered in deciding whether to make improvements in standstill and/or bankruptcy procedures for sovereigns a high priority? The costs of resorting to such measures have to be high if the credit mechanism is to work well. If creditors believe emerging market debtors will too easily use legal provisions to restructure debts, spreads will rise and capital flows to those countries will decline. That is why policymakers from emerging market countries generally oppose proposals to make it easier for them to restructure their payments, be it through collective action clauses [in bond contracts] or the creation of a sovereign bankruptcy procedure.

A number of other bolder—hence more controversial—proposals for financial reform have been suggested. These vary from the establishment of codes of conduct for global financial regulation to contingency finance mechanisms, a credit insurance agency, new rules for IMF lending with private sector involvement, and even a world central bank.[15]

11

Global Trade Issues

A central feature of globalization is the growing importance of international trade. The share of world trade for many developing countries has increased, but for the poorest countries the share has actually declined. For the "globalizers," their increase in trade and their gains from trade contribute to their gains from growth. Trade policy, however, affects the amount and distribution of the gains—both from trade and growth. Trade policy, in turn, is shaped to a large extent within the context of the GATT/WTO system. As nations undertake another round of trade negotiations under the new Doha Development Agenda (2001), the overriding challenge is to establish a global rule-based trade architecture that is more supportive of development.

TRADE NEGOTIATIONS

Future negotiations should deal with several crucial questions. If export promotion is a desired strategy for development, how can market access be enhanced? Can the rules of trade policy regarding market safeguards, subsidies, and antidumping be reformed? Is there a case for special and differential treatment for developing countries? Will "development-through-trade" efforts be influenced more by policy actions outside the GATT/WTO system than within?

The baseline for negotiations is the case for free trade—and its exceptions. With words, diagrams, mathematics, and the computer, economists have proved the logical validity of Ricardo's principle of comparative advantage on which the case for free trade rests. The Orthodox Reaction (chapter 5), with its emphasis on trade liberalization, reinforced the case. And empirical evidence also supports it.

An age-old exception, however, that appeals to developing countries is protection for an "infant industry." When properly put, the case for protecting an infant industry arises when there is a domestic market failure in which prices do not equal the future social benefit from the industry. The industry may confer a social benefit outside its own production but not be paid for this external benefit. By training labor, for example, an industry provides experienced labor to other industries at no cost. The essence of the case for government support is that the infant industry yields an external economy but cannot appropriate payment for it through the market price system. There is then justification for government intervention to promote a greater output from the industry that confers external benefits: the social gain is greater than the private profit, and more output should be encouraged. Although it is popular in less developed countries, the argument must be carefully circumscribed. When expressed in its precise modern form, its applicability is narrowly limited.

The validity of the protectionist argument rests on "dynamic learning effects," such that after a period of learning by experience, an industry that is not currently competitive may achieve comparative advantage through a temporary period of protection. Learning by doing may give rise to external economies; without protection there would then be underproduction from the social point of view. If the learning experience results in dynamic internal economies, in which the learning benefits remain wholly in the firm, the market failure may be in the imperfection of capital markets that makes the financing of such investment difficult or too expensive because capital markets are biased against this type of "invisible" investment in human capital, or because the rate of interest for such a long-term investment is too high, owing to private myopia. If capital markets are imperfect, the firm may not be able to borrow, so that even if a firm were to acquire a long-run comparative advantage in some product, it would not be privately feasible to produce it. The best policy would be to remove imperfections in capital markets. But if this cannot be implemented, a second-best case can be made for a protective trade policy.

It is necessary, however, to stress that the protection be limited in time and that it allow a sufficient decrease in economic costs such that the initial excess costs of the industry will be repaid with an economic rate of return equal to that earned on other investments. In a less developed country, a costly import-substituting industrialization policy that protects infant industries beyond the first easy stage of import substitution is only too likely to result in excessive costs to the economy and adverse spillover effects on agricultural development and export promotion.

When the narrow conditions for government intervention are met, a subsidy on the activity that gives rise to the external benefit would be the best feasible policy. This is because it induces more output but does not raise the price to consumers. The next-best policy would be a tariff. Third best would be a quota on imports. The quota is inferior to a tariff because it physically limits the amount of imports and completely paralyzes the price system, unlike the tariff. We must recognize, however, that whether the industry is subsidized directly or indirectly through a tariff or quota, infant industry protection will redistribute income from taxpayers and consumers to the owners, and probably also to the employees, of the industries protected. Given the opportunity to vote, would taxpayers and consumers endorse such a redistribution?

Another exception to free trade because of international market failure is based on the argument that a country may have sufficient market power to improve its terms of trade (raise its export prices relative to import prices). If, for example, the country is a monopoly exporter of a product, it may tax its export and increase its price to a foreign buyer. If, on the other hand, the country is the major importer and the supplier has to reduce its price f.o.b. in order to get under a tariff imposed by the country that is its largest market, the tariff-imposing country may again make the foreigner in effect pay the duty by lowering the price of its export. The tariff-imposing country's terms of trade would then improve.

The terms of trade argument can be traced back to J. S. Mill in the nineteenth century. But neither Mill nor successive generations of economists have seen much empirical validity in the argument. In general, these instances of market failure, whether domestic or international, are extremely limited. The necessary condition of possessing monopoly or monopsony power is rare for a developing economy.

If most development economists were listened to, free trade would be the rule of the global economy. National borders would not interfere with the best global allocation of resources. Exceptions would be few and confined to strictly limited conditions. Developing countries, along with all countries, would benefit—especially from the dynamic gains of trade.

Free trade, however, needs enforcement. Otherwise, for national political considerations, governments will frequently intervene in international markets. Absent an international mechanism for the enforcement of the rules of the game, national trade policies frequently conflict with the economist's prescription.

Developing countries can pursue trade liberalization at three levels: unilateral, regional, and multilateral. Export promotion is heavily dependent on policy reforms undertaken by the developing country itself—macroeconomic stabilization, exchange rate adjustment, removal of quotas and tariffs, capital market liberalization. Much attention has been given to the proper sequencing of policies that move a country from its distorted system to one that is liberalized (McKinnon, 1993).

INTER-LDC TRADE

It must also be recognized that there are considerable restrictions on inter-LDC trade. Developing-country tariffs in manufacturing for imports from other developing countries are on average four times higher than tariffs in industrial countries on imports from developing countries

(12.8 percent as opposed to 3.4 percent). Restrictions on services (finance, telecommunications, business services) are also more common than in industrial countries (World Bank 2002: xii). Unilateral trade reform in developing countries may allow the largest potential for policy-induced gains from trade. Developing countries should reduce their own trade barriers on imports from both advanced countries and other less developed countries. Although trade among the developing countries themselves accounts for less than 20 percent of the exports of LDCs, there is considerable potential for inter-LDC trade if restrictions are reduced.

The increasing number of regional or preferential trading arrangements (PTAs) is also cause for concern. Article 24 of the GATT has been used to form customs union or free trade areas. Developing countries have resorted to PTAs—such as in the (NAFTA), the Caribbean Community (CARICOM), the East African Community (EAC), and the South Asian Preferential Trade Agreement (SAPTA)—in order to give preferential reduction of trade barriers to a subset of countries without having to pursue a nondiscriminatory reduction on a multilateral basis. Some may believe that half a step toward free trade is better than none. The second best, however, may not be welfare enhancing: instead of trade creation, there may be trade diversion in the sense of importing from a preference-receiving country instead of from a lower cost outside country that confronts a common regional tariff. Such discrimination does not lead to efficient world integration, in contrast to nondiscriminatory multilateral liberalization, which involves equal treatment of all nations.

Studies of the empirical evidence on regionalism versus multilateralism are not conclusive (Winters 1996: 24). Neither theory nor evidence provides a definitive guide to the choice between regionalism and multilateralism. The most important lesson to be learned from efforts at regional integration is that, if the potential benefits of integration are to be fully realized, the regional association must be a strong one that is capable of coordinating trade policies, including exchange-rate policy, among the member countries. It must also provide some means for an equitable distribution of the costs and benefits among the members.

THE GATT/WTO SYSTEM

The forces of globalization intensify the need for a multilateral approach to trade policy. Imperfect as it was, the GATT was a step in the direction of liberalizing world trade through multilateral negotiations. Its basic principle of reciprocity, however, did not conform to the pure free trader's position of unilateral free trade but instead yielded to the necessary political inducement that a country negotiates to reduce its tariffs only on the condition that other countries reciprocate. Under GATT, tariff reduction was viewed politically as a "cost." Each country therefore insists on "reciprocity." Developing countries, however, believed that their "cost" should be less than that of more developed countries, hence that they should enjoy some special and differential treatment (Finger 1999). Differential treatment was rather limited, but article 18 of the original GATT did allow protection "to promote the establishment of a particular industry." Moreover, developing countries were allowed to impose trade restrictions to safeguard their external financial position, at the same time that the IMF supported fixed exchange rates. In the 1960s and 1970s, import-substitution policies were therefore followed with impunity as many developing countries failed to take advantage of the foreign market opportunities provided by the globalizing economy. In contrast were the East Asian globalizers, with their higher growth rates.

Establishment of the World Trade Organization is inducing more active participation by developing countries in trade negotiations and greater interest in other issues to be addressed in future negotiations. Over three-quarters of the WTO's members have self-elected the status of developing countries, of which 30 are the least developed. The launch of the Doha Development Agenda in 2001 gave new emphasis to trade and development issues.

How might the governance exercised by the GATT/WTO system now contribute more to development?

Of special concern to developing countries is the future of agreements with respect to market safeguards, antidumping policies, and subsidies. Also significant will be action with respect to textiles, agriculture, TRIPs (trade-related intellectual properties), and TRIMs (trade-related investment measures). Most of these issues in the "Development Round" are subsumed under the need for market access. Export promotion has now succeeded import substitution—not for mercantilistic reasons but to relax the foreign exchange constraint on the development process, realize the dynamic gains from trade based on comparative advantage, and allow the developing country to import more growth-promoting goods and services in which it has a comparative disadvantage.[1]

Under the old GATT system, the developing countries benefited to the extent that tariffs were reduced by successive rounds of multilateral trade negotiations. Although average tariff rates have declined, the developing countries still face some high rates on their export products—especially basic agricultural foods, textiles, clothing, and footwear. The escalation in tariff rates according to the degree of processing is a severe impediment to exports because the high effective rates of protection limit the developing country's ability to move from raw commodities to more processed products. The World Bank calculates that the average poor person selling into globalized markets confronts trade barriers approximately twice as high as those confronting a typical worker in industrialized countries (World Bank 2002: xii).

Negotiations in the Development Round should deal with these high tariff rates and nontariff barriers on exports from developing countries—not only in trade with developed countries but also in inter–developing country trade. Quantitative restrictions on textiles and clothing, as in the

Multi-Fibre Arrangement (MFA), should be phased out by 2005, as agreed in the Uruguay Round. Subsidies on agricultural output in the European Union, Japan, and the United States, as well as agricultural export subsidies, are a major cause for complaint.[2] The WTO estimates that if the Doha trade agenda could succeed in halving trade barriers in agriculture and textiles alone, developing countries would gain more than $200 billion a year in additional income by 2015.[3]

In thinking now about a new trade architecture, most economists focus on market access and the reform of some rules in the GATT/WTO system, especially those relating to market safeguards and escape clauses to limit imports in the more developed countries. The present practice of imposing market safeguards and involving escape clauses under the GATT, by national legislation and by executive discretion, lacks any rationale in welfare economics. How can the deficiencies in the present mixture of policies be overcome and a first-best remedial policy be established to monitor problems of trade adjustment?

First, the conditions of "market disruption" and "domestic injury" in the importing country must be more clearly established. If there are to be safeguards for the importing country, what are the different effects of protecting via the suspension of a tariff concession, introduction of a tariff on the imports that are found to cause "injury," the imposition of quantitative restrictions, or the institution of "voluntary export restraints?" What relevance does the principle of "nondiscrimination" have? In turn, as the exporting country loses exports, should it receive compensation? In what form—another tariff concession or financial compensation? If the latter, to the government or the exporting industry? From the importing country's government or a multinational fund? In this connection, do the legislative terms of "orderly marketing," "fair share," and "equitable share" have any economic meaning?

If, on the other hand, safeguards are disallowed, and the importing country instead chooses to undertake adjustment policies to ease the transformation costs, who should receive compensation in the importing country and in what amount? Should only workers? Or also owners of capital? In which industries and under what conditions?

Finally, because the market safeguards of one importing country will have an effect on another importing country (as exports are redirected to the other country), should there be some form of multilateral surveillance of these safeguards? Similarly, would not multinational coordination of domestic adjustment policies be welfare superior to only national policies taken independently?

These several questions indicate that the welfare states of all these various schemes need to be compared before the welfare superiority of a new set of policies can be established for trade adjustment. Although policies have been instituted in a piecemeal and ad hoc fashion, mainly designed for so-called emergency situations, new policy initiatives to meet the problem of trade adjustment require that policies be founded on systematic welfare analysis and be directed to the consequences of an ever-changing international division of labor. If this is not done, there will continue to be distortions in the patterns of comparative advantage, and the liberalization of trade will not be facilitated.

Although there is now no international agreement on measures that will permit short-term market safeguards while adjustment policies are undertaken, it has been suggested that new rules for these safeguards should be established in conformity with the following three principles. First, emergency protection should have a finite time limit and be progressively reduced over the period. Second, market safeguards must be accompanied by a definite effort by the importing country's government and industry to adjust, modernize, or diversify into competitive lines of production. Third, some multilateral organization, such as the WTO, should establish multilateral surveillance over both safeguard and adjustment measures.

SUBSIDIES

In turning to export promotion, a developing country is likely to institute incentive programs that entail subsidies on exports. Protective action against LDCs' exports that are subsidized is now common. But the practice should be reexamined in future trade negotiations. What types of subsidies are to be prohibited, actionable, or nonactionable?

The economic theory of optimal trade policy would allow subsidies under certain conditions. The infant industry argument for intervention can be expressed best in terms of external economies, hence as a case of a domestic divergence justifying an optimum subsidy.

If a pioneer firm incurs expenses on acquiring knowledge, which is then available free to later entrants, there is a case for an optimal subsidy to the learning process. Similarly, one firm's investment can give rise to an externality if, in accordance with "learning by doing," productivity in the capital goods industry is a function of cumulative gross investment, so that if a firm invests more today, the return on any given level of investment undertaken by any firm tomorrow will be higher. An optimal subsidy on investment would then be justified. These cases indicate that the private market may underestimate the future benefits of an investment in the acquisition of knowledge. It is also possible that the private capital market overestimates the time preference for returns, with private firms desiring returns within a shorter period of time than would society, which may have greater concern for the future than has the firm. The social rate of discount is then less than the current market rate of interest, and the investment may be socially profitable even though privately unprofitable. Again, subsidization of investment would be appropriate.

In factor markets there is a case for an optimum subsidy policy whenever there is a divergence between social and private marginal costs in factor use. A distortionary wage differential between activities for the same factor is a common instance of this in less developed countries. The market wage in the advanced manufacturing sector of the economy tends to be greater than the alternative opportunity cost of labor in agriculture. When labor migrates from the rural to the urban sector, the sacrifice in agricultural output is less than the value of the manufacturing wage. The market price of the factor does not reflect the social cost of the input: a true accounting or shadow wage would be less than the actual wage facing the manufacturing sector. The result is that the price ratio understates the profitability of transforming agriculture into manufactures. The manufacturing sector, which is an import-competing sector, employs less labor than would be socially desirable.

To offset the distortionary wage differential, the best policy would be a factor subsidy geared directly to the amount of labor employment provided by the import-competing firms. Second-best policy would be a subsidy on manufacturing production, and third-best a tariff to protect import-competing manufacturing firms. The production subsidy and tariff would shift production toward more manufacturing output, but it would not remove the wage differential, and therefore the economy would still operate on an inefficient production-possibility frontier. Moreover, the tariff would create an added consumption cost. A quota to protect the import-competing manufacturing firms would be fourth-best policy because of its additional consumption cost and physical limitation on imports.

In each of these cases, it is most desirable that the subsidy be directed as specifically as possible to the exact source of the externality. The optimal subsidy is geared to labor training or to investment in creation of knowledge or to labor employment—not simply a general subsidy to the firm. A general subsidy would not distinguish among production activities or type of factor inputs, hence would lead to some byproduct distortion.

Charges of "unfair trade" multiply as globalization intensifies international competition. In the interest of "fair trade," many now argue not only for reciprocity of market access for exports but also for protection against imports that are subsidized or dumped. A "level playing field" is wanted. But care must be taken not to equalize costs among nations, as some wish. For to do so would mean no trade. A plea for "fair trade" becomes only too easily a plea for protection.

Considering the issue of "fairness," economists maintain that it is wrong for foreign governments to pursue policies that violate a country's natural comparative advantage and competitive markets. The free competitive market is the standard that is normally adopted as fair trade: market economic principles should apply equally to all trading firms. Insofar as an export subsidy makes private costs less than social costs, and exporters acquire an artificially larger share of world markets, economists would deem such trade unfair.

Other economic and legal considerations, however, call for a complex exercise in line drawing between fair and unfair trade. This is apparent in an assessment of the major policies aimed at unfair trade—namely, countervailing duties on export subsidies and antidumping measures. These measures are good politics, but again, care must be taken that their misuse or overuse does not result in bad economics.

Agricultural subsidies are widespread in the United States, Japan, and the EU. For political reasons, these have not been subjected to counter-vailing action. The GATT Subsidies Code permits subsidies for agricultural products, as long as the subsidies do not result in the exporter obtaining "more than an equitable share of the world market." This has had little bite in practice. In the Uruguay round of trade negotiations, the United States sought multilateral agreement to eliminate farm sub-sidies over a 10-year period. But this met with opposition from the EU. Subsidies and other support to agriculture in high-income countries are roughly $1 billion a day—or more than six times all development assis-tance (World Bank 2002: xii). The potential welfare gains from further liberalizing agricultural markets are huge, both absolutely and relatively to gains from liberalizing textiles or other manufacturing (Anderson, Hoekman, and Strutt 2001).

When there is a finding of subsidization and injury, the remedial ac-tion is scaled to offset the subsidy, not the injury. A countervailing duty is calculated equivalent to the amount of the subsidy. This is a complex calculation that depends on the time profile of the subsidy, its duration, and its discount rate.

Regardless of what definition of subsidy is used, no consideration is given to the possibility that the subsidy might improve resource alloca-tion in the subsidizing country by correcting a market failure (an external economy as in R&D activity) in that country. Such a subsidy might also improve resource allocation in the world and increase the value of world output. An infant export industry might justify promotion by subsidi-zation when the social return is greater than the private return.

Moreover, in imposing countervailing duties, governments do not consider the costs imposed on consumers through higher prices, costs to the government of administering the law, and the lobbying expenditures of domestic producer groups that seek a rent from the protection. These may not be offset by benefits to producers or by duty revenues, and the cases in which countervailing duties can generate a net benefit to the economy are difficult to identify in practice. Foreign governments are also likely to retaliate.

Notwithstanding criticisms of existing trade law, and regardless of theoretical analyses of ideal trade policy, countervailing action against subsidized exports will undoubtedly become even more important in the future. As international competitiveness has intensified with globaliza-tion, the number of countervailing duty cases has risen rapidly. As long as firms do not like to surrender markets for any reason, action against foreign subsidies will remain a major trade issue in the competitive future.

DUMPING

Antidumping duties are another major weapon against so-called unfair trade. Antidumping actions hit developing countries disproportionately in both industrial country markets and in other developing countries. While the countervailing duty on subsidized exports reacts against action of a foreign government, the antidumping duty responds to the action of a foreign firm.

The traditional definition of dumping is selling at a lower price in one national market than in another—that is, price discrimination between national markets. One test of dumping is simply foreign price being less than home price for the goods. Another test is selling to country 2 at an export price f.o.b. lower than in country 3. Still another is foreign price being less than cost of production.

The practice of dumping represents price discrimination, which can be a common practice for maximizing profits when a firm faces a more elastic demand in foreign markets than at home and realizes economies of scale. During periods of slack demand, a firm that has high fixed costs and low variable costs will rationally produce in the short run if it can sell at any price above variable costs. It may then export to a country where firms have higher variable costs. But persistent sales at a loss tend to indicate a lack of comparative advantage, and if they continue over the longer run then it must be because of some assistance provided by government. The rationale of the antidumping law then merges with that of the countervailing duty law.

An antidumping duty is also rationalized by claiming that it prevents predatory dumping—that is, a temporary period of selling below marginal costs to either forestall the development of competition or eliminate competition in the importing country, followed by an increase in price above marginal cost. Even during the period of dumping there can be injury to import-competing producers who lose market share and to other domestic producers from whom demand has been diverted onto the dumped goods.

Proponents of countervailing and antidumping duties maintain that "free trade" is a mirage and that what matters is "fair trade." But when protectionist sentiment is strong, care must be taken not to overextend and overuse these restrictive policies. When duties are imposed, fairness to the producer means higher cost to the buyer. When a country imposes countervailing and antidumping duties, the action is trade restricting. These measures should not be used in trivial cases or as harassment of successful foreign competitors. Such action is likely in periods of intense international competition and as long as the petitioner has nothing to lose. Discipline and transparency are therefore required if the truly unfair cases are to be resolved without being protectionist for high-cost firms competing against imports. Given, however, that antidumping measures are discriminatory, can be politically manipulated, and are highly trade distorting, some advocate that in negotiations on refining article 6 of the GATT/WTO agreements relating to antidumping, the developing countries should propose that it ban their use altogether (Srinivasan 2002: 325).

Beyond the use of market safeguards, subsidies, and dumping, the LDCs are concerned with negotiations on TRIMs and the implementation of the TRIPs agreement. These measures are politically difficult to reform. There is now particular concern that the TRIPs agreement might price patent drugs beyond the capability of the poor.

Although labor and environmental standards are major issues in the backlash against globalization, proposals in trade and labor standards are viewed by developing countries as protectionist measures that diminish the comparative advantage of developing countries. The problem of labor standards is better left to the International Labor Organization (ILO) or other agencies. While there are many negotiating issues, the central ones of liberalization can be handled unilaterally and by the GATT/WTO reforms of market safeguards, subsidies, and dumping.

SPECIAL AND DIFFERENTIAL TREATMENT

The next round of multilateral trade negotiations should be development friendly. To what extent, however, does this call for special and differential treatment of the developing countries? Contrary to the multilateral most-favored-nation nondiscrimination view of trade policy, there has been a persistent minority view that developing countries should receive special treatment on the basis of "need" or "fairness."[4]

Under the old GATT system there were demands in the 1960s and 1970s for a new international economic order based on need or fairness that would exempt developing countries from GATT rules and favor the "periphery" in "North-South" trade. The first session of UNCTAD recommended that the GATT allow developing countries to retain their right to control imports, "implement measures designed to increase and stabilize primary commodity export earnings at equitable and remunerative prices," and grant "new preferential concessions, both tariff and non-tariff to developing countries as a whole and such preferences should not be extended to developed countries." Not only was it politically infeasible to implement these proposals but also the mainstream of development economists did not support the early recommendations of UNCTAD. What has existed in the past is some limited special and differential treatment for balance-of-payments purposes, infant industries, tariff preferences under the General System of Preferences, non-

reciprocity trade negotiations, exemptions on export subsidies for the
least developed countries, and a graduated threshold on safeguard measures against the least developed countries.

Now, however, the demand for special and differential treatment has
diminished. This is because the earlier practice of import substitution has
lost favor, and care must now be taken not to thwart the move to international integration by overdoing discriminatory protection. The developing countries stand to gain more by requiring reciprocal exchanges of
liberalization between both the less and more developed countries.[5]
"Fairness" now focuses on liberalization of agricultural trade, reduction
of tariffs that are especially adverse for developing countries, and reduction or elimination of nontariff barriers.

GOVERNANCE OF ECONOMIC GLOBALIZATION

Why does the question of governance arise for the global economy? Why
not simply rely on the market as the standard of economic conduct? Why
not leave the "rules of the game" with respect to international trade and
international finance to the operation of international market forces? Development economics has a strong component of welfare economics, and
the welfare economist immediately replies that there are international
market failures that merit remedial policy action. There are also global
public goods that cannot be provided adequately by the market. Among
these, knowledge and information, health, financial stability, peace, and
equity are especially relevant for development.

Beyond these welfare considerations, development practitioners recognize that in reality governments are frequently reluctant to rely on the
market and instead intervene with deliberate policy making. Governments intervene to affect the composition, direction, and terms of trade.
They intervene to manage the foreign exchange rate. Some collective
management—akin to an international public sector—is therefore necessary, not only to remedy international market failure but also to mitigate competitive policy making by national governments and to achieve
a better policy outcome through coordination of national policies.

As exemplified by trade issues and currency crises, a fundamental
problem of the globalized economy is that international economics, in
the sense of international integration, continues to be opposed by national politics, because governments desire to retain autonomy over their
economic policies. Economists applaud the process of globalization because it integrates economies, promotes competition, and yields a more
efficient allocation of resources on an international scale. To a national
policy maker, however, internationalization is troubling: it heightens the
vulnerability of a nation to external shocks and influences the course of
domestic policy. When the domestic economic objectives of different
nations clash, international tension and conflict arise, often resulting in

a zero-sum game among nations. There are conflicts over markets, the terms of trade, terms of foreign investment, balance-of-payments adjustment, stabilization policies, the common resources of the world, and the environment. The forces behind the globalization process are unlikely to wane, but as internationalization proceeds, the international community will have to seek better policy solutions for the avoidance of conflicts and for more effective structures of global governance. The crucial question for developing countries is how the increasing economic and technical interdependence can be subjected to collective management that will allow the less developed countries to gain more benefits from the globalization process. For developing countries, improvement in global governance is as vital as improvement in domestic governance, and both levels of governance call for institution building.

Better governance of the global economy is essential to promote standards of international economic conduct and establish international economic order. This is even more important for developing countries than the more developed. While the latter have strong states, the less developed tend to have weak states with weak domestic institutions of governance.

> Whether because of the artificial and partial grafting on of western institutions by colonial powers or the ravages of chronic public sector poverty, rule by corrupt leaders, or institutional incapacity and decay, government institutions in most developing countries have never worked particularly well. States have generally been highly centralized and inefficient at the same time that they have expanded to constrict the activities of nonstate actors, whether individuals or organizations; weak themselves, they also pursued policies and strategies that weakened their societies and economies. . . . Ambitious but weak institutions of governance are a primary reason why international financial institutions insist that governments undergoing stabilization and structural adjustment radically restructure their public sectors. (Grindle 2000: 188–189)

Insofar as weak developing countries are at a disadvantage in trade negotiations and in managing financial markets, there is all the more reason for institutions of global governance.

Rodrik (2001a: 348) summarizes as follows the implications of the discrepancy between global markets and institutions that remain national.

> On the one hand, the existence of jurisdictional boundaries, drawn largely along national lines, restricts economic integration. This inhibits efficiency. On the other hand, the desire by producers and investors to go global weakens the institutional base of national economies. This inhibits equity and legitimacy.
>
> Taken together, the two processes drive us toward a no-man's world. Exporters, multinationals, and financiers complain about impediments to trade and capital flows. Labor advocates, environmentalists, and consumer safety activists decry the downward pressures on national standards and

legislation. Broad sections of the populace treat globalization as a dirty word while happily devouring its fruits. And government officials vacillate, trying to please each group in turn while satisfying none.

Globalization of economic transactions requires that the international community search for a normative order that will accommodate conflicts, make better policy choices, and manage change. What rules, norms, or standards can be invoked to shape the behavior of nations in the world economy, with special attention to the developing countries?

The issues of inequality and financial crises in a global economy are stimulating considerable discussion about governance on behalf of development. The Bretton Woods order, as outlined in chapter 3, was notable for introducing some "rules of the game." During the half century since the establishment of the Bretton Woods institutions, however, a rapidly changing world economy has called for considerable modification of the Bretton Woods order and the establishment of more effective rules for the global economy.

In an evolutionary way, the World Bank and IMF have responded with some changes in their objectives and procedures. The IMF has modified its principle of treating all members in a uniform way by establishing new facilities designed for use by its less developed members. The World Bank has moved beyond project loans to program financing and to the functions of a "knowledge bank" that attempts to devise and implement appropriate policies. The GATT has been transformed into the WTO with additional powers.

Nonetheless, despite the reorientation that has occurred, many believe that the forces of globalization require additional measures of global governance in the interest of development. The central problem of governance is that policy is still made at the national level, while markets in goods, services, and assets have become global. As the requirements of development economics confronts national politics, the need for governance intensifies.

Can there be more effective mechanisms or structures of governance to shape the international economic conduct of private business and national governments? We cannot yet appeal to an international public sector that might engage in international economic management as extensively as does national economic management. There is no international central bank. There is no international fiscal policy, no international antitrust legislation, no international industrial policy, no international regulation of the natural environment. What then are the institutions and procedures for making decisions that might govern international order?

The need for an international reach in policy making is simply a corollary of the principle that the level at which a decision is taken should be high enough to cover the area in which the impact is nonnegligible. In order that the decisions regarding necessary policy instruments be optimal, there must not be "external" effects—that is, the influences exerted on the well-being of groups outside the jurisdiction of those who make the decision should be weak. The area in which the impact of the instrument will be felt determines what decision level will be optimal. For many issues that we have discussed, the nation-state is an inappropriate decision-making unit. Decisions taken at the national level are often far too low to be optimal. Governance must reach beyond national jurisdiction.

A system of functional federalism among nations or world federalism (Rodrik 2001b) might be the ideal of the far distant future. For the immediate future, however, intergovernmental cooperation and coordination will have to rely on action by the GATT/WTO system, IMF, World Bank, and specialized United Nations agencies.[6] These institutions make up the structure of an international public sector, rudimentary as it is. They have to devise programs that ensure that the benefits of global integration are more equally shared, competitive policy making is avoided, problems of international market failures are mitigated, and international public goods are adequately provided.

In the future, as in the past, agreement on some form of governance is most likely to emerge under conditions of crisis management. This aside, nations are more likely to submit to more governance the more frequent the attempts are to institute such governance, as in repeated games. The challenge is to recognize more strongly the interests of developing nations and to have these nations be more active in establishing an international economic order.

The previous discussions of trade issues and currency crises associated with globalization have advocated a strengthening of the GATT/WTO system and the IMF. It is also necessary for the World Bank to support the efforts of the WTO and IMF. Although the central focus of the Bank is on long-term development, while the Fund concentrates on short-term stabilization and balance-of-payments adjustment, the policies of one affect the other. In essence, the WTO, Bank, and Fund are all concerned with policies to relax the foreign exchange constraint on a country's development. New and enhanced actions by the IMF, WTO, and World Bank in concert would rejuvenate the Bretton Woods institutions and would strengthen the international public sector.

In the future, the degree and quality of global governance of the international monetary regime will be determined mainly by activities of the IMF, but greater collaboration with the World Bank and the WTO is desirable. A study of the Fund's historical evolution and the key issues in the future concludes as follows.

> The world faces an institutional choice between an order in which these aspects of surveillance (over management of global liquidity, adjustment policies, confidence, and trade policy) are fragmented and treated in separation, with a smaller IMF [as in figure 11.1], or, preferably, one in which the elements of surveillance are more effectively coordinated, with a stronger IMF [as in figure 11.2]. The case for greater coordination between international institutions rests on the substantial extent of the linkages that

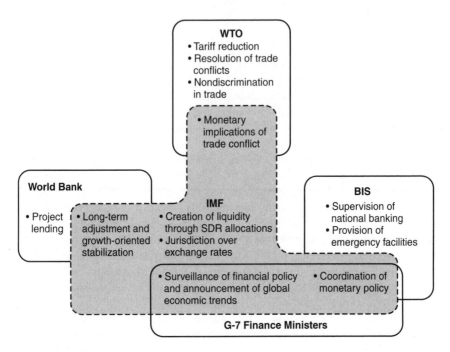

Figure 11.1 Small IMF

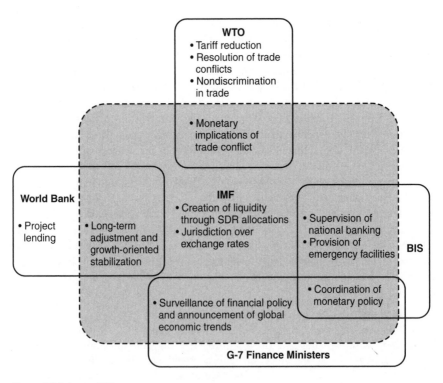

Figure 11.2 Large IMF

exists between different global economic problems. Issues such as interest rate levels, macro-economic orientation, debtor problems, and capital flows cannot be treated adequately in isolation from each other. (James 1996: 617–620)

For developing countries, it is especially important to add trade issues. Trade and finance issues are linked to the serious international problem of incomplete risk markets. With globalization, the risks from volatile price changes have increased. Added to the volatility in their international commodity prices, the repercussions of wide movements in exchange rates and interest rates have increased the risks for many developing countries. Although the solution is not to fix prices, some international measures—led by the IMF and World Bank—should be devised that would allow a better distribution of risk and permit it to be borne more efficiently.

The World Bank's influence on policy making in developing countries can be strong through its policy advice and allocation of loans. Together with the IMF, the World Bank can help debtor countries with their debt management. Not only can the Bank supplement the Fund in providing liquidity but, even more important, it can also promote the development of a stronger corporate and financial infrastructure to mitigate international financial crises. The Bank can also take the lead in promoting debt relief for the most highly indebted countries.

Moreover, the Bank should cooperate with the WTO. If market access in goods and services is to be sought in WTO negotiations, the Bank can complement the effort by supporting policies within the developing country that increase its trade capacity. Financial and technical assistance from the Bank may support supply-side initiatives to expand a country's trade capacity. This expansion of "Aid for Trade" can be the most important dimension of strengthening the international trade architecture (Hoekman 2001: 3, 21–26). This calls not only for loans and technical assistance for upgrading basic infrastructure, but also for meeting export market product standards, protecting intellectual property, and improving trade logistics and customs clearance. The export of goods can be especially stimulated by liberalization in services (transportation, insurance, finance, communication) (Deardorff 2001).

Adjustment loans and policy advice from the World Bank can also make trade liberalization more effective, especially by supporting macroeconomic stabilization and facilitating the allocation of resources to the export sector. The Bank will also have to give special attention to poverty alleviation, to the extent that the poor were formerly employed in the importable sector.[7]

If export-led development is to succeed, there must be not only a strong stimulus from the enhancement of the country's export capacity but also a strong response or diffusion mechanism within the domestic economy. The "carry-over" from exports or the integrative process will be stronger under the following conditions: the more developed the domestic structure of the economy the more robust market institutions, the stronger health and education services that support human capital, the greater the transformation capacity of the economy.[8] The World Bank's aid is vital in promoting these "behind the border" initiatives for a strong process of trade integration.

Although it is not difficult to outline actions by the Fund, Bank, and WTO to support development, the problem remains that the "strong" advanced states have more influence on the creation and enforcement of rules of the global economy than do the "weak" developing states (Woods 2000). Indeed, some have contended that the liberalizing economic reforms advocated by the Bank and Fund in the 1980s and 1990s actually constituted "coercive liberalization" (Wade 2001) and that this continues with "forced harmonization" in trade negotiations (Rodrik 1999: 148).[9]

Moreover, Rodrik (2001a: 31–32) argues that the GATT/WTO system is not development friendly, insofar as its "rules for admission into the world economy not only reflect little awareness of development priorities, they are often completely unrelated to sensible economic principles." Efforts at international integration may also be misdirected, insofar as "policy makers need to forge a domestic growth strategy, relying on domestic investors and domestic institutions. The most costly downside of the integrationist agenda is that it is crowding out serious thinking and efforts along such lines."

Further, as Stiglitz observes, there are

> real risks associated with delegating excessive power to international economic agencies. . . . Agency problems arise at several levels. Not only may an institution not serve the general interest and weight the welfare or perspectives of certain groups more than others, but the institution can actually become an interest group itself, concerned with maintaining its position and enhancing its power. This problem becomes particularly alarming when the power and prestige of an international organization is pitted against the weak position of a developing country that is appealing to the international community in a time of crisis. (1999: F583–F584)

Efforts are needed to counterbalance the power of the strong state and to make international economic agencies more accountable. Decision making in the Fund and Bank needs to be more transparent and subject to public criticism. The Fund took a step in this direction when it established in 2001 its new Independent Evaluation Office (IEO) that is to undertake independent evaluations of the IMF's various activities, with a view to strengthening the learning process.[10] To improve the negotiation capacity of the weak states, technical assistance and financial aid are needed. J. Michael Finger and P. Schuler (1999) estimate that a typical developing country would need budgetary outlays of at least $150 million to implement only three of the WTO's many agreements—namely, on intellectual property, customs valuation, and technical standards.

Moreover, NGOs and the institutions of civil society can play a stronger role in governance.

Governance of the global economy cannot, however, be reduced to a set of rules and regulations. Even though the GATT/WTO system looks legalistic, it is better described as "diplomat's jurisprudence." The GATT diplomats attempted to shape an approach to law that tried to reconcile, on their own terms, the regulatory objectives of a conventional legal system with the turbulent realities of international trade affairs (Hudec 1970). The same is true for the WTO. Although the dispute settlement process has been improved, it still remains ambiguous and uncertain. While the Fund and the Bank both impose conditionality on their operations, the conditions are also subject to considerable disagreement that can only be resolved by negotiation. Issues of global governance are more a matter of diplomacy than adjudication.

International economic diplomacy is complicated by not only the lack of legal norms but also the fact that the intellectual underpinning for mechanisms of global governance is ambiguous and subject to differing interpretations. Competing models of international economic behavior have different implications for the degrees and kinds of governance (Bryant 1995). When there is no consensus among economists about the single best model, international cooperation becomes all the more difficult. Moreover, insofar as "development" is a prescriptive—even an emotive—term, it raises implicitly questions of distributive justice and equity. As globalization continues, international institutions and national governments will have to show explicit concern for the effects on developing countries and for a more equitable distribution of the benefits of international integration. In the absence of international government, the extent to which this is achieved will depend largely on the future evolution and cooperative efforts of the IMF, World Bank, and WTO.

Moreover, along with Merilee S. Grindle (2000: 199–200), development economists are now realizing that

> the burden of finding ways to increase the capacity of developing countries to benefit from globalization does not fall only on the shoulders of the developing countries and their public leadership. Certainly the academic community must be part of such efforts. Increasingly, researchers are attempting to understand and map patterns of change from the most micro-levels of livelihoods and communities in poor countries to national policies and international markets and institutions as they are affected by insistent pressures of globalization. In this way, the problems of developing countries are being reinterpreted as global issues, relevant to the North as well as to the South. This kind of research is clearly contributing to a knowledge base about the dynamics of globalization and its impact can be useful to policy audiences internationally and domestically.

12

An Unfinished Biography

Fifty years on, the subject of economic development is very different from the pioneering time when Arthur Lewis walked down that road in Bangkok and threw away the neoclassical assumption of a fixed supply of labor. Two generations of economists have been responsible for the subsequent evolution of the subject in various dimensions. Other assumptions of the neoclassical competitive equilibrium model have been dropped, especially the imperfect information paradigm.

EXPERIENCE AND DEVELOPMENT ANALYTICS

The initial emphasis on growth in GDP has become subsidiary to reduction of poverty. And the reverse causation is now also recognized: reductions in poverty and inequality have positive effects on growth. The most significant addition to the subject has been the microeconomics of development based on the economics of information and the emphasis on institutions and incentives.

Another major advance is the attention to empirical observations. Data sets and case studies have become increasingly abundant. The lessons from development experience are now plentiful and are subject to more refined statistical and econometric techniques of analysis.

The development record over the past 50 years has been mixed, with a creditable overall advance and some outstanding country successes—but also failures. Population in developing countries grew rapidly from nearly 3 billion in 1970 to 5 billion in 2000. In the aggregate, however, more people in the world enjoyed an increase in their standard of living than ever before in history. Since 1965, average income per capita in developing countries (population weighted in 1995 dollars) rose from $989 in 1980 to $1,354 in 2000. In the past four decades, life expectancy in the developing world increased 20 years on average. Infant mortality was reduced by a half. Adult rate rose from an estimated 47 percent in 1970 to 73 percent in 2000 (World Bank 2002). Since 1965, the per capita GDP of the developing countries as a whole has increased by an average of some 2.2 percent per year, more than doubling the income of the average developing country resident.

Almost 1.2 billion, however, still live on less than $1 a day—especially in South Asia (40 percent of Asia's population) and Sub-Saharan Africa (46 percent). Although subject to various measurements,[1] the wide gap between average income in the richest countries and the poorest has tended to accelerate over the past 50 years. During the 1990s the number of people living on less than $1 a day barely changed. But given the population growth, the percentage living in extreme poverty fell from 29 percent in 1990 to 23 percent in 1999, and the number fell by 200 million from 1980 to 1998, with the greatest changes in East Asia and China. It appears that poverty rose a little from 1987 to 1998 but fell substantially from 1980 to 1998 (World Bank 2001). The gap between average income in the richest 20 countries and poorest 20 has doubled in the past 40 years, mainly because of lack of growth in the poorest countries. Some

Table 12.1 Major areas of the world: Growth rate of real GDP per capita (c. 1950–95), share of world population, and GDP per capita as a percentage of developed countries average (c. 1995)

	(1) Annual growth rate (percentage)	(2) Ratio: Per capita GDP at end to beginning	(3) Share of world population (percentage)	(4) 1995 GDP per capita (percentage of developed areas)
1. More developed areas	2.7	3.1	20	100
2. Less developed areas	2.5	2.9	80	18
a. China	3.8	5.0	21	17
b. India	2.2	2.5	17	10
c. Rest of Asia	3.7	4.6	21	23
d. Latin America	1.6	1.9	9	36
e. Northern Africa	2.1	2.4	2	18
f. Sub-Saharan Africa	0.5	1.2	11	8

Notes: In columns 1 and 2, lines 1 through 2b refer to the period 1952–95 and are calculated from Maddison (1998: 40); lines 2c–2f are for 1950–92, calculated from Maddison (1995: apps. A, C, D). Northern Africa is a weighted average of Egypt and Morocco, which together account for over half of the region's population; Sub-Saharan Africa is a weighted average of the rates for seven countries, accounting for about half of the region's population. The sources for column 4 are the same; lines 1 through 2b are ratios for 1995, lines 2c–2f for 1992. The values in 2e and 2f are based on all countries in each region. Column 3 is the medium variant projection for 2000 in United Nations (1998).
Source: Easterlin (2000: 35).

Sub-Saharan African countries have actually retrogressed, and progress in the reduction in poverty in Latin America has been disappointing. In some 30 countries, real per capita incomes have actually fallen over the past 35 years. (See appendix B for changes in income poverty during the recent period 1987–98.) Rising global inequality now comes from the growing divergence among developing countries themselves: some are the fastest growing in the world, while others are the slowest (Dollar 2001).

Tables 12.1–12.3 show changes in real GDP per capita, life expectancy, and adult literacy during the period 1950–95.

Table 12.2 Years of life expectancy at birth, major areas of the world, 1950–55 and 1990–95

	(1) 1950–55	(2) 1990–95	(3) Years Added
1. More developed areas	66.6	74.1	7.5
2. Less developed areas	40.9	61.9	21.0
a. China	40.8	68.4	27.6
b. India	38.7	60.3	21.6
c. Rest of Asia	39.4	62.0	22.6
d. Latin America	51.4	68.1	16.7
e. Northern Africa	41.8	62.2	20.4
f. Sub-Saharan Africa	35.3	47.0	11.7

Data: United Nations (1998: 12, 546–566)
Source: Easterlin (2000: 37).

Table 12.3 Adult literacy rate, major areas of the world, 1950 and 1995 (percentage)

	(1) 1950	(2) 1995	(3) Added percentage points
1. More developed areas	93	98	5
2. Less developed areas	40	70	30
a. China	48	82	34
b. India	19	52	33
c. Rest of Asia	24	72	48
d. Latin America	57	86	29
e. Northern Africa	12	53	41
f. Sub-Saharan Africa	17	56	39

Data: UNESCO (1957), World Bank (1999).
Source: Easterlin (2000: 42).

FUTURE CONTENT

What now of the future?

Policy recommendations have evolved in response to the lessons of experience and the evolution in the analytics of development. Development economists in the 1970s advised developing countries to "get prices right." Then in the 1980s and 1990s, they said "get macro policies right." Now they say "get institutions right."

Convergence between rich countries and poor is questionable for many poor countries over the next half century. Yet the world's population will grow by some two billion in the next 25 years, with 97 percent of that increase in developing countries (World Bank 2002: 1). In the same countries, 2.5 billion to 3 billion people now live on less than $2 a day.

The solution of development problems is likely to continue as the priority of the age. And the subject will continue to evolve as a function of future ideas and experience. Although we cannot anticipate the future content of the subject, we might proceed from our understanding of the past to some outstanding topics and issues that deserve future attention.

In an earlier review of the nature and scope of development economics, Stern (1989) divided the wide scope of the subject into the grand issues, analytical techniques, and micro studies. Much of the evolution of development economics has been based on the reductionist model of analysis—analyzing the problem in smaller and smaller constituent parts—going down from the aggregate economy to particular sectors to firms and to households. The subject, however, should also be synthetic and integrative to appreciate the relationships in the subject in a wider way. We should be aware of both approaches. Since the time of the early development economics, however, economists have slipped in failing to focus on the grand issues—on development as a dynamic process with attention to the interrelation of its parts. Consideration of the future may be most relevant for the grand issues in their modified and extended form.

The very meaning of "development" is expanding beyond narrow economic objectives to larger social and political goals. This requires attention to issues of human rights, global equity, gender fairness, freedom, and democracy. If development policies are to be goal driven, this broader set of goals will require clearer definition and greater understanding of their policy implications. While the noneconomic goals have intrinsic value, it will also be important to determine their instrumental value for improving living standards. Then it will be necessary to determine the sequencing of policies and—even more difficult—how the goals can be achieved simultaneously.

Although specific strategies will be necessary to achieve nonmonetary objectives, growth and change will undoubtedly remain central to any explanation of the determinants of development. The determinants of the sources of growth will still require more attention. Especially important will be further research to understand an increase in total factor productivity. Almost a half century ago, Abramovitz (1956) called the unexplained residual of early growth theory "some sort of measure of ignorance," but he advised that it was also "some sort of indication of where we need to concentrate our attention." This will still be true in the future. For as Stern (1991: 131) observes, "we seem to have too many theories claiming 'property rights' in the unexplained 'residual,' and have no reassurance that any of them, separately or together, really capture what is going on. Just as worrying is that they omit many issues which are probably crucial to growth in the medium run, including economic organization and the social and physical infrastructure."

Growth accounting still has to establish the interactions in the residual among technological progress, economies of scale and scope, tangible capital accumulation, human capital, knowledge capital, and institutional change. Beyond disaggregating the residual into recognizable elements and coming to understand the joint and interdependent action of the main sources of growth, the ultimate task will be to determine how these elements are to yield to policies. Many policies that have been considered in the past bear on the supply of inputs, but it will be more difficult to devise and implement policies to promote the income-raising forces that make up the residual.

To explain the residual and devise policies to increase total factor productivity, the next generation will have to refine and extend new growth theories. Especially fruitful could be the combination of endogenous growth theory with historical country studies. This potential is implicit in Paul Romer's recognition that "our knowledge of economic history, of what production looked like 100 years ago, and of current events convinces us beyond any doubt that discovery, invention and innovation are of overwhelming importance in economic growth and that the economic goods that come from these activities are different in a fundamental way from ordinary objects" (1993: 562).

Romer's endogenous growth theory (as outlined in chapter 6) yields increasing returns to capital accumulation through R & D innovations. This type of activity, however, is not significant for developing countries; the economics of ideas and knowledge will have to be extended in other directions. Endogenous growth theory will become more relevant if it incorporates institutions and government policy. Crafts (1997: 69) anticipates this.

> One of the most exciting avenues of research for economic historians and economists to pursue together using an endogenous innovation framework is the political economy of growth. This should aim for an understanding both of what the key effects of policy on growth have been and also of how the incentive structures facing politicians and private agents generate growth-retarding or growth-enhancing interventions. This will more likely be successfully achieved through a portfolio of detailed case studies of individual countries than through regressing growth rates against standard political variables.

Such studies might illuminate a number of central policy questions. What is the institutional design that will motivate behavior for the creation of knowledge? Can governments encourage the production and use of new knowledge? What is the search mechanism for the discovery of the most productivity-enhancing ideas? Can the sectors or locations be identified in which spillover effects may be large? Given the forces of globalization, what are the extensions of endogenous growth theory to international trade, international capital flows, and international diffusion of ideas?

Future attention to historical development also links to the need to understand more fully the admonition "get institutions right." What is the meaning of "right"? And how are high-quality institutions to be established? While the recognition that institutions matter has become widespread, operational guidance for the formation of desirable institutional arrangements lies in the future.

As North (2001: 491) says, "we know both the economic conditions and the institutional conditions that make for good economic performance. What we do not know is how to get them. For that, we need a body of theory that explores the process of economic, political, and social change. When we have such a theory, we will make much better progress toward solving problems of development."

North also emphasizes (as in chapter 7) that the incentive structure of society—which is fundamental for the process of change—is a function of the institutional structure of that society. But just as more research is needed to understand the sources of growth, so too is more research required to understand the process of economic change. In concentrating most recently on the microeconomics of development, economists have slipped since the time of the early development economics in failing to focus on development as a dynamic process with attention to the interrelation of the parts.

Future economists concerned with incomplete or missing institutions might do well to consider deepening the causation in the first generation's dual sector model. For institutions play a major role in determining the quantity and quality of capital accumulation. Early on, Myint (1985) suggested that dualism is preeminently a phenomenon of an underdeveloped organizational framework: there is incomplete development of not only the market network but also of the government's administrative and fiscal system. This perspective reinforces the requirement of appropriate institutions and the need to secure more policy-relevant information about the building of institutions that will promote growth.

Recognizing the fragmentation of the subject, Michael Lipton (1992: 417) complains:

> The alienation of development economics from its classical forebears is cause for alarm. Development economics is breaking up. Its once integrated components are joining other economic empires. Once, its central topics were set into the context of how individuals in communities develop out

of pervasive poverty. Now these topics are increasingly split up, into special studies of labor, agriculture, and so on. Such studies generalize about
all households (or firms), at all levels of income or production, any-
where. . . .

Development economists, formerly social scientists studying "developing countries," are becoming specialists in the pure economics of location-
less topics (agriculture, labor, etc.) conceived as requiring similar analytical
methods relevant everywhere. The prevailing ethos of the sub-empires of
global economics is more rigorous, theoretically and empirically, than that
of the developmentalist forerunner that they have colonized. However, the
new ethos often subverts understanding of the development *process*. The
ethos perceives success, scientific agreement and "frontier" progress as ly-
ing mainly in equilibrium microstatics. Dynamics are seen as doubtful,
especially if disequilibria persist. All this, however, misses out the very
core of development economics: the macro-dynamics of transformation
from poverty to sufficency. Such analysis is, of necessity, disequilibrated,
trans-sectoral, relevant to (and relating) progress *and* poverty—and probably multi-disciplinary.

Appreciation of the new development economics, however, would mod-
ify this complaint. So would the emphasis on institutional development.

ECONOMICS AND POLITICS

As it has been in the past, another major issue in development is the
determination of the respective roles of the state and the market. In the
early years of the subject, planning dominated, based on the belief in
extensive market failures. In the 1970s and 1980s, in turn, an orthodox
reaction set in against government failures and advocated minimalist
government. With the new development economists it has become apparent that there has been a reaction too far, and that government has
an important role to play, especially in a complementary fashion with
the market. The future task is not to determine whether government
action or the market gives a better outcome but rather how the two in
complementary fashion can improve the situation. How can state action
support the formation and deepening of markets? How can government
policy facilitate or complement private sector coordination—not replacing markets but instead enhancing their functions?[2]

The nexus of economics and politics therefore deserves more analysis.
The subject has changed from viewing government as autonomous and
an exogenous factor in any development analysis to making government
endogenous. If the subject is no longer to view government action and
the market as alternatives but rather as complements, then the task will
be to determine not whether one or the other gives a better outcome but
how the two in complementary fashion can improve the situation. Government policy should facilitate or complement private sector coordination—not replacing markets but instead enhancing their functions.
This task of blending public policies with the market will involve much

deeper conceptual issues than those policy makers have previously faced.

While the state should not be overextended, government will still have extensive functions in dealing with the market failures of the new development economics, protecting property rights, providing public goods, satisfying merit wants such as education and health, improving income distribution, providing physical infrastructure and social capital, and protecting the natural environment. How can these functions be best fulfilled? What public institutional arrangements are required?

If state and market are to be complementary in carrying out these functions, policy makers will have to determine how nonmarket institutions can make markets right. Various forms of market enhancement will have to be determined—from indirect rule making that affects incentives to direct government interventions that structure markets. As the new development economics implies, although the public sector is shrinking, it will still have to improve the functioning of markets through monitoring and regulation. The determination of getting specific policies right in particular countries will be a major obligation of national governance. Is a proposed policy necessary, sufficient, or the best to solve a problem?

This, in turn, will again call for an understanding of institutional foundations that foster or hinder the operation of existing and missing markets. To do this, it will be desirable to extend the new research agenda that considers the state to be an endogenous and political agent, a positive analysis of which requires an understanding of its institutional foundations and their specific characteristics in a particular society (Greif 2001: 338). The objective of blending public policies with the market will require involvement in much deeper conceptual issues than those that policy makers have confronted in the past. In many ways, it will be more difficult to be a policy maker, policy advisor, or policy administrator. More analysis will be necessary to determine why government does what it does and then to determine how its actions could be more effective in promoting development. Crucial for policy reform is an understanding of the reasons for the successes and failures of government policy. It is also necessary to understand what determines political entrepreneurship and what induces political innovations.

APPROPRIATE GOVERNANCE

Questions of political governance are also related to globalization and the international public sector. The future must supply answers to a number of questions about the impact of globalization. For macro policy, open economy models will have to be the rule. While trade policy will continue to merit attention, new attention will have to be given to determining the effects of international capital movements, South–North migration of labor, and technology transfer. All these effects will have to be related to the overriding question of whether globalization benefits the poor countries and whether it creates benefits for poor people within countries. Considering lessons of history, Williamson (2002) has asked:

> If gaps between rich and poor countries have widened, and if globalization is the cause, it is because poor countries have not gained from going global, or is it because they have actually lost? If the gaps between rich and poor within countries have widened, and if globalization is the cause, is it because poor citizens have not gained by their country going global, or is it because they have actually lost? To the extent that policy is driven by the *absolute* losses to vocal citizens and/or vocal nations, rather than relative losses, it is all the more amazing that so many contemporary economists insist on using relative inequality measures. Economic historians know better.

In future, development economists should also know better.

In sorting out the positive and negative impulses resulting from globalization, political economists in the future will have to answer more questions about "appropriate governance" (Bhagwati 2002). Recognizing the potential of a positive growth-poverty linkage, what policies of international governance can strengthen the linkage? What new programs can the World Bank, IMF, and the WTO devise to ensure that the benefits of global integration are equally shared, that competitive policy making among nations is avoided, and that problems of incomplete risk markets are mitigated as international integration becomes ever more complex? Not only will more attention have to be given to the powers of the international public sector, but the roles of the multinationals and NGOs will also have to be considered. Concern over new problems—such as managing the global commons—will also require new international institutions.

When development economists think about both national and international governance, they will have to adopt what might be termed a "constitutive type" of rationality. While the usual thinking about economic problems involves an instrumental type of rationality—that is, determining technical policy instruments that can be the means of achieving policy objectives—problems of governance require decisions about how decisions are to be made. A constitution is needed, and an institutional context for decision making has to be established. The resolution of many issues of governance will depend on the way decisions will be made and the boundary of the decisions.

We have considered only a few of the many questions for the future. According to one's interpretation of the past evolution of the subject, a number of other problems may call for future solutions. Clearly, there will continue to be a need for ideas to shape future policy and implementation.

The analytics of development economics have evolved with increasing rigor. And policy implications have become more definitive. The ultimate objective is to have appropriate ideas for development absorbed and implemented in the less developed countries—both ideas of development policy at the macro level and ideas that lead to a reduction of real costs at the micro or enterprise level. Beyond contributing to technical change and raising the growth rate, the absorption of ideas may also facilitate the structural transformation of the economy, allow better control of demographic changes, and improve the distribution of income. In an even deeper sense, scientific ideas and rationality can change a society's values and support modernization.

A deficiency of knowledge is a more pervasive handicap to development than is the scarcity of any other factor. Knowledge is, however, a global public good (Stiglitz 1998), and contact with more advanced economies provides an expeditious way to overcome this deficiency. The importation of technical knowhow and skills is an indispensable source of technical progress, and the importation of ideas in general is a potent stimulus to development. This is vital not only for economic change in itself but also for political and sociocultural advances that may be necessary preconditions of economic progress.

Although the creation of ideas is a necessary condition, their effectiveness depends on the absorptive capacity of the developing country. The local research capacity is significant for local knowledge and locally appropriate policies. If development economists and visiting missions are not listened to, their ideas will come to naught. Or if ideas of policy reform require political conditions for their implementation, and these conditions do not exist, then again the ideas come to naught. Or if the absorptive capacity depends on institutional change that is not forthcoming, the ideas will be without effect. In the organization of government and the design of information and an incentives system, the preconditions must be in place for the acceptance and implementation of ideas.

Moreover, the absorption of wrong ideas may require a reversibility or termination of policies—a difficult task. In general, ideas that become embedded as knowledge in human capital need to be "appropriate knowledge," just as appropriate technology is required. Indeed, inappropriate human capital may be more of a handicap than inappropriate physical capital because human capital cannot be scrapped. A bad practice is not conveniently ended, and a bad idea may drive out a good idea.

Whether ideas are used from abroad or produced within the developing countries, they should avoid the biases of ideology. Ideological beliefs have only too easily permeated development thought. The early references to "center" and "periphery" were emotive—not logical—categories. Being policy oriented and problem solving, the subject has also been colored by ideology from both the Left and Right. Disciplined thinking on the proper balance between state and market has all too often been neglected.

If ideas are to be more influential, they will have to evolve from rigorous analysis and empirical testing. To this end, multiple sources of analytic arguments and empirical evidence should be promoted in both the more and less developed countries. As in the past, so too in the future will ideas for development be improved by learning from experience and subjecting ideas to open debate. The emotive and ideological may then be reduced in favor of disciplined analysis that will strengthen the subject.

Much of the evolution of development economics has been based on the reductionist model of analysis—that is, analyzing a problem into smaller and smaller constituent elements, going down from the aggregate economy to particular sectors to firms and to households. The subject, however, also requires us to be synthetic and integrative so as to understand the relationships in the subject in a wider way.

As long as there is persisting poverty, the past is only prologue. The biography of the subject of development is not yet finished. A continuation of it remains to be written.

Appendix A: The Evolution of Development Thought

Lewis and Dualism

Fifty years ago, the subject matter of development was thrust upon economists. Ever since, the evolution of development thought has been wide and deep. It began in 1954 with W. Arthur Lewis's article "Development with Unlimited Supplies of Labor" and his book *The Theory of Economic Growth* (1955). Lewis wrote: "A book of this kind seemed to be necessary because the theory of economic growth once more engages world-wide interests and because no comprehensive treatise on the subject has been published for about a century. The last great book covering this wide range was John Stuart Mill's *Problems of Political Economy*, published in 1848" (5).

When he received his Nobel Prize in economic science in 1979, Lewis offered an autobiography in which he said that while half of his interest was in policy questions, the other half was in the fundamental forces determining the rate of economic growth. He recalled:

This was the subject of my so-called classic book of 1955, and also the origin of the model to which the Nobel citation refers.

From my undergraduate days, I had sought a solution to the question of what determines the relative prices of steel and coffee. The approach through marginal utility made no sense to me. And the Heckscher-Ohlin framework could not be used, since that assumes that trading partners have the same production functions, whereas coffee cannot be grown in most of the steel-producing countries.

Another problem that troubled me was historical. Apparently, during the first fifty years of the industrial revolution, real wages in Britain remained more or less constant while profits and savings soared. This could not be squared with the neoclassical framework, in which a rise in investment should raise wages and depress the rate of return on capital.

One day in August, 1952, walking down the road in Bangkok, it came to me suddenly that both problems have the same solution. Throw away the neoclassical assumption that the quantity of labour is fixed. An "unlimited supply of labour" will keep wages down, producing cheap coffee in the first case and high profits in the second case. The result is a dual (national or world) economy, where one part is a reservoir of cheap labour for the other. The unlimited supply of labour derives ultimately from population pressure, so it is a phase in the demographic cycle.

The publication of my article on this subject in 1954 was greeted equally with applause and with cries of outrage. In the succeeding 25 years, other scholars have written five books and numerous articles arguing the merits of the thesis, assessing contradictory data, or applying it to solving other problems. The debate continues.

Reviewing his extension of dualism, Lewis recalled:

So in three minutes I had solved two of my problems with one change of assumptions. Writing this up would take four articles from me, and further exploration by Fei and Ranis and others. The thing became for a time a growth industry, with a stream of articles expounding, attacking, testing, revising, denouncing, or approving. The upshot seems to be that the model is illuminating in some places at some times, but not in other places or other times. This was said when it was first presented. (1984a: 132)

In the 1950s, development economists formulated grand aggregate models—"magnificent dynamics"—and general strategies. Lewis's dual sector model was the richest and most instructive.

Many contributions extended or revised Lewis's work in the 1960s–1980s. Dale Jorgensen (1961) offered an alternative approach to the dual economy that was more neoclassical in spirit. By 1964, J. C. H. Fei and G. Ranis provided an elaborate discussion of dualism and transition in terms of various phases. Throughout the 1970s and 1980s, the subject matter of development quickly recognized that development involved growth plus change.

In 1991 Lewis died. His academic and professional honors, as listed in table A.1, had clearly been impressive in meeting demands by critics. A series of memorial lectures to celebrate the legacy of Lewis was later established by Eastern Caribbean Central Bank.

Table A.1 Arthur Lewis's Academic and Professional Honors

M.A.	Manchester	1951
L.H.D.	Columbia	1954
L.H.D.	Boston College	1972
L.H.D.	Wooster	1980
L.H.D.	De Paul	1981
L.H.D.	Brandeis	1982
L.H.D.	Princeton	1988
LL.D.	Toronto	1960
LL.D.	Williams	1960

LL.D.	Wales	1961
LL.D.	Bristol	1961
LL.D.	Dakar	1962
LL.D.	Leicester	1964
LL.D.	Rutgers	1965
LL.D.	Atlanta	1980
LL.D.	Hartford	1981
LL.D.	York	1981
LL.D.	Bard	1982
LL.D.	Tuskegee	1984
LL.D.	Harvard	1984
LL.D.	Howard	1984

Honorary Doctor	Brussels	1969
Honorary Doctor	Open University	1974

Litt.D.	West Indies	1966
Litt.D.	Lagos	1974
Litt.D.	Northwestern	1979
D.Sc.	Manchester	1973
D.Sc. (Econ.)	London	1982
	Syracuse	1983
D. Soc. Sc.	Yale	1983
D. Pub. Ser.	Maryland	1983

Hon. Fellow, London School of Economics, 1959
Hon. Fellow, Weizman Institute, 1961
Hon. Foreign Member, American Academy of Arts and
   Sciences, 1962
Knight Bachelor, 1963
Noble Prize in Economics (Jointly), 1979
Hon. Fellow, American Geographical Society, 1987

Sir Arthur Lewis and Development Economics—Fifty Years On

A series of Memorial Lectures were later held for Lewis. In November 2002, Gerald Meier presented in St. Vincent and the Grenadines the Seventh Sir Arthur Lewis Memorial Lecture, entitled "Sir Arthur Lewis and Development Economics—Fifty Years On." Excerpts follow.

Some fifty years ago Lewis became the leading pioneer in development economics. He was the first to establish the subject on a worldwide basis through his large ideas and policy insights. To Lewis, the study of why development occurs was not simply to satisfy intellectual curiosity but was to be useful in meeting "the practical needs of contemporary policy makers" (Lewis 1955: 5).

Lewis immediately recognized that "output may be growing, and yet the mass of the people may be becoming poorer." He also did not venture whether growth meant welfare, satisfaction, or happiness; the book concentrates only on the processes by which more goods and services become available. In an appendix, however, Lewis notes that "the advantage of economic growth is not that wealth increases happiness, but that it increases the range of human choice. . . . The case for economic growth is that it gives man greater control over his environment, and thereby increases his freedom" (1955: 420–421).

Most economists then concentrated for decades on growth in GNP, but in recent years the latest Nobel laureate in development—Amartya Sen— has returned to an emphasis on freedom. One of the worst "unfreedoms" is poverty. Sen's new book is *Rationality and Freedom* (2003).

Celebrated as the dual model is, and optimistic as it seemed, Lewis himself later in the 1980s listed "the principal errors of omission and commission that have prevented the developing countries from fully exploiting their economic potential. Here [he said] is what we have failed to do."

First, we have failed to get the balance of industry and agriculture right. "The agricultural deficit has meant that large sections of the population do not get enough food, or the importation of food puts a strain on the balance of payments. Moreover, food prices rise. And the farmer's marketable surplus provides too small a market for industrialization, so LDC industry is forced into dependence on exporting manufactures to the developed countries, where they are not welcome."

Second, "we failed to get on top of population growth early enough. . . . Population explosion reduces the growth rate of output per person; reduces the savings ratio; eats up capital for providing houses and equipment for extra hands instead of better equipment for fewer persons; and in these ways widens the gap of income per head between the industrial and the developing countries."

Moreover, "population pressure in the countryside forces young people to move off the family farms. . . . In overpopulated countries, the surplus spills over into the towns if the towns display an expanding demand for labor. The faster employment grows in the towns, the bigger the spillover. The movement of the last three decades is unprecedented. Most developing countries do not have the capital to absorb 5 to 6 percent per annum increase in the urban population, so the result is either an explosion of foreign debt, or a vast multiplication of urban slums."

Lewis then recognizes the duality of the modern sector—now the urban sector—into a formal well-organized subsector and the small-scale low-productivity informal subsector. The excessive migration results in earnings in the informal sector not substantially different from rural earnings, and in underemployment and open unemployment. But Lewis contends that "even with the population explosion, unemployment would be smaller if LDCs could attain two objectives—less capital-intensive technology and more rural development."

A third error in the 1950s, according to Lewis, was that "it took us quite some time to learn that foreign exchange can be a separate bottleneck in economic growth. . . . The principal danger is not to recognize the connection between the balance of payments and domestic expenditure; that the net balance is part of an overall equation, so that domestic imbalance turns up as foreign exchange imbalance; that inflation leads directly to loss of reserves; that in making a development plan the question 'which industries will produce the required foreign exchange' is at least as important as any other; and that in carrying out the plan a precondition of success is to have the right exchange rate, defined very roughly as the rate that makes it possible for exports to grow at 6 percent a year."

And fourth, Lewis concludes, "we failed to do enough to improve the condition of the poor." Lewis contends: "We know pretty well but not completely what needs doing to eliminate absolute poverty. The diet is a mixture of land, jobs, and social services. . . . What lacks is the will of governments to proceed, rather than a programme. . . . The trick here is to get more for the poor and also more for capital formation, both at the expense of consumption by the nonpoor. This is hard to do in practice, because of the political power of the nonpoor" (1955).

While Lewis in the 1950s had followed classical economists in emphasizing physical capital as the fundamental source of growth, some neoclassical economists later proceeded to generalize capital to include not only physical tangible capital but also now human capital, knowledge capital, and social capital. They have done so because econometric analysis of an economy's aggregate production function shows that output is not a function of only an increase in inputs. Output can increase in greater proportion than inputs. There is "something left over"—an unexplained residual. This is interpreted as total factor productivity— more simply, an increase in the efficiency with which inputs are used. What, however, causes this increase in output per unit of input? Initially, the explanation was merely "technological progress."

But the explanation of what determines technological progress was not to be found in the economist's model. The increase in total factor productivity was simply left as "manna from heaven." This was unsatisfying because total factor productivity is too influential to be left unexplained: it forestalls diminishing returns and provides continual growth. Improving the efficiency with which resources are used will often make a greater difference to growth than investing more heavily.

Economists then turned to human capital for more of an explanation. Improvements in education, training, and health would make managers and labor more productive. Moreover, attention to human capital means that the original trade-off between consumption and investment for the intertemporal balancing of welfare must be modified. Social consumption is emphasized in the form of education, health care, and nutrition to increase productivity and well-being.[1]

More recently, going beyond human capital, the new growth theory now emphasizes knowledge capital. Lewis's early chapter on "knowledge," in his *Theory of Economic Growth*, is related to this, but the new growth theory articulates the high importance of new ideas or knowledge capital in terms of formal models. Knowledge is a very special factor of production that is scarce but is the one factor that is not subject to diminishing returns. It is like a public good, can be used repeatedly with no additional cost, and has positive spillovers. These models demonstrate that investment in knowledge yields economies of scale and external economies, persists indefinitely, and sustains growth more than physical capital or human capital can.

Lewis also considered human behavior, and economists now accept that behavioral patterns do differ among countries and that they do matter for development. The link to development, however, should not be through a questionable appeal to "culture" but instead through the recognition of differences in the quantity and quality of "social capital."

Social capital can be divided into "civil social capital" and "government social capital." At the micro level, civil social capital relates to individual values, attitudes, and norms of behavior. These embody in civil society such attributes as trust, reciprocity, and social cooperation. At the macro level, government social capital relates to rules, procedures, and organization. These embody the rule of law, a strong judiciary, contract enforcement, the absence of corruption, transparency in decision making, an efficient administrative system—in short, the existence of state capability and credibility.

Attributes of social capital are absent or weak in many developing countries. As a result, high information costs, transaction costs, and risk affect managerial capability in both the public and private sectors.

The question now is how more productive social capital can be accumulated. And this comes down to the ultimate question of how high-quality institutions can be formed. Lewis initially recognized the importance of economic institutions in a chapter in his *Theory of Economic Growth* (1955). There he wanted to consider the scope that the community's institutions offer to encourage people to make the effort required for economic growth. This early emphasis on incentives has now become a central part of development economics.[2]

By "institution" we mean an established way of acting. Civil social capital embodies informal institutions, while government social capital relates to formal institutions. The institutions establish the rules of the game—the constraints on behavior and the incentives for patterns of behavior. The players in the game are organizations—firms, political bodies, unions, the central bank. They react to the opportunities and incentives offered by institutions.

Institutions, however, can be good or bad for a country's development. Good institutions shape the right incentives for development performance: they promote social capital and thereby facilitate information flows, reduce transaction costs, avoid or resolve conflict, and yield mutually beneficial collective action.

Development economists in the 1970s advised developing countries to "get prices right." Then in the 1980s and 1990s they said "get macro policies right." Now we say "get institutions right." But the appropriate policies to accomplish this are, sadly, not yet much better known than when Lewis recognized the historical importance of institutions.

The new development economics interprets a country's financial sector as different from other sectors in being characterized by a combination of information asymmetries—namely, providers of funds know less about their ultimate use than do the borrowers, and the giving of credit involves intertemporal exchange of future claims on resources for present ones. There is an inherent element of uncertainty. The fact that information in credit markets is imperfect and costly to obtain also gives rise to problems of adverse selection because of hidden information and to moral hazard because of hidden action. High transaction costs may limit trade or prevent the creation of a market. Moreover, efficient intermediation requires diversification, but many developing countries are too small to make this possible.

To minimize these problems—not to mention financial crises—there is a need for supervision and monitoring by both markets and nonmarket supervisory institutions. Given the unique character of finance and the range of market failures to which financial markets are subject, government actions are commonly needed to create new financial institutions and regulate financial market instruments. Government interventions may be especially needed to improve the efficiency of the banking system and secondary markets. Necessary research is now being done on prudential standards. In addition, based on the new development economics, more research is being devoted to the effects of various kinds of institutional arrangements for insuring individuals in developing countries against various types of risk and facilitating their access to credit and investment (e.g. land reform, rural credit markets, and microcredit).

In terms of social objectives, government actions may provide consumer protection, ensure bank solvency, improve macroeconomic stability, promote competition, stimulate growth, and improve the allocation of resources. Public actions themselves, however, are also subject to constraints and limitations, so that the essential problem of public regulatory policy is to determine when government action improves market performance and when, in contrast, private action can take better advantage of information and incentives within the marketplace (Stiglitz 1994: 36).

Through public and private action together, better and deeper financial systems support higher rates of growth. Recent studies by the World Bank show that countries with deeper financial systems have been more successful in taking credit away from loss-making firms and reallocating to profitable investments.

Moreover, if we are to follow Lewis's interest in the context of world economic history, we also now need more analysis of how financial liberalization, in the sense of expanding, diversifying, and modernizing financial services, connects greater participation in the global economy.[3]

Changes in Development Thinking

Fifty years on, the new development economies represents the major change in development thinking. Many of Lewis's insights have been refined and extended over the past half century. But the most significant addition is the microeconomics of development, based on the economics of information, and the emphasis on institutions and incentives.

With the emphasis on the microeconomics of development and the theory of organization, analysis has become partial and reductionist in the sense of going down to particular sectors and to firms and to households.

The subject, however, also requires us to be synthetic and integrative so as to understand the relationships of the parts in a wider way, as did Lewis. The large ideas, grand design, and vision of the 1950s are missing.

A second major change is the attention to empirical observations. Data sets and case studies have become much more abundant.

There have been more than 50 years of lessons from development experience and a vast accumulation of data unknown to Lewis. And statistical and econometric techniques of analysis have become ever more refined. The original challenge, however, remains: this generation of development economists still needs to formulate a relevant theoretical framework to bring some logical order to the data. Most important, a conjuncture with policy making has to be established.

This leads to the third major change—the interpretation of the respective roles of the state and the market. In the 1950s and 1960s, planning dominated, on the basis of the belief in extensive market failures. In the 1970s and 1980s, in turn, an orthodox reaction set in against government failures and advocated minimalist government. Since the 1990s, it is apparent that there has been a reaction too far, and that government has an important role—especially in a complementary fashion with the market.

In 1983, in his presidential address to the American Economic Association, Lewis said that the appeal to government should not imply that government action in the market always gives a better answer than the uncontrolled market, whether in allocation or in distribution. It is often the case that the imperfect solution of the market could be better than that of the government. The government needs to be modernized just as much as the market. And the assumption that the government "represents" the people may not hold.

This leads Lewis to conclude that we need "a theory of government." In this connection, we have now changed from viewing government as autonomous and an exogenous factor in any development analysis to making government endogenous. That is, we must now not take government action as simply "given" but must analyze why government does what it does and then determine how its actions could be more effective in promoting development. The "new political economy" attempts this. Crucial for policy reform are an understanding of the reasons for the successes and the failures of government policy. We must also understand what determines political entrepreneurship and what induces political innovations.

As Lewis threw away one neoclassical assumption to build his famous dual sector model, so too now—in applying the new development economics—we must throw away other neoclassical assumptions of a competitive equilibrium model. And as political economists, we must improve the complementary roles of the state and market.

Development economists have slipped since the time of Lewis and the 1950s in two respects: (1) the failure to extend the analysis of development in the context of world history, as Lewis did, and (2) the failure to focus on development as a dynamic process with attention to the interrelation of its parts, as did Lewis.

One notable effort is Kevin H. O'Rourke and Jeffrey G. Williamson's book *Globalization and History* (1999). For many now the central concern of development economics is how globalization affects inequality among nations and within a nation.

Lucas (2000) has also asked:

How did the world economy of today, with its vast differences in income levels and growth rates, emerge from the world of two centuries ago, in which the richest and the poorest societies had incomes differing by perhaps a factor of two, and in which no society had ever enjoyed sustained growth in living standards? I have sketched an answer to this question in this note, an answer that implies some very sharp predictions about the future. If you are reading this in the year 2100, in a retrospective issue of the *Journal of Economic Perspectives*, I ask you: Who else told you what the macroeconomics of your century would look like, in advance, with such accuracy and economy? (167)

Indeed, Jeffrey Williamson's past attention to globalization and his new Harvard course deserve much attention.

Jeffrey Williamson and His Response to Lewis

Professor Williamson is the Laird Bell Professor of Economics and Faculty Fellow at the Center for International Development at Harvard University. He has served as president of the Economic History Association (1994–95), from which he received the Hughes Prize for outstanding teaching in 2000; chairman of the Economics Department at Harvard (1997–2000); and master of Mather House at Harvard (1986–93). In addition, he has twice been recipient of the Galbraith Prize for the best teacher in Harvard's economics program.

Academic Background

B.A., Wesleyan University, June 1957 (Mathematics); M.A., Stanford University, Fall 1959 (Economics); M.A., Harvard University, February 1984 (Honorary); Ph.D., Stanford University, June 1961 (Economics).

Williamson is the author of more than 20 scholarly books and almost two hundred articles on economic history, international economics, and economic development. His most recent books include *The Age of Mass Migration* (1998, with T. Hatton), *Growth, Inequality, and Globalization* (1998, with P. Aghion), *Globalization and History* (1999, with K. O'Rourke), and *Globalization in Historical Perspective* (2002, with M. D. Bordo and A. M. Taylor). He is currently doing research on world migration issues and on the globalization agenda dealing with the less developed countries raised by Lewis.

A list of Lewis-related publications by Williamson is provided here.

Other publications by Williamson cover issues that have had an impact on global inequities. His lecture on September 5, 2002, at the University of Copenhagen is notable for discussing historical and contemporary topics relating to "winners and losers in two centuries of globalization." His Harvard course on world development (Economics 2325) has been important in analyzing globalization, inequality, and poverty.

Professor Williamson teaches and does research on economic history and the contemporary developing World. Some topics he has explored recently include: the growth and distributional implications of the demographic transition in Asia, 1950–2025, and the Atlantic economy, 1820–1940; the impact of international migration, capital flows, and trade on factor price convergence in the greater Atlantic economy since 1830; the sources of globalization backlash before World War I; the causes of the cessation of convergence during the deglobalization years between 1914 and 1950; a detailed analysis of both the sources and consequences of the mass migrations prior to the 1920s and after the 1950s; the economic implications of 1492.

Beyond his Lewis-related publications, Williamson has supported other measures to extend the subject of development. He concentrates on a wide range of historical and contemporary topics, including growth, trade migration, living standards, and inequality. These themes were prominent in Williamson's 2002 WIDER Annual Lecture, entitled "Winners and Losers in Two Centuries of Globalization." The period from 1950 until the present day constitutes the second globalization era. Williamson's teaching and research efforts illuminate the significance of globalization, especially in answer to the question "Did the Second Global Century Make the World More Unequal?"

Some recent articles by Williamson listed on the World Wide Web are as follows.

"Globalization in Latin America Before 1940." With Luis Bertola. Draft date: April 2003.
"Was It Stolper-Samuelson, Infant Industry or Something Else? World Tariffs 1879–1938." Draft date: April 2003.
"Explaining U.S. Immigration 1971–1998." With Ximena Clark and Timothy J. Hatton. Draft date: December 2002.

"What Fundamentals Drive World Migration?" With Timothy J. Hatton. Presented as the WIDER Conference on Migration, Helsinki, September 27–28, 2002. National Bureau of Economic Research paper no. 9159. Draft date: September 2002.

"The Roots of Latin American Protectionism: Looking Before the Great Depression." With John H. Coatsworth. National Bureau of Economic Research paper no. 8999. Draft date: June 2002.

"Where Do U.S. Immigrants Come From, and Why?" With Ximena Clark and Timothy J. Hatton. National Bureau of Economic Research Paper no. 8998. Draft date: June 2002.

"Does Globalization Make the World More Unequal?" With Peter H. Lindert. Revised version of National Bureau of Economic Research paper no. 8228. Draft date: October 2001.

"Is Protection Bad for Growth? Will Globalization Last? Looking for Answers in History." Presented at the thirteenth IEHA Congress, Buenos Aires, August 22–26, 2002.

"Out of Africa? Using the Past to Project Future African Demand for Emigration." With Timothy J. Hatton. Forthcoming in the *Review of International Economics*. Presented at the May 2000 Globalization Conference, Athens, Greece: Draft date: April 27, 2000.

Especially interesting for world development over the past two centuries are the following readings suggested for Williamson's course Economics 2325: World Development (spring 2003):

Kavin H. O'Rourke and Jeffrey G. Williamson. 1999. *Globalization and History: The Evolution of a Nineteenth-Century Atlantic Economy*. Cambridge, Mass.: MIT Press.

F. Bourguignon and C. Morrison. "Inequality Among World Citizens 1820–1992." *American Economic Review* 92 (September 2002): 727–744.

J. Williamson. 1991. *Inequality, Poverty and History: The Kuznets Memorial Lectures*. Oxford: Blackwell.

J. Williamson. "Globalization, Labor Markets and Policy Backlash in the Past." *Journal of Economic Perspectives* 12, no. 4 (fall 1998): 51–72.

J. Williamson. "Land, Labor and Globalization in the Third World 1870–1940." *Journal of Economic History* 62, no. 1 (March 2002): 55–85.

Appendix B: The Contours of World Development*

World economic performance was very much better in the second millennium of our era than in the first. Between 1000 and 1998 population rose 22-fold and per capita income 13-fold. In the previous millennium, population rose by a sixth and per capita GDP fell slightly.

The second millennium comprised two distinct epochs. From 1000 to 1820 the upward movement in per capita income was a slow crawl—for the world as a whole the rise was about 50 percent. Growth was largely "extensive" in character. Most of it went to accommodate a fourfold increase in population. Since 1820, world development has been much more dynamic, and more "intensive." Per capita income rose faster than population; by 1998 it was 8.5 times as high as in 1820; population rose 5.6-fold.

There was a wide disparity in the performance of different regions in both epochs. The most dynamic was Group A: Western Europe, Western Offshoots (the United States, Canada, Australia and New Zealand) and Japan. In 1000–1820, their average per capita income grew nearly four times as fast as the average for the rest of the world. The differential continued between 1820 and 1998, when per capita income of the first group rose 19-fold and 5.4-fold for the second.

There are much wider income gaps today than at any other time in the past. Two thousand years ago the average level for Groups A and B was similar. In the year 1000 the average for Group A was lower as a result of the economic collapse after the fall of the Roman Empire. By 1820, Group A had forged ahead to a level about twice that in the rest of the world. In 1998 the gap was almost 7:1. Between the Western Offshoots and Africa (the richest and poorest regions) it is 19 to one.

*Excerpts from *The World Economy: A Millennial Perspective* by Angus Maddison, pp. 27–28, 126. OECD Copyright, 2001.

Economic performance since 1820 within Group B has not been as closely clustered as in Group A. Per capita income has grown faster in Latin America than Eastern Europe and Asia, and nearly twice as fast as in Africa. Nevertheless, from a Western standpoint, performance in all these regions has been disappointing.

There have been big changes in the weight of different regions. In the year 1000, Asia (except Japan) produced more than two-thirds of world GDP, Western Europe less than 9 percent. In 1820 the proportions were 56 and 24 percent, respectively. In 1998, the Asian share was about 30 percent, compared with 46 percent for Western Europe and Western Offshoots combined.

Table B.1 Level and rate of growth of population: World and major regions, 0–1998 A.D.

	Population in millions				Annual average compound growth rate		
	0	1000	1820	1998	0–1000	1000–1820	1820–1998
Western Europe	24.7	25.4	132.9	388	0.00	0.20	0.60
Western Offshoots	1.2	2.0	11.2	323	0.05	0.21	1.91
Japan	3.0	7.5	31.0	126	0.09	0.17	0.79
Total Group A	28.9	34.9	175.1	838	0.02	0.20	0.88
Latin America	5.6	11.4	21.2	508	0.07	0.08	1.80
Eastern Europe & former USSR	8.7	13.6	91.2	412	0.05	0.23	0.85
Asia (excluding Japan)	171.2	175.4	679.4	3390	0.00	0.17	0.91
Africa	16.5	33.0	74.2	760	0.07	0.10	1.32
Total Group B	202.0	233.4	866.0	5069	0.01	0.16	1.00
World	230.8	268.3	1041.1	5908	0.02	0.17	0.98

Table B.2 Level and rate of growth of GDP per capita: World and major regions, 0–1998 A.D.

	1990 international dollars				Annual average compound growth rate		
	0	1000	1820	1998	0–1000	1000–1820	1820–1998
Western Europe	450	400	1232	17921	−0.01	0.14	1.51
Western Offshoots	400	400	1201	26146	0.00	0.13	1.75
Japan	400	425	669	20413	0.01	0.06	1.93
Average Group A	443	405	1130	21470	−0.01	0.13	1.67
Latin America	400	400	665	5795	0.00	0.06	1.22
Eastern Europe & former USSR	400	400	667	4354	0.00	0.06	1.06
Asia (excluding Japan)	450	450	575	2936	0.00	0.03	0.92
Africa	425	416	418	1368	−0.00	0.00	0.67
Average Group B	444	440	573	3102	−0.00	0.03	0.95
World	444	435	667	5709	−0.00	0.05	1.21

Table B.3 Level and rate of growth of GDP: World and major regions, 0–1998 A.D.

	Billion 1990 international dollars				Annual average compound growth rate		
	0	1000	1820	1998	0–1000	1000–1820	1820–1998
Western Europe	11.1	10.2	163.7	6961	−0.01	0.34	2.13
Western Offshoots	0.5	0.8	13.5	8456	0.05	0.35	3.68
Japan	1.2	3.2	20.7	2582	0.10	0.23	2.75
Total Group A	12.8	14.1	198.0	17998	0.01	0.32	2.57
Latin America	2.2	4.6	14.1	2942	0.07	0.14	3.05
Eastern Europe & former USSR	3.5	5.4	60.9	1793	0.05	0.29	1.92
Asia (excluding Japan)	77.0	78.9	390.5	9953	0.00	0.20	1.84
Africa	7.0	13.7	31.0	1939	0.07	0.10	1.99
Total Group B	89.7	102.7	496.5	15727	0.01	0.19	1.96
World	102.5	116.8	694.4	33726	0.01	0.22	2.21

Table B.4 Growth of per capita GDP, population, and GDP: World and major regions, 1000–1998 (annual average compound growth rates)

	1000–1500	1500–1820	1820–1870	1870–1913	1913–1950	1950–1973	1973–1998
Per capita GDP							
Western Europe	0.13	0.15	0.95	1.32	0.76	4.08	1.78
Western Offshoots	0.00	0.34	1.42	1.81	1.55	2.44	1.94
Japan	0.03	0.09	0.19	1.48	0.89	8.05	2.34
Asia (excluding Japan)	0.05	0.00	−0.11	0.38	−0.02	2.92	3.54
Latin America	0.01	0.15	0.10	1.81	1.42	2.52	0.99
Eastern Europe & former USSR	0.04	0.10	0.64	1.15	1.50	3.49	−1.10
Africa	−0.01	0.01	0.12	0.64	1.02	2.07	0.01
World	0.05	0.05	0.53	1.30	0.91	2.93	1.33
Population							
Western Europe	0.16	0.26	0.69	0.77	0.42	0.70	0.32
Western Offshoots	0.07	0.43	2.87	2.07	1.25	1.55	1.02
Japan	0.14	0.22	0.21	0.95	1.31	1.15	0.61
Asia (excluding Japan)	0.09	0.29	0.15	0.55	0.92	2.19	1.86
Latin America	0.09	0.06	1.27	1.64	1.97	2.73	2.01
Eastern Europe & former USSR	0.16	0.34	0.87	1.21	0.34	1.31	0.54
Africa	0.07	0.15	0.40	0.75	1.65	2.33	2.73
World	0.10	0.27	0.40	0.80	0.93	1.92	1.66
GDP							
Western Europe	0.30	0.41	1.65	2.10	1.19	4.81	2.11
Western Offshoots	0.07	0.78	4.33	3.92	2.81	4.03	2.98

(continued)

Table B.4 (continued)

	1000–1500	1500–1820	1820–1870	1870–1913	1913–1950	1950–1973	1973–1998
Japan	0.18	0.31	0.41	2.44	2.21	9.29	2.97
Asia (excluding Japan)	0.13	0.29	0.03	0.94	0.90	5.18	5.46
Latin America	0.09	0.21	1.37	3.48	3.43	5.33	3.02
Eastern Europe & former USSR	0.20	0.44	1.52	2.37	1.84	4.84	−0.56
Africa	0.06	0.16	0.52	1.40	2.69	4.45	2.74
World	0.15	0.32	0.93	2.11	1.85	4.91	3.01

Table B.5 Levels of per capital GDP and interregional spreads, 1000–1998 (1990 international dollars)

	1000	1500	1820	1870	1913	1950	1973	1998
Western Europe	400	774	1232	1974	3473	4594	11534	17921
Western Offshoots	400	400	1201	2431	5257	9288	16172	26146
Japan	425	500	669	737	1387	1926	11439	20413
Asia (excluding Japan)	450	572	575	543	640	635	1231	2936
Latin America	400	416	665	698	1511	2554	4531	5795
Eastern Europe & former USSR	400	483	667	917	1501	2601	5729	4354
Africa	416	400	418	444	585	852	1365	1368
World	435	565	667	867	1510	2114	4104	5709
Interregional Spreads	1.1:1	2:1	3:1	5:1	9:1	15:1	13:1	19:1

Notes

Chapter 1

1. These are the World Bank's frequently quoted summary estimates of income poverty based on 1993 purchasing power parity (PPP) or U.S. international dollars (as explained in the next section). Measurement is, however, inexact and complex, as is noted in several World Bank publications, such as *World Development Indicators* (annual) and *World Development Report* (annual beginning in 1990). For a critical discussion of the current methods used by the World Bank, see Deaton (2001).

2. In the 1970s the International Comparison Project, under the direction of Irving B. Kravis, Alan Heston, and Robert Summers (1982), collected price data for a number of countries and estimated per capita GDP for these countries measured in "international dollars." National price levels for the same commodity were made equal by converting to a common currency that reflects purchasing power parity. Summers and Heston subsequently extended their data sets, and the World Bank continues to measure per capita GNP in international dollars.

3. See also an extension of the capabilities approach by Nussbaum (2000).

4. For an extended rebuttal of the contrary view that political freedoms are irrelevant in face of the priority of urgent economic needs, see chapter 6. In particular, Sen emphasizes that political freedoms have intrinsic importance, an instrumental role, and a constructive role in the conceptualization of "needs."

5. At Oxford, Hla Myint introduced a seminar, "Economics of Underdeveloped Countries," in 1949–50, and other lectures in development were presented in the early 1950s at Oxford by Peter Ady and Ursula Hicks. W. Arthur Lewis was appointed reader in colonial economics in the University of London (London School of Economics) in 1947 and in 1948 went to Manchester where be began lecturing systematically on development economics from about 1950. At Yale, Henry Wallich introduced a development course in 1952–53, and the following year Henry Bruton also taught a graduate development course. In 1953–54, John Kenneth Galbraith began a seminar at Harvard on economic and political de-

velopment. Others who started teaching in the development field during the 1950s at Harvard were Alexander Eckstein, A. J. Meyer, R. E. Baldwin, David Bell, E. S. Mason, and Gustav Papanek. A seminar on theories of economic development, with a special effort to integrate economic and psychological theories, was offered by G. M. Meier and David McClelland at Wesleyan University in 1955. McClelland was to draw on this seminar for his book *The Achieving Society* (1961). Meier was at the same time writing, with R. E. Baldwin, *Economic Development: Theory, History, Policy* (1957).

Throughout the 1950s, there was also an expansion in the number of journals devoted to economic development. The *Ceylon Economist* began publication in 1950; *Economic Development and Cultural Change*, 1952; *Pakistan Economic and Social Review*, 1952; *Indian Economic Review*, 1952; *Indian Economic Journal*, 1953; *Social and Economic Studies* (University of West Indies), 1953; *East African Economic Review*, 1954; *Middle East Economic Papers*, 1954; *Malayan Economic Review*, 1956; *Nigerian Journal of Economic and Social Studies*, 1959. The number of articles in development theory and development policy as reported in the *Index of Economic Articles* tripled in the decade between 1950–54 and 1960–64.

Chapter 2

1. For the prehistory (to 1945), see Arndt (1981, 1987: ch. 2). Illuminating analyses of the growth aspects of classical economics are presented by Robbins (1968), Hollander (1973), Samuelson (1978), Eltis (2000), Rostow (1990). Hicks (1985: ch 4) presents a modern analysis of the "primitive growth models" of Smith and Ricardo.

2. Adam Smith (1723–1790) was born in Scotland, entered the University of Glasgow at the age of 14, and then spent six years at Oxford. Twenty-five years before he published the *Wealth of Nations*, he was elected professor of logic at Glasgow in 1751 and then professor of moral philosophy. Smith's earlier work, *Theory of Moral Sentiments*, was never intended as a preamble to the *Wealth of Nations*. But it did give rise to "Das Adam Smith Problem," in which sympathy as the motor of social order in the *Theory of Moral Sentiments* conflicts with human self-interest in the *Wealth of Nations* and its relation to the progress of commercial society in originating and creating wealth. See Ross (1995).

3. As discussed by O'Brien (1975: 208–209).

4. For an expanded discussion of the place of knowledge, invention, and innovation in the classical theory, see Robbins (1968: 70–94).

5. Thomas Robert Malthus (1766–1834) was arguably the most famous social scientist of the nineteenth century, on the basis of his *Essay on the Principle of Population, As It Affects the Future Improvement of Society* (1798). The Reverend Malthus was variously described as cheerful, with a mild and easy temper. The literary editor Sydney Smith wrote this description to a friend:

> Philosopher Malthus came here last week. I got an agreeable party for him of unmarried people. There was only one lady who had had a child; but he is a good-natured man, and, if there are no appearances of approaching fertility, is civil to every lady. . . . Malthus is a real moral philosopher, and I would almost consent to speak as inarticulately, if I could think and act as wisely.

And the author Harriet Martineau wrote of him:

> A more simple-minded, virtuous man, full of domestic affections, than Mr. Malthus could not be found in all England. . . . Of all people in the world, Malthus was the one whom I heard quite easily without my trumpet;—Malthus, whose speech was hopelessly imperfect, from defect in the palate. I dreaded meeting him. I was delightfully wrong. His first sentence—slow and gentle with the vowels sonorous, whatever might become of the consonants—set me at ease completely. I soon found that the vowels are in fact all that I ever hear. His worst letter was *L*, and when I had no difficulty with his question—"Would not you like to have a look at the lakes of Killarney?" I had nothing more to fear.

In 1804, Malthus became the recipient of the earliest chair in political economy to be established in England, with no less a prodigious title than "Professor of General History, Politics, Commerce, and Finance." Interestingly enough, the position was at the newly established East India College at Haileybury—an institution for the training of administrators in the East Indian Company. He was, however, no longer the center of controversial pamphleteering. His students called him "Pop," and he had three children while writing his second book on *The Principles of Political Economy, Considered with a View to Their Practical Application.*

6. For an excellent analysis of Malthus and the classical theory of growth, see Eltis (2000: chs. 4, 5, 9).

7. David Ricardo (1772–1823) was a one-time stockbroker from the early age of 14, gentleman farmer, member of Parliament, and the avid author of *The Principles of Political Economy and Taxation* (1817). He left an estate valued at £750,000 (the equivalent of nearly £100 million today). Ricardo may or may not be the greatest economist who ever lived, but he was certainly the richest (Blaugh 1986: 201).

8. Mill (1806–1873) learned about these classical forces at an early age. When only 13 years old, he received lectures on political economy from his father, James Mill. From the lectures during their daily walks, the son prepared abstracts of the lessons that served as notes for the father as he wrote his *Elements of Political Economy.* About the same time, the young Mill wrote that "Mr. Ricardo invited me to his house and to walk with him in order to converse upon the subject." At age 16, he was publishing articles in defense of the Ricardian analysis. And the last thing Ricardo wrote on the day he was stricken with his fatal illness was a letter in which he corrected an essay written by the 17-year-old Mill.

9. Karl Marx (1818–1883) was born in Prussia, studied at the Universities of Bonn and Berlin, and finally settled in London in 1848. Friedrich Engels introduced him to the writings of Smith and Ricardo. Marx and Engels published *The Communist Manifesto* in 1848, and Marx published volume 1 of his *Capital* in 1867. See Mandel (1987).

10. Karl Marx, "The Future Results of British Rule in India," *New York Daily Tribune*, August 8, 1953, reprinted in Avineri (1968: 125–131).

Chapter 3

1. See ECLA, *An Introduction to the Technique of Programming*, first presented at an ECLA session in 1953 and printed in 1955. See also Cardoso (1979).

2. The first group of experts was composed of John Maurice Clark, Nicholas Kaldor, Arthur Smithies, Pierre Uri, and E. Ronald Walker. The group who wrote the second report included Alberto Baltra Cortez (Chile), D. R. Gadgil (India), George Hakim (Lebanon), W. Arthur Lewis (England), and T. W. Schultz (United States).

3. Criticisms of this report were expressed by Frankel (1952) and Bauer (1953).

4. This third group of experts was composed of James W. Angell, G.D.A. McDougall, Hla Myint, Trevor W. Swan, and Javier Marquez.

5. For a comprehensive history, Kapur, Lewis, and Loebb (1997).

6. For an exposition and assessment of project lending, see Kapur et al. (1997: 35–46).

7. See Kapur et al. (1997: ch. 5).

8. In 1946, the Professorship of Colonial Economic Affairs was created at Oxford. In 1956, the chair was renamed the Professorship of Commonwealth Economic Affairs, and it was eventually changed in 1963 to the Professorship of the Economics of Underdeveloped Countries.

Chapter 4

1. These were a sentence comparing the steady improvement in Western living standards with "more backward nations, two-thirds of whose inhabitants were badly undernourished"; a descriptive paragraph on the International Bank for Reconstruction and Development; and the statement that the infant industry or "young economy" argument "has more validity for present-day backward nations than for those who have already experienced the transition from an agricultural to an industrial way of life. In a sense such nations are still asleep; they cannot be said to be truly in equilibrium."

2. Lewis was born in 1915 in St. Lucia (British West Indies), and his state funeral took place there in 1991. After finishing secondary school at the age of 14, Lewis became a St. Lucia Island scholar at age seventeen. By the age of 33 he was a full professor of economics at the University of Manchester. In 1979 he was awarded the Nobel Prize in economic science. Ironically, Lewis's choice of economics as a career was accidental. He recalls: "I had never meant to be an economist. . . . I had no idea of what economics was, but I did well in the subject from the start, and when I graduated in 1937 with first class honours, ISE gave me a scholarship to do a PhD in industrial economics" (Lewis 1989:).

3. H. W. Arndt was Rosenstein-Rodan's research assistant and in 1942 wrote a study that contributed to Rodan's *Economic Journal* article. The study—"Agricultural Surplus Population in Eastern and Southeastern Europe"—is reprinted in Arndt (1993: 3–13).

4. See also Rosenstein-Rodan's (1984) later review of his analysis.

5. For various formulations of dependency theory, see Furtado (1963), Sunkel (1969), Frank (1967), and Baran (1957).

Chapter 5

1. An informative recollection is made by Clark (1984).

2. Rostow (1960).

3. See "The Stages of Economic Growth: A Non-Communist Manifesto" in Spengler (1949).

4. Rostow (1961) responded to his critics with some clarifications, refinements, and amendments.

5. For just one illustrative manual of techniques for programming, see U.N. (1960).

6. The balanced growth approach was recognized early in Indian planning. See Mahalanobis (1955). The four-sector model of Mahalanobis was used in drawing up the draft second five-year plan of India.

7. For the pioneers' retrospective interpretations of why they said what they did in the late 1940s and 1950s, see Meier and Seers (1984). Rostow (1990: ch. 17) also considers the views of the pioneers.

8. See, however, a discussion of the difference between Western and non-Western political systems in Almond and Colemon (1960).

Chapter 6

1. The "resurgence of neoclassical economics" is emphasized by Little (1982: p. 3).

2. Remark attributed to Harberger in *New York Times*, February 7, 1993.

Chapter 7

1. In articulating his macrodynamic theory of growth and fluctuations, J. R. Hicks (1950–59) introduced the concept of "autonomous investment" that occurs in direct response to inventions. Although exogenous, this provided a basis for a rising trend in his "regularly progressive economy."

2. For a comprehensive survey of endogenous growth theory and knowledge-based growth, see Aghion and Howitt (1998).

3. For an instructive empirical study, see Barro (1991).

4. As Arrow observes,

> Trust has a very important pragmatic value. . . . Trust is an important lubricant of a social system. It is extremely efficient. . . . Unfortunately this is not a commodity which can be bought very easily. . . . Trust and similar values, loyalty or truth-telling, are examples of what the economist would call 'externalities.' They are goods, they are commodities; they have real, practical, economic value; they increase the efficiency of the system, enable you to produce more goods or more of whatever values you hold in high esteem. But they are not commodities for which trade on the open market is technically possible or even meaningful.
>
> It follows from these remarks that, from the point of view of efficiency as well as from the point of view of distributive justice, something more than the market is called for. Other modes of governing the allocation of resources occur. . . .
>
> Societies in their evolution have developed implicit agreements to certain kinds of regard for others, agreements which are essential to the survival of the society or at least contribute greatly to the efficiency of its working. It has been observed, for example, that among the properties of many societies whose economic development is backward is a lack of mutual trust. Collective undertakings of any kind, not merely governmental, become difficult or impossible not only because A may

betray B, but because even if A wants to trust B, he knows that B is unlikely to trust him. And it is clear that this lack of social consciousness is in fact a distinct economic loss in a very concrete sense as well, of course, as a loss in the possible well-running of a political system. (1974: 23, 26)

5. An illuminating initial attempt to measure various components of social capital is made by Collier at www.worldbank.org/poverty/scapital. See also Woolcock and Narayan (2000: 239–241); Temple and Johnson (1998).

6. For some initial suggestions, see Woolcock (1998).

7. From a review of growth accounting results for individual countries, Easterly and Levine (2001) demonstrate that the TFP residual accounts for most of the crosscountry and crosstime variation in growth.

8. For a textbook exposition of trade theory, see Krugman and Obstfeld (2003). For a fuller explanation of Porter- and Krugman-type goods, see Porter (1990: 77).

9. See Sala-I-Martin (1997).

10. After critiquing formal models of growth of the assembly of statistics of average behavior, Rostow (1990: 372) concludes that "it is only by getting to know these stories [in analytical histories of national growth] in their uniqueness and complexity, including the critical role of noneconomic variables, and the sequences of increasingly sophisticated leading sectors through which the major specific technologies were absorbed, and their changing relationship to the world economy, that we will be able to round out our knowledge of the growth process and its dynamics."

11. For a fuller discussion, see Greif (1997).

Chapter 8

1. Other prominent expositors are Hoff (2000, 2001) and Ray (2000).

2. Besides the several articles by Stiglitz listed in the references, see Mookherjee and Ray (2001), a textbook containing other articles on the new development economics, and Bardhan and Udry (2000).

3. For a more detailed discussion, see Hoff, Braverman, and Stiglitz (1993).

4. Easterley (2001) attributes many wrong governmental policies to incentives that divert and distort proper actions.

5. Stiglitz (2002) provides an excellent description of the change in thinking.

6. A fuller discussion of this connection is provided in Stiglitz (1995).

Chapter 9

1. For a review of the use of culture to explain economics, see Dasgupta (2000: 373–380) and Harrison and Huntington (2000).

2. Recall Abramovitz's earlier emphasis on the growth role of "social capability" (chapter 6) and see Adelman and Morris (1968).

3. Coleman (1990) and Putnam (1993) have been most influential in introducing the concept of "social capital" into social theory.

4. For a database of articles, see the World Bank's social capital website: www.worldbank.org/poverty/scapital/library.

5. Social capital does not conform, however, to some other attributes of physical capital: it is not tangible; some associational relationships may entail no cost; measurement is ambiguous. See Arrow (1999) and Solow (1999). For critical commentaries on the concept of social capital from the political economy perspectives of class, power, and conflict, see Harriss (2002) and Fine (2001).

6. For an economic sociology discussion of the extent to which economic action is embedded in structures of social relations, see Granovetter (1985).

7. See also Easterly (2001: ch.13). Good institutions mitigate polarization between factions in ethnically diverse countries. Progrowth policies are more likely when class conflict and ethnic tensions are absent—when there is a middle-class consensus.

Chapter 10

1. Globalization also raises other issues associated with the migration of labor, technology transfer, and global rules of competition. These deserve treatment in their own right, but this chapter is selective in focusing on international trade and finance.

2. See, among others, Dollar (1992), Sachs and Warner (1995), Edwards (1998), Ben-David and Nordstrom (2000), and Frankel and Romer (1999).

3. Similar evidence is provided in Dollar (1992). Edwards (1998) also provides econometric results that establish the robustness of the relationship between openness and total factor productivity growth.

4. For a penetrating critique of Rodrik's positions, see Srinivasan and Bhagwati (1999).

5. Much of this section has been based on Cooper (2001), which offers a more detailed assessment of the debate.

6. The data are available at www.worldbank.org/research/growth.

7. Ravallion (2001: 23) says that "while growth-promoting policies may well have close to zero average impact on inequality, this is perfectly consistent with sizable distributional impacts in specific countries, albeit in different directions." Explanation of the variance calls for more micro, country-specific research on the factors determining why some poor people are able to take up the opportunities afforded by growth while others are not.

8. See Krueger and Berg (2002) for a larger survey of the theory and empirics of foreign trade leading to growth and reducing absolute poverty. Their survey extracts three main propositions: (1) poverty reduction is mainly about growth in average per capita income, (2) trade openness is an important determinant of growth, and (3) the growth that is associated with trade liberalization is as propoor as growth in general.

9. Foreign investment as well as trade is a dimension of "openness" and globalization. But it is difficult to generalize about the direct distributional impact of foreign investment. The effects on commodity prices and factor prices are project specific and country specific. To the extent, however, that foreign investment stimulates growth, it is likely to reduce poverty.

For theoretical analyses of the possible influence of foreign investment on distribution, see Cooper (2001: 13–17), and Meier (1968: 137–143). In an empirical way, Moran (2002) focuses on the impact of foreign companies and their contribution to the development of host countries.

10. Floating is unlikely to be effective if the country's financial markets are incomplete and domestic investments have either a currency mismatch or a maturity mismatch (Eichengreen and Hausmann 1999; Cooper 1999).

11. For excellent discussions of reform of the international financial system, see Fischer (2002) and Cooper (2002).

12. This is advocated by De Gregorio, Eichengreen, Ito, and Wyplosz (2000), Williamson (2000), and Gilbert, Irwin, and Vines (2001).

13. For an evaluation of this Report, see Collier and Mayer (1989).

14. Sachs (1995) and Raffer (1990) have also proposed establishment of an international bankruptcy court. For criticisms, see Rogoff (1999: 30) and the discussion by Kenen (2002: 144–150) on the problems posed by standstills.

15. For a summary and evaluation of various proposals, see Eichengreen (1999: 123–132) and Kenen (2002).

Chapter 11

1. The emphasis here is on development through trade—not on trade as an end in itself. Rodrik (2000), however, cautions that the emphasis on trade liberalization is "at the cost of neglecting other goals of development policy that may potentially clash with it," and "the benefits of trade openness should not be oversold." Rodrik (2001) also maintains that "policymakers need to forge a domestic growth strategy by relying on domestic investors and domestic institutions. The costliest downside of the [global economic] integrationist faith is that it crowds out serious thinking and efforts along such lines" (55). Moreover, Rodrik contends, "the rules of admission into the world economy not only reflect little awareness of development priorities, they are often completely unrelated to sensible economic principles. For instance, WTO agreements on anti-dumping, subsidies and countervailing measures, agriculture, textiles, and trade-related intellectual property rights lack any economic rationale beyond the mercantilist interests of a narrow set of powerful groups in advanced industrial countries."

2. For a detailed account of these limitations on exports from developing countries, see World Bank, (2001).

3. *Financial Times*, February 18, 2002, p. 15.

4. For an elaboration of "the idea of need as a basis for entitlement" in the evolving international law of development, see Meier (1977: 517–523).

5. For an emphasis on how, in contrast to special treatment, the WTO should support reform of developing countries' own policies, see Finger and Winters (1998).

6. The focus here is on issues of trade and finance, but what Bhagwati (1999) calls "appropriate governance" at the international level is also required for other issues of labor standards, international migration, and the environment. Such governance would involve the ILO, UNICEF, NGOs, and creation of new organizations rather than the WTO.

On the problems of labor standards and environmental rules, see also Lawrence, Rodrik, and Whalley (1996).

7. For an emphasis on behind-the-borders actions to help countries to benefit from deeper integration, see Hoekman (2002).

8. Meier (1995: 466–469) offers a more detailed analysis of the need to remove

the domestic impediments that may cut short the stimulus from exports. See also Hoekman (2002: 5–9, 27–28).

9. Although most international rules of governance are based on a uniformity principle of equal treatment for all countries, Rodrik argues for more extensive exceptions for developing countries that would allow them to opt out and exercise more domestic autonomy in their policies, including a diverse range of institutional arrangements (Rodrik 2000: 28–31, 2001a). In Rodrik's criticism of the "foundation of an augmented Washington Consensus," however, it is not clear which of the various interpretations of the Washington Consensus is being made. See Williamson (2000).

10. For details of the IEO, see *IMF Survey* 31, 1 (January 14, 2002): 1–5.

Chapter 12

1. Measurements of inequality between rich and poor countries differ according to the methodology and data used. See Sala-I-Martin (2002) and the many different articles cited there.

2. The market-enhancing view and comparative institutional analysis have been introduced by Aoki, Kim, and Okuno-Fujiwara (1997).

Appendix A.

1. See Sen (1997: 10) and citations there.

2. This is the main theme of the recent bestselling book by William Easterley (2001).

3. In this connection, attention may be directed to a new database of financial sector indicators that measure the size, activity, and efficiency of financial intermediaries and markets across countries and over time: see Beck, Demirguc-Kunt, and Levine (2000).

References

Chapter 1

Arndt, H. W. 1981. "Economic Development: A Semantic History." *Economic Development and Cultural Change* (April): 457–466.

———. 1987. *Economic Development: The History of an Idea.* Chicago: University of Chicago Press.

Arrow, Kenneth. 1974. *The Limits of Organization.* New York: Norton.

Bauer, Peter, and Basil Yamey. 1957. *The Economics of Under-Developed Countries.* Chicago: University of Chicago Press.

Bliss, Christopher. 1989. "Trade and Development." In Hollis Chenery and T. N. Srinivasan (eds.), *Handbook of Development Economics,* vol. 2. Amsterdam: North Holland, 1187–1240.

Chenery, Hollis, et al. 1974. *Redistribution with Growth,* London: Oxford University Press.

Currie, Lauchlin. 1967. *Obstacles to Development.* East Lansing: Michigan State University Press.

Deaton, Angus. 2001. "Counting the World's Poor: Problems and Possible Solutions." *World Bank Research Observer* 16, no. 2 (fall): 125–47.

Heilbroner, Robert. 1953. *The Worldly Philosophers.* New York: Simon & Schuster.

Hicks, John. 1981. *Wealth and Welfare.* Cambridge, Mass.: Harvard University Press.

Kravis, Irving B., Alan Heston, and Robert Summers. 1982. *World Product and Income: International Comparisons of Real Gross Product.* Baltimore, Md.: Johns Hopkins University Press.

Lewis, Arthur W. 1955. *The Theory of Economic Growth.* Homewood, Ill.: R. D. Irwing.

McNamara, R. S. 1972. *Address to the Board of Governors.* Washington, D.C.: World Bank.

———. 1973. *One Hundred Countries, Two Billion People: The Dimensions of Development.* New York: Praeger.

Nussbaum, Martha C. 2000. *Women and Development: The Capabilities Approach.* New York: Cambridge University Press.

Romer, Paul M. 1992. "Two Strategies for Economic Development: Using Ideas and Producing Ideas." *Proceedings of the World Bank Annual Conference on Development Economics*, 63–91. Washington, D.C.: World Bank.

Schultz, Theodore. 1980. "Nobel Lecture: The Economics of Being Poor," *Journal of Political Economy* (August).

Sen, Amartya. 1999a. *Development as Freedom*. New York: Knopf.

———. 1999b. "The Possibility of Social Choice." *American Economic Review*, (June): 349–78.

Stiglitz, Joseph E. 1998b. "Knowledge as a Global Public Good." In Inge Kaul, (eds.), *Global Public Goods*. New York: Oxford University Press, 308–25.

———. 1998b. "Knowledge for Development." *Annual World Bank Conference on Development Economies*.

Summers, Lawrence. 1991. "Research Challenges for Development Economists." *Finance and Development* (September).

Trager, Frank N., 1958. "A Selected and Annotated Bibliography of Economic Development, 1953–57." *Economic Development and Cultural Change* (July).

Viner, Jacob. 1953. *International Trade and Economic Development*. New York: Oxford University Press.

Chapter 2

Avineri, Shlomo, ed. *Karl Marx on Colonialism and Modernization*. New York: Doubleday Anchor.

Eltis, Walter. 2000. *The Classical Theory of Economic Growth*. 2nd ed. New York: Palgrave.

Hicks, John. 1966. "Growth and Anti-Growth." *Oxford Economic Papers* 288.

———. 1979. *Causality in Economics*. New York: Basic Books.

———. 1985. *Methods of Dynamic Economics*. Oxford: Clarendon Press.

Hollander, Samuel. 1973. *The Economics of Adam Smith*. Toronto: University of Toronto Press.

Jevons, W. S. 1879 *Theory of Political Economy*. 2nd ed. London: Macmillan.

Lenin, Vladimir I. 1916. *Imperialism, The Highest Stage of Capitalism*. New York: International Publishers.

Lewis, W. K. 1988. "The Roots of Development Theory." In Hollis Chenery and T. N. Srinivasan (eds.), *Handbook of Development Economics*, vol. 1. Amsterdam: North Holland, ch. 2.

Malthus, Thomas Robert. 1798/2004. *An Essay on the Principle of Population*. Ed. Philip Appleman. New York: Norton.

Mandel, Ernest. 1987 "Karl Marx." In *The New Palgrave Dictionary of Economics*. London: Macmillan Press.

Marx, Karl. 1848. *Manifesto of the Communist Party*. Translated by Friedrich Engels. Chicago: C. H. Kerr.

———. 1853. "The British Rule in India" and "The Future Results of British Rule in India." Reprinted in Shlomo Avineri, *Karl Marx on Colonization and Modernization*. New York: Doubleday, 1968, 125–131.

Mill, John Stuart. 1848. *Principles of Political Economy* (Boston: Little, Brown).

Myint, Hla. 1948. *Theories of Welfare Economics*. Cambridge, Mass.: Harvard University Press.

O'Brien, D. P. 1975. *The Classical Economists*. Oxford: Oxford University Press.

Place, Francis. 1822/1930. *Illustrations and Proofs of the Principle of Population*. London: Allen & Unwin.

Rae, John. 1834. *Statement of Some New Principles on the Subject of Political Economy* Boston: Hillard, Gray.

Robbins, Lionel. 1968. *The Theory of Economic Development in the History of Economic Thought*. London: Macmillan.

Rosenberg, Nathan. 1994. *The Emergence of Economic Ideas*. Aldershot, England: Elgar.

Ross, Ian Simpson. 1995. *The Life of Adam Smith*. Oxford: Clarendon Press.

Rostow, W. W. 1990. *Theories of Economic Growth from David Hume to the Present*. New York: Oxford University Press.

Samuelson, Paul A. 1978. "The Canonical Classical Model of Political Economy." *Journal of Economic Literature* 16, no. 4 (December): 1415–1434.

Chapter 3

Bauer, P. J. 1953. "The United Nations Report on the Economic Development of Under-Developed Countries." *Economic Journal* 63, no. 249 (March): 210–222.

Cardoso, Fernando Henrique. 1979. "The Originality of the Copy: The Economic Commission for Latin America and the Idea of Development." In *Toward a New Strategy for Development*, Rothko Chapel Colloquium, New York: Pergamon.

Frankel, S. Herbert. 1952. "United Nations Primer for Development." *Quarterly Journal of Economics* 66, no. 3 (August): 301–326.

Gavin, M., and D. Rodrik. 1955. "The World Bank in Historical Perspective." *American Economic Review*, Papers and Proceedings, 85: 329–334.

Gilbert, Christopher L., and David Vines, eds. 2000. *The World Bank: Structure and Policies*. New York: Cambridge University Press.

Kapur, Devesh, John Lewis, and Richard Loebb. 1997. *The World Bank: Its First Half Century*. Vol. 1. *History*. Washington, D.C.: Brookings Institution Press.

Keynes, John Maynard. 1980. *The Collected Writings of John Maynard Keynes*, edited by Donald Moggridge. London: Macmillan.

Martin, K., and J. Knapp, Eds. 1967. *The Teaching of Development Economics: Its Position in the Present State of Knowledge*. London: Frank Cass.

Stern, Nicholas, and Francisco Ferreira. 1997. In D. Kapur, J. P. Lewis, and R. Webb (eds.), *The World Bank: Its First Half Century*. Vol. 2, *Perspectives*. Washington D.C.: Brookings Institution, 523–609.

United Nations Department of Economic Affairs. 1951. *Measures for the Economic Development of Under-Developed Countries* New York: United Nations.

Chapter 4

Arndt, H. W. 1993. *Fifty Years of Development Studies*. Canberra, ACT: National Centre for Development Studies. Australian National University.

Baran, Paul. 1957. *The Political Economy of Growth*. New York: Monthly Review Press.

Bruno, Michael, and Hollis B. Chenery. 1962. "Development Alternatives in an Open Economy." *Economic Journal* 72, no. 285: 79–103.

Fei, J.C.H., and G. Ranis. 1961. *Development of the Labor Surplus Economy: Theory and Policy*. Homewood, Ill.: Richard D. Irwin.

Frank, Andre Gunder. 1967. *Capitalism and Underdevelopment in Latin America*. New York: Monthly Review Press.

Furtado, Celso. 1963. *The Economic Growth of Brazil*. Berkeley: University of California Press.

———. 1987. "Underdevelopment: To Conform or Reform?" In Gerald M. Meier (ed.), *Pioneers in Development*. 2nd series. New York, Oxford University Press, 205–227.

Hirschman, Albert O. 1958. *The Strategy of Economic Development*. New Haven: Yale University Press.

Jorgensen, D. W. 1996. "The Development of a Dual Economy." *Economic Journal* 71, no. 282: 309–334.

Lewis, W. Arthur. 1954. "Economic Development with Unlimited Supplies of Labor." *Manchester School*, May 1954.

———. 1966. *Development Planning*. London: Allen and Uniwn.

Myrdal, Gunnar. 1956. *Development and Underdevelopment*. Cairo: National Bank of Egypt.

———. 1957. *Rich Lands and Poor: The Road to World Prosperity*. New York: Harper & Row.

Nurkse, Ragnar. 1953. *Problems of Capital Formation in Underdeveloped Countries*. Oxford: Blackwell.

Prebisch, Raul. 1950a. *The Economic Development of Latin America and Its Principal Problems*. New York: United Nations Economic Commission for Latin America.

———. 1950b. *Theoretical and Practical Problems of Economic Growth*. Mexico City: United Nations.

———. 1984. "Five Stages in My Thinking on Development." In Gerald M. Meier and Dudley Seers (eds.), *Pioneers in Development*. New York: Oxford University Press.

Ranis, Gustav. 1988. "Analytics of Development: Dualism." In Hollis Chenery and T. N. Srinivasan (eds.), *Handbook of Development Economics*, vol. 1. New York: Elsevier Science.

Rosenstein-Rodan, Paul. 1984. "Natura Facit Saltum: Analysis of the Disequilibrium Growth Process." In Gerald M. Meier and Dudley Seers (eds.) *Pioneers in Development*. New York: Oxford University Press, pp. 205–221.

Schultz, T. W. 1956. "The Role of Government in Promoting Economic Growth." In L. D. White (ed.), *The State of the Social Sciences*. Chicago: University of Chicago Press.

Singer, Hans. 1950. "The Distribution of Gains Between Investing and Borrowing Countries." *American Economic Review* 40 (May): 473–485.

Spengler, J. J. 1949. "Theories of Socio-Economic Growth." In *Problems in the Study of Economic Growth*. New York: National Bureau of Economic Research, pp. 47–114.

Stern, Nicholas. 1989. "The Economics of Development: A Survey." *Economic Journal* 99, no. 397 (September): 597–685.

Sunkel, O. 1969. "National Development and External Dependence in Latin America." *Journal of Development Studies* 6, no. 1 (October): 23–48.

Young, Allyn. 1928. "Increasing Returns and Economic Progress," *Economic Journal* 38, no. 152: 527–542.

Chapter 5

Adelman, Irma, and Cynthia Taft Morris. 1967. *Society Politics and Economic Development: A Quantitative Approach.* Baltimore: Johns Hopkins University Press.

Almond, G. A., and J. S. Coleman, eds. 1960. *The Politics of the Developing Areas.* Princeton: Princeton University Press.

Bauer, P. T., and Basil Yamey. 1957. *The Economics of Under-Developed Countries.* Chicago: University of Chicago Press.

Bourguignon, Francois, and Christian Morrison. 2002. "Inequality Among World Citizens, 1820–1992." *American Economic Review* 92, no. 4 (September): 727–745.

Chenery, Hollis B., and Michael Bruno. 1962. "Development Alternatives in an Open Economy: The Case of Israel." *Economic Journal* 72 (March): 79–103.

Chenery, Hollis B., and Alan M. Strout. 1966. "Foreign Assistance and Economic Development." *American Economic Review* 56 (September): 679–733.

Clark, Colin. 1940. *Conditions of Economic Progress.* London: Macmillan.

———. 1951. *Conditions of Economic Progress.* 2nd ed., completely rewritten. London: Macmillan.

———. 1957. *Conditions of Economic Progress.* 3rd ed., largely rewritten. London: Macmillan.

———. 1984. In Gerald M. Meier and Dudley Seers (eds.), *Pioneers in Development.* New York: Oxford University Press, 57–84.

Clark, Colin, and M. R. Haswell. 1964. *The Economics of Subsistence Agriculture.* London: Macmillan.

Domar, Evsey. 1947. "Expansion and Employment." *American Economic Review* 37 (March): 34–35.

Easterlin, Richard A. 2000. "The Worldwide Standard of Living Since 1800." *Journal of Economic Perspectives* 14, no. 1 (winter): 7–26.

Fields, Gary S. 2000. *Distribution and Development.* Cambridge, Mass.: MIT Press.

Fishlow, Albert. 1965. "Empty Economic Stages?" *Economic Journal* 75, no. 297 (March): 112–125.

Gerschenkron, Alex. 1962. *Economic Backwardness in Historical Perspective.* Cambridge, Mass.: Harvard University Press.

Habbakuk, H. J. 1961. "Review of Rostow's Stages of Economic Growth." *Economic Journal* 71 (September): 601–604.

Haberler, Gottfried. 1959. *International Trade and Economic Development.* Cairo: National Bank of Egypt.

Harrod, Roy. 1939. "An Essay in Dynamic Theory." *Economic Journal* 49 (March): 14–33.

Hicks, J. R. 1959. *Essays in World Economics.* Oxford: Clarendon Press.

Hoselitz, Bert F. 1960. *Sociological Aspects of Economic Growth.* Glencoe, Ill.: Free Press.

Johnson, Harry G. 1958. "Planning and the Market in Economic Development." *Pakistan Economic Journal* (June).

Kravis, I. B., A. W. Heston, and R. Summers. 1978. "Real GDP Per Capita for More Than One Hundred Countries." *Economic Journal* 88 (June): 215–242.

Kuznets, Simon. 1956. "Quantitative Aspects of the Economic Growth of Nations: I. Levels and Variability of Rates of Growth." *Economic Development and Cultural Change* 5, no. 1 (October).

———. 1959. "On Comparative Study of Economic Structure and Growth of

Nations." In National Bureau of Economic Research, *The Comparative Study of Economic Growth and Structure.* New York, pp. 162–176.

———. 1963. "Quantitative Aspects of the Economic Growth of Nations: V III. Distribution of Income by Size." *Economic Development and Cultural Change* 11, no. 2, p. 2 (January): 1–80.

———. 1966. *Modern Economic Growth: Rate, Structure, and Demand.* New Haven: Yale University Press. Especially ch. 1, 8, 9.

Lewis, W. Arthur. 1952. *The Principles of Economic Planning: A Study Prepared for the Fabian Society.* London: Allen & Unwin.

———. 1966. *Development Planning.* London: Allen and Unwyn.

———. 1984. "The State of Development Theory." *American Economic Review* 74, no. 1 (March): 1–10.

———. 1989. "Sir Arthur Lewis: The Simplicity of Genius." *May 1989 Annual Conference of the Caribbean Studies Association.*

Maddison, Angus. 2001. *The World Economy: A Millennial Perspective.* Paris: Development Centre of the Organisation for Economic Co-operation and Development.

Mahalanobis, P. C. 1955. "The Approach of Operational Research to Planning in India." *Sankhya* 16, nos. 1 and 2 (December): 3–130.

Mallon, Richard D., and Joseph J. Stern. 1989. *The Political Economy of Trade and Industrial Policy Reform in Bangladesh.* Cambridge, Mass.: Harvard Institute for International Development.

Myint, Hla. 1954–55. "Gains from International Trade and Backward Countries." *Review of Economic Studies* 22, no. 58: 129–142.

Notestein, F. W. 1953. "Economic Problems of Population Change." In *Proceedings of the Eighth International Conference of Agricultural Economists.* London: Oxford University Press, 13–31.

Rostow, W. W. 1960. *The Stages of Economic Growth.* Cambridge: Cambridge University Press.

Rostow, W. W., ed. 1963. *The Economics of Take-off into Sustained Growth.* Proceedings of the International Economic Association (Konstanz). London: Macmillan.

Schultz, Theodore W. 1987. "Tensions Between Economics and Politics in Dealing with Agriculture." In Gerald M. Meier (ed.), *Pioneers in Development.* 2nd series. New York: Oxford University Press, pp. 17–38.

Schultz, T. Paul. 1988. "Inequality in the Distribution of Personal Income in the World: How It Is Changing and Why." *Journal of Population Economics* 11, no. 3: 307–344.

Spengler, Joseph J. 1949. "Theories of Socio-Economic Growth." In National Bureau of Economic Research (NBER), *Problems in the Study of Economic Growth.* New York: NBER, pp. 46–115.

Summers, R., and A. Heston. 1988. "A New Set of International Comparisons of Real Product and Price Level Estimates for 130 Countries, 1950–1985." *Review of Income and Wealth* 34, no. 1:1–25.

United Nations. 1960. Report by Group of Experts. *Programming Techniques for Economic Development* (with special reference to Asia and the Far East). New York: United Nations.

Viner, Jacob. 1953. *International Trade and Economic Development.* Oxford: Clarendon Press.

Chapter 6

Abramovitz, Moses. 1956. "Resource and Output Trends in the United States since 1870." *American Economic Review* 46, no. 2 (May): 5–23.

Aghion, Philippe, and Peter Howitt. 1992. "A Model of Growth Through Creative Destruction." *Econometrica* 60, no. 2 (March): 322–352.

Askari, Hossein, and John T. Cummings. 1977. "Agricultural Supply Response with the Nerlove Model: A Survey." *International Economic Review,* 18, no. 2 (June): 257–292.

Barber, William J. 1995. "Chile con Chicago: A Review Essay." *Journal of Economic Literature,* 33 (December) 1941–1949.

Bates, Robert. 1981. *Markets and States in Tropical Africa.* Berkeley: University of California Press.

Bauer, P. T. 1957. *Economic Analysis and Policy in Underdeveloped Countries.* Durham, N.C.: Duke University Press.

Bhagwati, Jagdish N. 1988. "Export Promoting Trade Strategy: Issues and Evidence." *World Bank Research Observer* 3, no.1 (January): 27–57.

Bhagwati, Jagdish, and Anne O. Krueger. 1973. "Exchange Control, Liberalization, and Economic Development." *American Economic Review, Papers and Proceedings* 63, no. 2 (May): 418–427.

Binswanger, Hans, and Mark Rosenzweig, eds. 1984. *Contractual Arrangements, Employment, and Wages in Rural Labour Markets in Asia.* New Haven: Yale University Press.

Birdsall, Nancy. 2002, December. *From Social Policy to an Open-Economy Social Contract in Latin America.* Washington, D.C.: Center for Global Development working paper no. 21.

Birdsall, Nancy, and John Nellis. 2002, May. *Winners and Losers: Assessing the Distributional Impact of Privatization.* Washington, D.C.: Center for Global Development, working paper no. 6.

Braverman, Avishay, and Joseph E. Stiglitz. 1982. "Sharecropping and the Interlinking of Agrarian Markets." *American Economic Review* 72, no. 4 (September): 695–715.

Bruno, Michael. 1972. "Domestic Resource Costs and Effective Protection." *Journal of Political Economy* 80, no. 1 (January–February): 16–33.

Bruton, Henry. 1970. "Import Substitution Strategy of Economic Development." *Pakistan Development Review* (summer): 123–146.

Colclough, Christopher, and James Manor, eds. 1991. *States or Markets? Neo-Liberalism and the Development Policy Debate.* Oxford: Clarendon Press.

Collins, Susan, and Barry P. Bosworth. 1996. "Economic Growth in East Asia: Accumulation versus Assimilation." In William C. Brainard and George L. Perry, eds., *Brookings Papers on Economic Activity,* vol. 1996, no. 2 (1996), 135–203.

Curry, S., and J. Weiss. 2000. *Project Analysis in Developing Countries.* London: MacMillan.

Faber, M.L.O., and Dudley Seers, eds. 1972. *The Crisis in Planning.* London: Chatto and Windus.

Fischer, Stanley. 1993. "The Role of Macroeconomic Factors in Growth." *Journal of Monetary Economics* 32: 485–512.

Ginswanger, Hans P., and Mark R. Rosenzweig. 1984. *Contractual Arrangements,*

Employment and Wages in Rural Labor Markets in Asia. New Haven, Conn.: Yale University Press.

Griliches, Zvi. 1996. "The Discovery of the Residual: An Historical Note." *Journal of Economic Literature,* 34 (September): 1324–1330.

Grossman, G., and E. Helpman. 1991. *Innovation and Growth in the World Economy.* Cambridge, Mass.: MIT Press.

Hayami, Yujiro, and Vernon Ruttan. 1985. *Agricultural Development: An International Perspective.* Baltimore: John Hopkins University Press.

Hirschman, Albert. 1982. "The Rise and Decline of Development Economics." In Mark Gersovitz, Carlos F. Diaz-Alejandro, Gustav Ranis, and Mark R. Rosenzweig, eds., *The Theory and Experience of Economic Development.* London: Allen and Unwin.

Kapur, Devesh, John P. Lewis, and Richard Webb. 1997. *The World Bank. Vol. 2, History.* Washington, D.C.: Brookings Institution.

Killick, Tony. 1989. *A Reaction Too Far.* London: Overseas Development Institute.

Kim, Jong-Il, and Lawrence Lau. 1994. "The Sources of Economic Growth of the East Asian Newly Industrialized Countries." *Journal of the Japanese and International Economies* 8: 235–271.

Kreinin, M., and L. Officer. 1978. *The Monetary Approach to the Balance of Payments: A Survey.* Princeton Studies in International Finance no. 43. Princeton: Princeton University Press.

Krueger, Anne O. 1980. "Trade Policy as an Input to Development." *American Economic Review, Papers and Proceedings* 70, no. 2 (May): 288–292.

———. 1997. "Trade Policy and Economic Development: How We Learn." *American Economic Review* 87, no. 1 (March): 1–22.

Krugman, Paul. 1993. "Towards a Counter-Counterrevolution in Development Theory." In *Proceedings of the World Bank Annual Conference on Development Economics 1992.* Washington, D.C.: World Bank.

———. 1994. "The Fall and Rise of Development Economics." In *Rethinking the Development Experience: Essays Provoked by the Work of Albert Hirschman.* Washington, D.C.: Brookings Institution, 39–58.

Kuznets, Simon. 1966. *Modern Economic Growth.* New Haven: Yale University Press.

Lall, Sanjaya, and Morris Teubal. 1998. " 'Market-Stimulating' Technology Policies in Developing Countries: A Framework with Examples from East Asia." *World Development* 26 no. 8: 1369–1385.

Lipton, Michael. 1968. "The Theory of the Optimizing Peasant." *Journal of Development Studies* (April): 327–351.

———. 1977. *Why Poor People Stay Poor: Urban Bias in World Development.* Cambridge, Mass.: Harvard University Press.

———. 1984. "Urban Bias Revisited." *Journal of Development Studies* (April).

Little, Ian M. D. 1982. *Economic Development.* New York: Basic Books.

Little, Ian M D., and J. A. Mirrlees. 1969. *Manual of Industrial Analysis in Developing Countries II: Social Cost Benefit Analysis.* Paris: Organisation for Economic Co-operation and Development..

———. 1974. *Project Appraisal and Planning for Developing Countries.* London: Heinemann.

———. 1990. "Project Appraisal and Planning: Twenty Years On." In *Proceedings of the World Bank Annual Conference on Development Economics.* Washington, D.C.: International Bank for Reconstruction and Development, pp. 351–82.

Little, Ian, Tibor Scitovsky, and Maurice Scott. 1970. *Industry and Trade in Some Developing Countries: A Comparative Study*. London: Oxford University Press.

Lucas, Robert E. 1988. "On the Mechanics of Economic Development." *Journal of Monetary Economics* 22, no. 1 (July): 3–42.

Mankiw, N. G., D. Romer, and D. Weil. 1992. "A Contribution to the Empirics of Economic Growth." *Quarterly Journal of Economics* 107, no. 2 (May): 407–437.

Murphy, Kevin M., Andrei Shleifer, and Robert W. Vishny. 1989. "Industrialization and the Big Push." *Journal of Political Economy* 97, no. 5: 1003–1026.

Nelson, Richard, and Howard Pack. 1999. "The Asian Growth Miracle and Modern Growth Theory." *Economic Journal* 109, no. 457 (July): 416–436.

Nerlove, Mark. 1999. "Theodore W. Schultz, 1902–1998." *Economic Journal* 109 (November): 726–748.

Reynolds, Lloyd. 1985. *Economic Growth in the Third World, 1850–1980*. New Haven, Conn.: Yale University Press.

Rodrik, Dani. 1997, February. *TFPG Controversies, Institutions, and Economic Performance in East Asia*. National Bureau of Economic Research, working paper no. 5914. Cambridge, Mass.: National Bureau of Economic Research.

Romer, Paul M. 1986. "Increasing Returns and Long-Run Growth." *Journal of Political Economy* 94 (October): 1002–1037.

———. 1990. "Endogenous Technological Change." *Journal of Political Economy* 98 (October): 71–102.

———. 1993a. "Idea Gaps and Object Gaps in Economic Development." *Journal of Monetary Economics* 32 (December): 543–573.

———. 1993b. "Two Strategies for Economic Development: Using Ideas and Producing Ideas." In *Proceedings of the World Bank Annual Conference on Development Economics 1992*. Washington, D.C.: World Bank, 63–98.

———. 1994. "The Origins of Endogenous Growth." *Journal of Economic Perspectives* 8,. no. 1 (winter): 3–22.

Schultz, Theodore W. 1964. *Transforming Traditional Agriculture*. Chicago: University of Chicago Press.

———. 1978. *Distortions of Agricultural Incentives*. Bloomington: University of Indiana Press.

Solow, Robert M. 1956. "A Contribution to the Theory of Economic Growth." *Quarterly Journal of Economics* 70 (February): 65–94.

———. 1957. "Technical Change and the Aggregate Production Function." *Review of Economics and Statistics* 39: 312–320.

Srinivasan, T. N. 2002. "Economic Reforms and Global Integration." Unpublished paper.

Streeten, Paul, and Michael Lipton, eds. 1969. *The Crisis of Indian Planning*. London: Oxford University Press.

Temple, Jonathan. 1997. "St Adam and the Dragons: Neoclassical Economics and the East Asian Miracle." *Oxford Development Studies* 25, no. 3: 279–300.

———. 1999. "The New Growth Evidence." *Journal of Economic Literature* 37 (March): 112–56.

Timmer, C. Peter. 1973. "Choice of Techniques in Rice Milling in Java." *Bulletin of Indonesian Economic Studies* 9, no. 2 (July): 57–76.

United Nations Industrial Development Organization. 1972. Amartya Sen, Partha Daspypta, and Stephen Marglin, *Guidelines for Project Evaluation*. New York: United Nations.

Williamson, John. 1990. "What Washington Means by Policy Reform." In John

Williamson (ed.), *Latin American Adjustment: How Much has Happened.* Washington, D.C.: Institute for International Economics.

World Bank. 1991–92. *The Political Economy of Agricultural Pricing Policy.* Washington, D.C.: World Bank.

———. 1993. *The East Asian Miracle: Economic Growth and Public Policy.* New York: Oxford University Press.

Young, A. 1995. "The Tyranny of Numbers: Confronting the Statistical Realities of the East Asian Growth Experience." *Quarterly Journal of Economics* 110, no. 3 (August): 641–680.

Chapter 7

Abramovitz, Moses. 1956. "Resource and Output Trends in the United States since 1870." *American Economic Review* 46, no. 2 (May): 5–23.

———. 1995. "The Elements of Social Capability." In Bon Ho Koo and Dwight H. Perkins (eds.), *Social Capability and Long-Term Economic Growth.* New York: St. Martin's Press, ch. 3.

Abramovitz, Moses, and Paul A. David. 1996. "Convergence and Deferred Catch Up." In Ralph Landau, Timothy Taylor, and Gavin Wrights (eds.), *The Mosaic of Economic Growth.* Stanford, Calif.: Stanford University Press.

Aghion, Philippe, and Peter Howitt. 1998. *Endogenous Growth Theory.* Cambridge, Mass.: MIT Press.

Arrow, Kenneth J. 1962. "The Economic Implications of Learning by Doing." *Review of Economic Studies* 29, no. 3: 155–173.

———. 1974. *The Limits of Organization.* New York: Norton.

———. 1995. "Returns to Scale, Information and Economic Growth." In Bon Ho Koo and Dwight H. Perkins (eds.), *Social Capability and Long-Term Economic Growth.* New York: St. Martin's Press.

Amsden, Alice H. 1985. "The Division of Labour Is Limited by the Rate of Growth of the Market: The Taiwan Machine Tool Industry in the 1970s." *Cambridge Journal of Economics* 9, no. 3 (271–284).

Barro, Robert J. 1991. "Economic Growth in a Cross-Section of Countries." *Quarterly Journal of Economics* 106 no. 2 (May): 407–43.

———. 1997. *Determinants of Economic Growth: A Cross-Country Empirical Study.* Cambridge, Mass.: MIT Press.

Barro, Robert J., and X. Sala-I-Martin. 1995. *Economic Growth.* New York: McGraw-Hill.

Baumol, William. 1986. "Productivity Growth, Convergence, and Welfare: What the Long-Run Data Show." *American Economic Review* 76, no. 5: 1072–1085.

Baumol, Williams, and James Tobin. 1989. "Communication. The Optimal Cash Balance Proposition: Maurice Allais' Priority." *Journal of Economic Literature* 27, no. 3 (1160–1162).

Clark, J. M. 1923. *Studies in the Economics of Overhead Costs.* Chicago: University of Chicago Press.

Collier, Paul 1998. "Social Capital and Poverty." The World Bank Social Capital Initiative Working Paper No. 4 (November).

Collins, Susan, and Barry P. Bosworth. 1997. "Economic Growth in East Asia: Accumulation versus Assimilation." In William C. Brainard and George L. Perry, eds., *Brookings Papers in Economic Activity,* vol. 2. Washington, D.C.: Brookings Institution, 135–203.

Crafts, Nicholas. 2001. "Historical Perspectives on Development." In Gerald M. Meier and Joseph E. Stiglitz (eds.), *Frontiers of Development Economics*. New York: Oxford University Press, 301–334.

Dasgupta, Partha, and Ismail Serageldin, eds. 2000. *Social Capital: A Multifaceted Perspective*. Washington, D.C.: World Bank.

Easterly, William, and Ross Levine. 2001. "What Have We Learned from a Decade of Empirical Research on Growth? It's Not Factor Accumulation-Stylized Facts and Growth Models." *World Bank Economic Review* 15, no. 2: 177–219.

Fagenberg, Jan. 1994. "Technology and International Differences in Growth Rates." *Journal of Economic Literature* (September): 1147–1175.

Fischer, Stanley. 1993. "The Role of Macroeconomic Factors in Growth." *Journal of Monetary Economics* 32: 485–512.

Greif, Avner. 1997 "Cliometrics After Forty Years." *American Economic Review, Papers and Proceedings*, 87 (May): 400–403.

Griliches, Zvi. 1996. "The Discovery of the Residual: An Historical Note." *Journal of Economic Literature* 34, (September): 1324–1330.

Hall, Robert E., and Charles I. Jones. 1999. "Why Do Some Countries Produce So Much More Output per Worker Than Others?" *Quarterly Journal of Economics* 114, no. 1 (February): 83–116.

Harberger, Arnold C. 2001. "The View from the Trenches." In Gerald M. Meier and Joseph E. Stiglitz (eds.), *Frontiers of Development Economics*. New York: Oxford University Press, 541–562.

Helpman, E., and P. Krugman. 1985. *Market Structure and Foreign Trade: Increasing Returns, Imperfect Competitions, and the International Economy*. Cambridge, Mass.: MIT Press.

Hicks, J. R. 1950. *A Contribution to the Theory of the Trade Cycle*. Oxford: Clarendon Press.

———. *Essays in World Economics*. Oxford: Clarendon Press.

Howitt, Peter. 2000. "Endogenous Growth and Cross-Country Income Differences." *American Economic Review* (September): 829–846.

Howitt, Peter, and Philippe Aghion. 1998. "Capital Accumulation and Innovation as Complementary Factors in Long-Run Growth." *Journal of Economic Growth* 3, no. 2 (June): 111–130.

Jensen, Bjarne S., and Kar-yiu Wong. 1997. *Dynamics, Economic Growth, and International Trade*. Ann Arbor: University of Michigan Press.

King, Mervyn A., and Mark Robson. 1989. "Endogenous Growth and the Role of History." National Bureau of Economic Research Working Paper no. 3151. Cambridge, Mass.: National Bureau of Economic Research.

Knack, Stephen, and Philip Keefer. 1995. "Institutions and Economic Performance: Cross-Country Tests Using Alternative Institutional Measures." *Economics and Politics* 7, no. 3 (November): 207–227.

Krugman, Paul, 1980. "Scale Economies Differentiation and the Pattern of Trade." *American Economic Review* 70: 950–959.

Krugman, Paul, and Maurice Obstfeld. 2003. *International Economics: Theory and Policy*. 6th ed. Boston: Addison Wesley.

Lau, Lawrence J. 1999. "The Sources of East Asian Economic Growth." In Gustav Ranis, (eds.), John CH Fei, Sheng-Cheng Hu, Ÿun-Peng Chu *The Political Economy of Comparative Development into the Twenty-first Century*. Northampton, Mass.: Edward Elgar, ch. 2.

Levine, Ross, and David Renelt. 1992. "A Sensitivity Analysis of Cross-Country

Growth Regressions." *American Economic Review* 82, no. 4 (September): 942–963.

Lucas, Robert E., Jr. 1988. "On the Mechanics of Economic Development." *Journal of Monetary Economics* 22, no. 1 (July): 3–42.

———. 2000. "Some Macroeconomics for the Twenty-first Century." *Journal of Economic Perspectives* (winter): 159–68.

Mill, J. S. 1848. *Principles of Political Economy*. Boston, Mass.: Little & Brown.

Myint, Hla. 1958. "The Classical Theory of International Trade and the Underdeveloped Countries." *Economic Journal*.

———. 1971. *Economic Theory and the Underdeveloped Countries*. New York: Oxford University Press.

———. 1985. "Organizational Dualism and Economic Development." *Asian Development Review*. 3, no. 1: 25–42.

Nelson, Richard, and Howard Pack. 1999. "The Asian Miracle and Modern Growth Theory." *Economic Journal* 209 (July): 416–436.

North, Douglass C. 1990. *Institutions, Institutional Change and Economic Performance*. New York: Cambridge University Press.

———. 1997. "The Process of Economic Change." World Institute for Development Economics Research, Paper 128.

Nurkse, Ragnar. 1953. *Problems of Capital Formation in Underdeveloped Countries*. Oxford: Blackwell.

Porter, Michael E. 1990. *The Competitive Advantage of Nations*.

Pritchett, Lant. 1997. "Divergence, Big Time." *Journal of Economic Perspectives* 11, no. 3 (summer): 3–17.

Rodrik, Dani. 1997, February. "TFPG Controversies, Institutions, and Economic Performance in East Asia." National Bureau of Economic Research, working paper no. 5914. Cambridge, Mass.: National Bureau of Economic Research.

Romer, David. 1996. *Advanced Macroeconomics*. New York: McGraw Hill.

Romer, Paul M. 1986. "Increasing Returns and Long-Run Growth." *Journal of Political Economy* 94, no. 5 (October): 1002–1037.

———. 1990. "Endogenous Technological Change." *Journal of Political Economy* 98, no. 5 (October): S71–S102.

———. 1993a. "Idea Gaps and Object Gaps in Economic Development." *Journal of Monetary Economics* 32, (December): 543–573.

———. 1993b. "Two Strategies for Economic Development: Using Ideas and Producing Ideas." In *Proceedings of the World Bank Annual Conference on Development Economics 1992*. Washington, D.C.: World Bank, 63–98.

———. 1994. "The Origins of Endogenous Growth." *Journal of Economic Perspectives* 8, no. 1 (winter): 3–22.

Rostow, W. W. 1990. *Theorists of Economic Growth from David Hume to the Present*. New York: Oxford University Press.

Sala-I-Martin, Xavier X. 1991. "I Just Ran Two Million Regressions." *American Economic Review*, Papers and Proceedings, 87 (May): 178–183.

Solow, Robert M. 1956. "A Contribution to the Theory of Economic Growth." *Quarterly Journal of Economics* 70 (February): 65–94.

———. 1957. "Technical Change and the Aggregate Production Function." *Review of Economics and Statistics* 39: 312–320.

———. 1994. "Perspectives on Growth Theory." *Journal of Economic Perspectives* 8, no. 1: 45–54.

———. 2000. "Toward a Macroeconomics of the Medium Run." *Journal of Economic Perspective.* 14, no. 1: 151–158.

Temple, Jonathan. 1997. "St Adam and the Dragons: Neoclassical Economics and the East Asian Miracle." *Oxford Development Studies* 25, no. 3 279–300.

———. 1999. "The New Growth Evidence." *Journal of Economic Literature* 37 (March): 112–156.

Temple, Jonathan, and Paul A. Johnson. 1998. "Social Capability and Economic Growth." *Quarterly Journal of Economics* 113, no. 3 (August): 965–990.

Woolcock, Michael, and Deepa Narayan. 2000. "Social Capital: Implications for Development Theory, Research, and Policy." *World Bank Research Observer* 15, no. 2 (August): 225–249.

Empirical Studies

Kim, Jong-Il, and Lawrence J. Lau. 1994. "The Sources of Economic Growth of the East Asian Newly Industrialized Countries." *Journal of the Japanese and International Economies* 8: 235–271.

World Bank 1993. *The East Asian Miracle, Economic Growth and Public Policy.* Oxford: Oxford University Press.

Young, A. 1995. "The Tyranny of Numbers: Confronting the Statistical Realities of the East Asian Growth Experience." *Quarterly Journal of Economics* 110, no. 3 (August): 641–680.

Chapter 8

Bardhan, Pranab, and Christopher Udry, eds. 2000. *Readings in Development Microeconomics.* Cambridge, Mass.: MIT Press.

Binswanger, Hans P., and Mark R. Rosenzweig. 1981. *Contractual Arrangements, Employment and Wages in Rural Labor Markets: A Critical Review.* New York: Agricultural Development Council.

Braverman, Avishay, and Joseph E. Stiglitz. 1982. "Sharecropping and the Interlinking of Agrarian Markets." *American Economic Review* 72, no. 4 (September): 695–715.

Greenwald, Bruce C., Meir Kohn, and Joseph E. Stiglitz. 1990. "Financial Markets Imperfections and Productivity Growth." *Journal of Economic Behavior and Organization* 13, no. 3 (June 1990): 321–345.

Hayami, Yujiro, and Keijiro Otsuka. 1993. *The Economics of Contract Choice.* Oxford: Oxford University Press.

Hoff, Karla. 2000. "Beyond Rosenstein-Rodan: The Modern Theory of Coordination Problems in Development." In *Washington, D.C., Annual Bank Conference of Development Economics.* Washington, D.C.: World Bank.

Hoff, Karla, Avishay Braverman, and Joseph E. Stiglitz. 1993. *The Economics of Rural Organization.* New York: Oxford University Press.

Hoff, Karla, and Joseph E. Stiglitz. 2001. "Modern Economic Theory and Development." In Gerald M. Meier and Joseph E. Stiglitz (eds.), *Frontiers of Development Economics.* New York: Oxford University Press, pp. 389–459.

Leibenstein, Harvey. 1957. *Economic Backwardness and Economic Growth.* New York: Wiley.

Mookherjee, Dilip, and Debraj Ray. 2001. *Readings in the Theory of Economic Development.* Oxford: Blackwell.

Murphy, Kevin M., Andrei Shleifer, and Robert W. Vishny. 1989. "Industrialization and the Big Push." *Journal of Political Economy* 97, no. 5: 1003–1026.

Ray, Debraj. 1998. *Development Economics.* Princeton, N.J.: Princeton University Press.

———. 2000. "What's New in Development Economics?" *American Economists* 44, no. 2 (fall): 3–16.

Rodrik, D. 1995. "Getting Interventions Right—How South Korea and Taiwan Grew Rich." *Economic Policy* 20, no. 20 (April 1995): 53–97.

Stiglitz, Joseph E. 1974. "Incentive and Risk Sharing in Sharecropping," *Review of Economic Studies* 4 (April): 219–255.

———. 1985, February. *Economics of Information and Theory of Economic Development.* National Bureau of Economic Research working paper no. 1566. Cambridge, Mass.: National Bureau of Economic Research.

———. 1986. "The New Development Economics." *World Development* 14, no. 2: 257–265.

———. 1989. "Financial Markets and Development." *Oxford Review of Economic Policy* 5, no. 4 (winter): 55–68.

———. 1994. "The Role of the State in Financial Markets." In *Proceedings of the World Bank Annual Conference on Development Economics 1993.* Supplement to the *World Bank Economic Review* and the *World Bank Researcher Observer.* Washington, D.C.: International Bank for Reconstruction and Development/World Bank. 19–52.

———. 1995. "Social Absorption Capability and Innovation." In Bon Ho Koo and Dwight H. Perkins (eds.), *Social Capability and Long-Term Economic Growth.* New York: St. Martin's Press, 48–81.

———. 2002. "Information and the Change in the Paradigm of Economics." *American Economic Review* 92, no. 3 (June): 460–501.

Chapter 9

Adelman, Irma, and Cynthia Taft Morris. 1968. "Performance Criteria for Evaluating Economic Development Potential: An Operational Approach," *Quarterly Journal of Economics,* 82: 260–280.

Aoki, Masahiko. 2000. *Toward a Comparative Institutional Analysis.* Cambridge, Mass.: MIT Press.

Aron, Janine. 2000. "Growth and Institutions: A Review of the Evidence." *World Bank Research Observer* 15, no. 1 (February): 99–135.

Arrow, Kenneth J. 1974. *The Limits of Organization.* New York: Norton.

———. 1995. "Returns to Scale, Information and Economic Growth." In Ben-Ho Koo and Dwight H. Perkins(eds.), *Social Capability and Long-Term Economic Growth.* New York: St. Martin's Press.

———. 1999. "Observations on Social Capital." In Partha Dasgupta and Ismail Serageldin (eds.), *Social Capital.* Washington, D.C.: World Bank, pp. 3–5.

Barro, Robert J. 1996. "Democracy and Growth." *Journal of Economic Growth* 1, no. 1: 1–27.

Coleman, James S. 1990. *Foundations of Social Theory.* Cambridge, Mass.: Harvard University Press.

Collier, Paul, and Jan Willem Gunning. 1999a. "Explaining African Economic Performance." *Journal of Economic Literature* 37 (March): 64–111.

———. 1999b. "Why Has Africa Grown Slowly?" *Journal of Economic Perspectives* 13, no. 3: 3–22.

Dasgupta, Partha. 1990. "Well-Being and the Extent of Its Realization in Poor Countries." *Economic Journal* 100, supplement: 1–32.

———. 1999. "Economic Progress and the Idea of Social Capital." In Partha Dasgupta and Ismail Serageldin (eds.), *Social Capital*. Washington, D.C.: World Bank.

———. 2000. "Wealth and Welfare." In P. J. Hammond and G. Myles (eds.), *Incentives, Organization, And Public Economies: Papers in Honour of Sir James A. Mirrlees*. Oxford: Clarendon Press.

———. 2001. *Human Well-Being and the Natural Environment*. New York: Oxford University Press.

Dasgupta, Partha, and Ismail Serageldin, eds. 1999. *Social Capital*. Washington, D.C.: World Bank.

Dasgupta, Partha, and Martin Weale. 1992. "On Measuring the Quality of Life." *World Development* 20, no. 1: 119.

Easterly, William. 2001. *The Elusive Quest for Growth*. New York: Basic Books.

Evans, Peter. 1996. "Government Action, Social Capital and Development: Reviewing the Evidence on Synergy," *World Development* 24, no. 6: 1119–1132.

Fine, Ben. 2001. *Social Capital versus Capital Theory*. London: Routledge.

Granovetter, Mark. 1985. "Economic Action and Social Structure: The Problem of Embeddedness." *American Journal of Sociology* 91, no. 3 (November): 481–510.

Greif, Avner. 2000. "The Fundamental Problem of Exchange: A Research Agenda in Historical Institutional Analysis." *European Review of Economic History* 4, no. 3: 251–84.

Hagen, Everett. 1968. *The Economics of Development*. Homewood, Ill.: R. D. Irwin.

Hall, Robert E., and Charles I. Jones. 1999. "Why Do Some Countries Produce So Much More Output per Worker than Others?" *Quarterly Journal of Economics* 114 (February): 83–116.

Harrison, Lawrence E., and Samuel P. Huntington, eds. 2000. *Culture Matters*. New York: Basic Books.

Harriss, John. 2002. *Depoliticizing Development*. London: Anthem Press.

Hoselitz, Bert F. 1960. *Industrialization and Society*. Paris: UNESCO.

Knack, Stephen. 1999. *Social Capital, Growth, and Poverty: A Survey of Cross-Country Evidence*." World Bank, Social Capital Initiative, working paper no. 7. Washington, D.C.: World Bank.

Knack, Stephen, and Philip Keefer. 1997a. "Does Social Capital Have an Economic Payoff? A Cross-Country Investigation." *Quarterly Journal of Economics* 112 (November): 1251–1288.

———. 1997b. "Why Don't Poor Countries Catch Up? A Cross-National Task of an Institutional Explanation." *Economic Inquiry* 35 (July): 590–602.

Kreps, D. 1990. *Game Theory and Economic Modelling*. Oxford: Clarendon Press.

Landes, David S. 1998. *The Wealth and Poverty of Nations: Why Some Are So Rich and Some So Poor*. New York: Norton.

McClelland, David. 1961. *The Achieving Society*. Princeton, N.J.: Van Nostrand.

McKinnon, Ronald I. 1993. "Liberalizing Foreign Trade in a Socialist Economy: The Problem of Negative Value Added." In Kazimierz Z. Poznanski (ed.), *Stabilization and Privatization in Poland: An Economic Evaluation of the Shock Therapy Program*. Boston: Kluwer Academic.

Myint, H. 1985. "Organizational Dualism and Economic Development." *Asian Development Review* 3, no. 1: 25–42.

Narayan, Deepa, and Lant Pritchett. 1996. *Cents and Sociability: Household Income and Social Capital in Rural Tanzania*. Washington, D.C.: World Bank.

North, Douglass C. 1990. *Institutions, Institutional Change and Economic Performance*. Cambridge: Cambridge University Press.

———. 1994. "Economic Performance Through Time." *American Economic Review* 84, no. 3 (June): 359–368.

———. 1995. "The New Institutional Economics and Third World Development." In John Harriss, Janet Hunter, and Colin M. Lewis (eds.), *The New Institutional Economics and Third World Development*. London: Routledge.

———. 1997. "Institutions, Economic Growth and Freedom." In *The Economic Foundations of Property Rights: Selected Readings*. Cheltenham, England: Elgar.

———. 2000. "Where Have We Been and Where Are We Going?" In Avner Ben-Ner and Louis Putterman (eds.), *Economics, Values, and Organization*. Cambridge: Cambridge University Press, ch. 19.

Nugent, Jeffrey B. 1993. "Between State, Market, and Households: A Neoinstitutional Analysis of Local Organizations and Institutions." *World Development* 12, no. 4: 623–632.

Ostram, Elinor. 1995. "Incentives, Rules of the Game, and Development." In *Proceedings of World Bank Annual Conference on Development Economics*: Washington, D.C.: International Bank for Reconstruction and Development/World Bank, 207–234.

Putnam, Robert D. 1993. *Making Democracy Work: Traditions in Modern Italy*. Princeton: Princeton University Press.

Rauch, J., and P. Evans. 2000. "Bureaucratic Structure and Bureaucratic Performance in Less Developed Countries." *Journal of Public Economics* 75, no. 3: 49–71.

Rodrik, Dani. 1997 February. *TFPG Controversies, Institutions, and Economic Performance in East Asia*. National Bureau of Economic Research working paper series 5914. Cambridge, Mass.: National Bureau of Economic Research.

———. 1999. Where Did All the Growth Go? External Shocks, Social Conflicts, and Growth Collapses." *Journal of Economic Growth* 14, no. 4: 385–412.

Ruttan, V. W. 1989. "Institutional Innovation and Agricultural Development." *World Development* 17, no. 9: 1375–1387.

Sachs, Jeffrey. 2000. "Notes on a New Sociology of Economic Development." In Lawrence E. Harrison and Samuel P. Huntington (eds.), *Culture Matters*. New York: Basic Books, ch. 3.

Sen, Amartya. 1999. *Development as Freedom*. New York: Knopf.

Solow, Robert M. 1995. "But Verify." *New Republic*, September 11.

———. 1999. "Notes on Social Capital and Economic Performance." In Partha Dasgupta and Ismail Serageldin (eds.), *Social Capital*. Washington, D.C.: The World Bank, pp. 6–10.

Townsend, Robert M. 1994. "Risk and Insurance in Village India." *Econometrica* 62, no. 3: 539–591.

Unger, Roberto Mangabeira. 1998. *Democracy Realized: The Progressive Alternative*. London, Verso.

Uphoff, Norman. 2000a. "Demonstrated Benefits from Social Capital: The Productivity of Former Organizations in Gal Oya, Sri Lanka." *World Development*
   28, no. 11: 1875–1890.
———. 2000b. "Understanding Social Capital: Learning from the Analysis and
   Experience of Participation." In Partha Dasgupta and Ismail Serageldin (eds.),
   Social Capital. Washington, D.C.: World Bank, 215–249.
Williamson, Oliver. 1994. "The Institutions and Governance with Economic Development and Reform." In *Proceedings of the World Bank Annual Conference on
   Development Economics.* Washington, D.C.: International Bank for Reconstruction and Development/World Bank, 171–197
———. 1998. "The Institutions of Governance." *American Economic Review, Papers
   and Proceedings* 88, no.2: 75–79.
———. 2000. "The New Institutional Economics: Taking Stock, Looking Ahead."
   Journal of Economic Literature 38, no. 3 (September): 595–613.
Woolcock, Michael. 1998. "Social Capital and Economic Development: Toward
   a Theoretical Synthesis and Policy Framework." *Theory and Society* 27: 151–
   208.
Woolcock, Michael, and Deepak Aryan. 2000. "Social Capital: Implications for
   Development Theory, Research, and Policy." *World Bank Research Observer* 15
   no. 2 (August): 225–249.
World Bank. 2002. *World Development Report 2002: Building Institutions for Markets.*
   New York: Oxford University Press.

Chapter 10

Alesina, Alberto, Enrico Spolaore, and Romain Wacziarg. 2002. *Trade, Growth, and
   Size of Countries.* Research paper no. 1774. Stanford, Calif.: Stanford Graduate
   School of Business.
Citrin, Daniel, and Stanley Fischer. 2000. "Strengthening the International Finan-
   cial System." *Work Development* 28, no. 6 (June).
Collier, Paul, and D. Dollar. 2001. "Can the World Cut Poverty in Half? How
   Policy Reform and Effective Aid Can Meet International Development Goals."
   World Development 29, no. 11 (November): 1787–1802.
Collier, Paul, and Colin Mayer. 1989. "The Assessment: Financial Liberalization,
   Financial Systems, and Economic Growth." *Oxford Review of Economic Policy*
   5, no. 4: 1–12.
Cooper, Richard N. 2001. "Growth and Inequality: The Role of Foreign Trade and
   Investment". Unpublished paper.
———. 2002. "Reforming the International Financial System." Unpublished pa-
   per.
Crockett, Andrew. 1997. "The Theory and Practice of Financial Stability." *The
   Economist* 144, no. 4: 531–568.
David, D., and Hakan Nordstrom. 2000. "Trade, Income Disparity and Poverty."
   Special Studies 5. Geneva: World Trade Organization.
De Gregorio, J., Barry Eichengreen, Takatoshi Ito, and Charles Wyplosz. 1999. *An
   Independent and Accountable IMF.* Geneva Reports on the World Economy, no.1.
   Geneva: International Center for Monetary and Banking Studies.
Dollar, David. 1992. "Outward-Oriented Developing Economies Really Do Grow
   More Rapidly: Evidence from 95 LDC's, 1976–1985." *Economic Development and
   Cultural Change* 40, no. 3 (April): 523–544.

Dollar, David, and Aart Kraay. 2001a. *Growth Is Good for the Poor.* World Bank policy research working paper no. 2587. Washington D.C.: World Bank.

———. 2001b. "Trade, Growth and Poverty." *Finance & Development* 38, no. 3 (September): 16–19.

Edwards, Sebastian. 1998. "Openness, Productivity and Growth: What Do We Really Know?" *Economic Journal* 108 (March): 383–398.

Eichengreen, Barry, and Ricardo Hausmann. 1999, November. *Exchange Rates and Financial Fragility.* National Bureau of Economic Research working paper no. 7418. Cambridge, Mass.: National Bureau of Economic Research.

Fischer, Stanley. 1999. "Reforming the International Financial System." *Economic Journal* (November): F557–F576.

———. 2002, October. *Financial Crises and Reform of the International Financial System.* National Bureau of Economic Research working paper no. 9297. Cambridge, Mass.: National Bureau of Economic Research.

Frankel, Jeffrey, and David Romer. 1999. "Does Trade Cause Growth?" *American Economic Review* 89, no. 3: 379–399.

Gilbert, C., G. Irwin, and D. Vines. 2001. "Capital Account Convertibility, Poor Developing Countries, and International Financial Architecture." *Development Policy Review* 19, no. 1 (March): 121–141.

Kenen, P. B. 2002. "The International Financial Architecture: Old Issues and New Initiatives." *International Finance* 5, no. 1 (spring): 23–45.

Krueger, Anne, and Andrew Berg. 2002, April 29–30. "Trade, Growth, and Poverty: A Selective Survey." World Bank, Annual Bank Conference of Development Economics (Washington, D.C.).

Krugman, Paul. 1979. "A Model of Balance of Payments Crises." *Journal of Money, Credit, Banking* 11, no. 3: 311–325.

Lindert, Peter H., and Jeffrey G. Williamson. 2001. "Does Globalization Make the World More Unequal?" In M. Bordso A. M. Taylor, and J. G. Wiliamson (eds.), *Globalization in Historical Perspective.* Chicago: University of Chicago Press.

McKinnon, Ronald I. 1993. *The Order of Economic Liberalization.* 2nd ed. Baltimore: Johns Hopkins University Press.

Meier, Gerald M. 1968. *The International Economics of Development.* New York: Harper and Row.

Moran, Theodore H. 2002. *Beyond Sweatshops: Foreign Direct Investment and Globalization in Developing Countries.* Washington, D.C.: Brookings Institution Press.

Myint, H. 1971. *Economic Theory and the Underdeveloped Countries.* New York: Oxford University Press.

Obstfeld, Maurice. 1996. "Models of Currency Crises with Self-Fulfilling Features." *European Economic Review* 40, nos. 3–5: 1037–1048.

O'Rourke, Kevin H., and Jeffrey G. Williamson. 1999. *Globalization and History.* Cambridge, Mass.: The MIT Press.

Radelet, Steven, and Jeffrey Sachs. 2000. "The Onset of the East Asian Financial Crisis." In Paul Krugman (ed.), *Currency Crises.* Chicago: University of Chicago Press, ch. 4.

Raffer, Kunibert. 1990. "Applying Chapter 9 Insolvency to International Debts." *World Development* 18: 301–311.

Ravallion, Martin. 2001. "Growth, Inequality and Poverty: Looking Beyond Averages." *World Development* 29, no. 11: 1803–1815.

Rodriguez, Francisco, and Dani Rodrik. 2000, May. "Trade Policy and Economic Growth: A Skeptic's Guide to the Cross-National Evidence."

Rodrik, Dani. 1999. *Making Openness Work: The New Global Economy and Developing Countries.* Washington, D.C.: Overseas Development Council.

———. 2000, June 26–28. "Can Integration into the World Economy Substitute for a Development Strategy?" Note for the World Bank, Annual Bank Conference of Development Economics Europe Conference (Paris).

Rogoff, Kenneth. 1999. "Institutions for Reducing Global Financial Instability." *Journal of Economic Perspectives* 13, no. 3, (summer): 21–42.

Romer, Paul. 1993. "Idea Gaps and Object Gaps in Economic Development." *Journal of Monetary Economics* 32 (December): 543–573.

Rostow, Walt W. 1987. *Rich Countries and Poor Countries: Reflections on the Past, Lessons for the Future.* Boulder, Colo. Westview Press.

Sachs, Jeffrey. 1995. "Russia's Struggle with Stabilization: Conceptual Issues and Evidence." Proceedings of the Annual Bank Conference on Developmental Economics, March 1994.

———. 1998. "International Economics: Unlocking the Mysteries of Globalization." *Foreign Policy* 110 (Spring): 97–112.

Sachs, Jeffrey, and Steven Radelet. 1998. *The East Asian Financial Crisis.* Brookings Papers on Economic Activity no. 1. Washington, D.C.: Brookings Institution.

Sachs, Jeffrey D., and Wing Thye Woo. 2000. "Understanding the Asian Financial Crises." In Wing Thye Woo, Jeffrey D. Sachs, and Klaus Schwab, *The Asian Financial Crises: Lessons for a Resilient Asia.* Cambridge, Mass.: MIT Press.

Sachs, Jeffrey D., and Andrew Warner. 1995. *Economic Reform and the Process of Global Integration.* Brookings Papers on Economic Activity no., 1. Washington, D.C.: Brookings Institution.

Sarno, Lucio, and Mark P. Taylor. 1999. "Moral Hazard, Asset Price Bubbles, Capital Flows, and the East Asian Crisis: The First Tests." *Journal of International Money Finance* 18, no. 4: 637–657.

Srinivasan, T. N., and Jagdish Bhagwati. 1999. "Outward-Orientation and Development: Are Revisionists Right?" New Haven, Conn.: Yale University, Economic Growth Center, Yale Station.

Stern, Nicholas. 2000. *Globalization and Poverty.* Jakarta: Institute of Economic and Social Research, University of Indonesia.

Stiglitz, Joseph. 2002a. "Globalism's Discontents," *American Prospect,* January 14, 2002.

———. 2002b. "The Way Ahead." In *Globalization and Its Discontents.* New York: Norton, ch. 9.

Williamson, John. 2000. *The Role of the IMF: A Guide to the Reports.* Mimeograph, Institute for International Economics.

World Bank. 1989. *World Development Report.* Washington, D.C.: World Bank.

———. 2002. *Globalization, Growth, and Poverty.* Washington, D.C.: World Bank.

Chapter 11

Anderson, Kym, Bernard Hoekman, and Anna Strutt. 2001. "Agriculture and the WTO: Next Steps." *Review of International Economics* 9 no. 2: 192–214.

Ben-David, Dan, and L. Alan Winters. 2000. *Trade, Income Disparity, and Poverty.* Geneva: World Trade Organization.

Borensztein, E., J. De Gregorio, and J.-W. Lee. 1998. "How Does Foreign Direct Investment Affect Economic Growth?" *Journal of International Economics* 45 (June): 115–136.

Bryant, Ralph C. 1995. "International Cooperation in the Making of National Macroeconomic Policies: Where Do We Stand?" In Peter B. Kenen (ed), *Understanding Interdependence.* Princeton: Princeton University Press, ch. 11.

Citrin, Daniel, and Stanley Fischer. 2000. "Strengthening the International Financial System: Key Issues." *World Development* 28, no. 6: 1133–1142.

Cooper, Richard N. 1999. "Exchange Rate Choices." Boston: Federal Reserve Bank of Boston.

Crafts, Nicholas. 2001. "Historical Perspectives on Development." In Gerald M. Meier and Joseph E. Stiglitz, (eds.), *Frontiers of Development Economics.* New York: Oxford University Press, 301–344.

Deardorff, Alan V. 2001. "International Provision of Trade Services, Trade, and Fragmentation." *Review of International Economics* 9, no. 2: 233–248.

Dollar, David, and Aart Kraay. 2001. "Globalization, Inequality, and Poverty Since 1980." Washington D.C.: World Bank.

Dollar, David, Lant Pritchett, and others. 1998. *Assessing Aid: What Works, What Doesn't, and Why.* New York: Oxford University Press.

Finger, J. Michael. 1999. "Development Economics and the General Agreement on Tariff and Trade." In Jaime De Melo and André Sapir (eds.), *Trade Theory and Economic Reform.* Cambridge, Mass.: Blackwell.

Finger, J. Michael, and P. Schuler. 1999. "Implementation of Uruguay Round Commitments." *World Economy* 23: 511–526.

Finger, J. Michael, and L. Alan Winters. 1998. "What Can the WTO Do for Developing Countries?" In Ann O. Krueger (ed.), *The WTO as an International Organization.* Chicago: University of Chicago Press, ch. 14.

Grindle, Merilee S. 2000. "Ready or Not: The Developing World and Globalization." In Joseph S. Nye, Jr., and John D. Donahue (eds.), *Governance in a Globalizing World.* Washington, D.C.: Brookings Institution Press, ch. 8.

Hoekman, Bernard. 2001. *Strengthening the Global Trade Architecture for Development: The Post Doha Agenda.* Washington, D.C.: World Bank.

———. 2002, June. *Economic Development and the WTO After Doha.* World Bank Policy Research working paper 2851. Washington, D.C.: World Bank.

James, Harold. 1996. *International Monetary Cooperation since Bretton Woods.* New York: Oxford University Press.

Lawrence, Robert Z., Dani Rodrik, and John Whalley. 1996, December. *Emerging Agenda for Global Trade: High Stakes for Developing Countries.* Policy essay no. 20 Washington, D.C.: Overseas Development Council.

Meier, Gerald M. 1977. "Externality Law and Market Safeguards: Applications in the GATT Multilateral Negotiations." *Harvard International Law Journal* 18 no. 3 (summer): 491–524.

———. 1984. *Emerging from Poverty.* New York: Oxford University Press.

———. 1998. *International Environment of Business.* New York: Oxford University Press.

Mishkin, Frederic S. 1999. "Global Financial Instability: Framework, Events, Issues." *Journal of Economic Perspective* 13, 3 (summer): 3–20.

Robinson, Joan. 1952. *The Rate of Interest and Other Essays.* London: Macmillan.

Rodrik, Dani. 2000, April 18–20. "Development Strategies for the Next Century."

World Bank, Annual Bank Conference on Development Economics (Washington, D.C.).

———. 2001a. *The Global Governance of Trade as if Development Really Mattered.* Report submitted to United Nations Development Plan.

———. 2001b. "Governance of Economic Globalization." In Joseph S. Nye and John D. Donahue (eds), *Governance in a Globalizing World.* Washington, D.C.: Brookings Institution Press, ch. 16.

———. 2001c. "Governing the World Economy: Does One Architectural Style Fit All?" Brookings Trade Policy Forum, Washington, D.C.

———. 2001d. "Trading in Illusions." *Foreign Policy* (March/April): 55–62.

Srinivasan, T. N. 2002. "Developing Countries and the Multilateral Trading System After Doha." New Haven, Conn.: Yale Economic Growth Center discussion paper.

Stiglitz, Joseph. 1999. "The World Bank at the Millennium." *Economic Journal* 109 (November): F577–F597.

Wade, Robert. 2001. "National Power, Coercive Liberalism and 'Global Finance.' " In Robert Art and Robert Jervis (eds.), *International Politics: Enduring Concepts and Contemporary Issues.* Ithaca, N.Y.: Cornell University Press.

Williamson, John. 2000. "What Should the World Bank Think About the Washington Consensus?" *World Bank Research Observer* 15, no. 2 (August): 251–264.

Winters, L. Alan. 1996. *Regionalism Versus Multilateralism.* World Bank Policy Research working paper series, no. 1687. Washington, D.C.: World Bank.

Woods, Ngaire. 2000. *The Political Economy of Globalization.* Basingstoke, England: Macmillan.

World Bank. 1999. *World Development Indicators 1999.* Washington, D.C.: World Bank.

———. 2002. *Global Economic Prospects and the Developing Countries.* Washington, D.C.: World Bank.

Chapter 12

Abramovitz, Moses. 1956. "Resource and Output Trends in the United States since 1870." *American Economic Review* 46, no. 2 (May): 5–23.

Aoki, Masahiko, Hyung-Ki Kim, and Masahiro Okuno-Fujiwara, eds. 1997. *The Role of Government in East Asian Economic Development: Comparative Institutional Analysis.* Oxford: Oxford University Press.

Bhagawati, Jagdish. 2002. *Globalization and Appropriate Governance.* Annual Lecture 4.

Crafts, N.F.R. 1997. "Endogenous Growth: Lessons for and from Economic History." In David M. Kreps and Kenneth F. Wallis (eds.), *Advances in Economics and Econometrics: Theory and Applications,* vol. 2. Cambridge, England: Cambridge University Press.

Dollar, David. 2001, November. "Globalization, Inequality, and Poverty since 1980." Washington, D.C.: Development Research Group, World Bank.

Easterlin, Richard A. 2000. "The Globalization of Human Development." *Annals.* (July): 32–48.

Greif, Avner. 2001. "Comment: Historical Perspectives in Development." In Gerald M. Meier and Joseph E. Stiglitz, (eds.), *Frontiers of Development Economics.* Washington, D.C.: World Bank.

Lipton, Michael. 1992. "Review of *Handbook of Development Economics, vol. 1.*" *Journal of Development Economics* 38 2, no. 2 (April): 415–434.

Maddison, Angus. 1995. *Monitoring the World Economy 1820–1992.* Paris: Development Centre of the Organisation for Economic Co-operation and Development.

———. 1998. *Chinese Economic Performance in the Long Run.* Paris: Development Centre of the Organisation for Economic Co-operation and Development.

Meier, Gerald M., and Joseph E. Stiglitz, eds. 2001. *Frontiers of Development Economics.* Washington, D.C.: World Bank.

Myint, H. 1985. "Organizational Dualism and Economic Development." *Asian Development Review* 3, no. 1: 25–42.

North, Douglass C. 2002. "Needed: A Theory of Change." in Gerald M. Meier and Joseph E. Stiglitz (eds), *Frontiers of Development Economics.* Washington, D.C.: World Bank.

Romer, Paul. 1993. "Idea Gaps and Object Gaps in Economic Development." *Journal of Monetary Economics* 32, no. 3 (December): 543–573.

Sala-I-Martin, Xavier. 2002. *The Disturbing 'Rise' of Global Income Inequality.* New York: National Bureau of Economic Research working paper.

Stern, Nicholas. 1989. "Economics of Development: A Survey." *Economic Journal* 99 (September): 597–685.

———. 1991. "The Determinants of Growth." *Economic Journal* 101 (January): 122–133.

Stiglitz, Joseph E. 1998. "Knowledge as a Global Public Good." In Inge Kaul et al. (eds)., *Global Public Goods.* New York: Oxford University Press, 308–325.

United Nations. 1998. *World Population Prospects: The 1998 Revision.* Vol. 1. *Comprehensive Tables.* New York: United Nations.

United Nations Educational, Scientific, and Cultural Organization (UNESCO). 1957. *World Illiteracy at Mid-Century.* Paris: UNESCO.

Williamson, Jeffrey. 2002. *Winners and Losers in Two Centuries of Globablization.* Annual Lecture. World Institute for Economic Research.

World Bank. 1999. *World Development Report 1998/99: Knowledge for Development.* New York: Oxford University Press.

———. 2002. *Sustainable Development in a Dynamic World.* World Development Report. Washington, D.C.: World Bank.

Appendix A

Beck, Thorsten, Ash Demirguc-Kunt, and Ross Levine. 2000. "A New Data Base on the Structure and Development of the Financial Structure." *World Bank Economic Review* 14, no. 3 597–605.

Easterly, William. 2001. *Elusive Quest for Growth.* New York: Basic Books.

Jorgenson, Dale W. 1961. "The Development of a Dual Economy." *The Economic Journal* 71, no. 282 (June): 309–334.

Levitt, Kari Polanyi. 2000. "The Right to Development." Fifth Sir Arthur Lewis Memorial Lecture.

Lewis, W. Arthur. 1952. *The Principles of Economic Planning.* London: Allen and Unwin.

———. 1954. "Development with Unlimited Supplies of Labor." *Manchester School of Economics and Social Studies* (May): 139–191.

———. 1955. *The Theory of Economic Growth.* London: Allen and Unwin.

————. 1980. "The Slowing Down of the Engine of Growth." Nobel Lecture. *American Economic Review* 70 no. 4 (September): 555–564.

Lewis, A. 1984a. "Development Economics in the 1950s." In G. M. Meier and D. Seers (eds.), *Pioneers in Development*. New York: Oxford University Press, 119–138.

————. 1984b. "The State of Development Theory." *American Economic Review* 7 (March): 1–10.

Lucas, Robert E. 2000. "Some Macroeconomics for the Twenty-first Century." *Journal of Economic Perspectives* 14, no. 1 (winter): 159–168.

Meier, Gerald M. 1994. "Review of Development Research in the UK: Report to the Development Studies Association." *Journal of International Development* 6, no. 5: 465–517.

Meier, G. M., and Dudley Seers, eds. 1984. *Pioneers in Development*. New York: Oxford University Press.

Ranis, G., and J.C.H. Fei. 1982. "Lewis and the Classicists." In M. Gersovitz, C. Diaz-Alejandro, G. Ranis, and M. Rosenzweig (eds). *The Theory and Experiences of Economic Development: Essays in Honor of Sir W. Arthur Lewis*. London: Allen and Unwin.

Sen, Amartya. 1997. *Development Thinking at the Beginning of the Twenty-first Century*. Development Economics Research Program, London School of Economics.

————. 1999. *Development as Freedom*. New York: Knopf.

————. 2000, June 26. *Development Thinking at the Millennium*. Annual World Bank Conference on Development Economics (Paris).

"Sir Arthur Lewis: The Simplicity of Genius." 1989. May 23–26. Issued on the occasion of the Fourteenth Annual Conference of the Caribbean Studies Association (Barbados).

Stern, Nicholas. 2000, December 15. "Globalization and Poverty." Address at the University of Indonesia.

Stiglitz, Joseph. 1986. "The New Development Economics." *World Development*, no.2: 257–265.

————. 1994. "The Role of the State in Financial Markets." In *Proceedings of the World Bank Annual Conference on Development Economics*. Washington, D.C.: World Bank, 19–52.

————. 2002. *Globalization and Its Discontents*. New York: Norton.

Index

Abramovitz, Moses, 112–113, 184, 210*n*
Absolute poverty, 5, 47
Adelman, Irma, 79
Afghanistan, 7, 46
Aggregate production function, 96, 102, 117
Agriculture, 45, 69, 194
   classical economics and, 18–20, 28, 30, 32
   revision of policies affecting, 86–88
   subsidies, 168, 169
Alliance for Progress, 46, 60
Antidumping duty, 170–171
Antiplanning, 83–85
Argentina, financial crisis in, 153
Arndt, H.W., 208*n*
Aron, Janine, 137
Arrow, Kenneth J., 100, 140, 209–210*n*
Arusha Initiative, 50
Asian financial crisis, 49, 50, 153–156, 158
Assimilation theories, 101
Association of Southeast Asian Nations (ASEAN), 146
Atlantic Charter, 41

Backwardness, advantage to hypothesis, 71, 111–113
Balanced growth strategy, 61–64, 73, 76, 123, 209*n*
Balance-of-payments crises, 49–51, 74, 75, 84, 90, 154

Bangladesh, 134, 135
Barber, William J., 83
Bauer, Peter, 6, 77, 82
Bhagwati, Jagdish, 84, 151
Big push, advocacy of, 60–61, 63, 73, 76, 94, 123
Birth control, 31, 35
Birth rates, 68
Bliss, Christopher, 13
Bolivia, 42
Border prices, 86
Bourgeoisie, 35, 36
Bourguignon, Francois, 78
Brazil, 42
   financial crisis in, 153
Bretton Woods Conference (1944), 41–44, 50, 174, 175
Bruton, Henry, 205*n*
Buffer Stock Facility, 49
Burma
   independence of, 41
   national development planning in, 46

Capital, Das (Marx), 207*n*
Capital accumulation, 184
   classical economics and, 17–19, 21–22, 25, 28, 32, 33, 53, 57, 59
   development economics and, 54, 56, 60–63, 75
   growth theory and, 96, 97, 101
Capital flows, types of, 153–154